Company's Coming ®

Healthy in a Hurry

Eat better in under 30 minutes

Jean Paré
LIFESTYLE SERIES

Healthy
in a Hurry

Healthy in a Hurry

Divider Photo

1. Honey Ginger Salmon, page 93
2. Fragrant Rice, page 134
3. Tropical Peppers, page 124

We gratefully acknowledge the following suppliers for their generous support of our Test and Photography Kitchens:

Broil King Barbecues
Corelle®
Hamilton Beach® Canada
Lagostina®
Proctor Silex® Canada
Tupperware®

Our special thanks to the following businesses for providing props for photography:

Anchor Hocking Canada
Canhome Global
Cherison Enterprises Inc.
Danesco Inc.
Emile Henry
Linens 'N Things
Mikasa Home Store
Out of the Fire Studio
Pfaltzgraff Canada
Pier 1 Imports
The Bay

Cooking tonight?

A selection of
feature recipes
is only a
click away—
absolutely ***FREE!***

Table of contents

foreword

For many of us, the thought of preparing a meal that's healthy *and* quick is a contradiction in terms, like jumbo shrimp or diet ice cream. We think wholesome eating means lots of scrubbing, peeling and slow cooking, while fast food can only equal high levels of fat, salt and sugar. How is it possible to put speed and nutrition on one plate?

Easy, with *Healthy in a Hurry*, the latest in Company's Coming's Lifestyle series. Every one of our nourishing recipes can be on the table in 30 minutes or less—and that includes the preparation and cooking times!

Our secret? We've used many commercially prepped ingredients, such as frozen veggies, fresh stir-fry vegetable mixes and ready-sliced beef strips, to help get you in and out of the kitchen fast. And while we've pared down ingredients for each recipe, we've carefully selected high-impact flavour boosters—balsamic vinegar, citrus juices, zests, low-sodium broth, no-salt seasoning and sesame oil, for example—to make each dish a success.

To help you use your time effectively, we'll occasionally nudge you along to the next step of a recipe even as it's simmering on the stove or baking in the oven. We'll also share our time-saving tips on everything from shopping to freezing, so meal-planning can become an effortless part of your life.

As with all our Lifestyle cookbooks, we've worked hard to cut down the sodium and fat in these dishes, while pumping up the flavour. And we've scattered extra health-related tips and facts through the book as FYIs.

Healthy in a Hurry has nutritious suggestions from breakfast and brunch to dinner and desserts. Surprising but delicious ingredient combinations will please family and friends.

A batch of Yam And Eggs, for instance, is the perfect breakfast comfort food, while Tuna Mango Wraps will soon be favourites at office lunches or Sunday picnics. Our Pear Chutney Pork Chops are fast enough for a weeknight supper, but just the thing for a weekend get-together.

Once you've tried a few of our recipes, you'll see that fast, nutritious food doesn't have to be an impossible contradiction. It's easy to get *Healthy in a Hurry*!

Jean Paré

Nutrition Information Guidelines

Each recipe is analyzed using the most current version of the Canadian Nutrient File from Health Canada, which is based on the United States Department of Agriculture (USDA) Nutrient Database.

- If more than one ingredient is listed (such as "butter or hard margarine"), or if a range is given (1 – 2 tsp., 5 – 10 mL), only the first ingredient or first amount is analyzed.

- For meat, poultry and fish, the serving size per person is based on the recommended 4 oz. (113 g) uncooked weight (without bone), which is 2 – 3 oz. (57 – 85 g) cooked weight (without bone)—approximately the size of a deck of playing cards.

- Milk used is 1% M.F. (milk fat), unless otherwise stated.

- Cooking oil used is canola oil, unless otherwise stated.

- Ingredients indicating "sprinkle," "optional," or "for garnish" are not included in the nutrition information.

- The fat in recipes and combination foods can vary greatly depending on the sources and types of fats used in each specific ingredient. For these reasons, the amount of saturated, monounsaturated and polyunsaturated fats may not add up to the total fat content.

Vera C. Mazurak, Ph.D.
Nutritionist

Keeping it Healthy When You're in a Hurry

Perfect your planning

Sorry to say, but the biggest time-saver is the one people have the hardest time with—planning. Avoid the daily routine of staring into your refrigerator, hoping for inspiration, and take the few extra minutes a week needed to make mealtime a breeze.

- **Have a running grocery list.** Get a magnetic shopping list and place it on your fridge. When you run low on something, or feel a little bit inspired, add the necessary ingredients to the list.

- **Plan your meals a week in advance.** This will make grocery shopping a snap. Just check the recipes to make sure you have everything you need. After all, there's nothing worse than getting halfway through a recipe and realizing you're missing an essential ingredient!

- **Take meat out the night before to thaw in the fridge.** The benefits of this are twofold: you won't be tempted to opt for takeout when you know you have something waiting to be cooked up; and you won't have to deal with those rubbery edges that mysteriously appear when you defrost meat in the microwave.

- **Double recipes and freeze extras.** Make a big dish and then freeze the leftovers in meal-sized portions that you can quickly heat up when you're extra low on time.

- **Double staple ingredients and freeze extras.** Consider cooking up extra ground beef, ground chicken, beans, rice and whole grains. They freeze well and, because they are already cooked, will help to reduce the cooking times of any future recipes.

- **Stock up on often-used ingredients.** Whole wheat pasta, prepackaged low-sodium stock, rice and your favourite spices should all be at the ready when you're ready to cook.

Fighting the snack attack

When you're on the go and hunger hits, it's easy to surrender and give in to the allure of the junk food counter of your nearest convenience store. But fear not, it's unlikely you'll have to raise a white flag if you have prepared, healthy snacks on hand.

Prepare your snacks at home, put them in individual baggies and have them waiting in your fridge when you need to grab-and-go. Or you can buy healthy prepackaged snacks in the produce or dairy section of your local grocer's. And don't underestimate the convenience of buying prewashed baby carrots and sugar snap peas—no fuss, no muss, just pop them in a baggie and your snack is ready. Consider the following foods as potential snack items in your battle against processed, fatty junk food.

- **100% fruit leather**
- **100% juice boxes**
- **Applesauce**
- **Bottled water**
- **Dried fruit (raisins, apricots, apples, prunes)**
- **Individual portions of low-fat cheese**
- **Low-fat yogurt & cottage cheese**
- **Pre-cut fruit**
- **Pre-cut veggies**

- **Raw nuts & seeds (almonds, sunflower seeds, peanuts)**
- **Rice cakes & baked rice crackers**
- **Soy nuts (in smaller amounts)**
- **Whole-grain crackers**

Learning to love the light

Shaving off a little bit of fat here and a few calories there will add up to big health benefits over time. Consider this: if you use reduced–fat ranch dressing, you'll save 40 calories and 5 grams of total fat per tablespoon; and if you use fat-free ranch dressing, you'll save 56 calories and 7 grams of total fat per tablespoon! By the end of the year you'll have literally cut out thousands of calories in salad dressing alone!

Healthy eating does not have to take longer. It can be done simply by shopping smarter. Easily cut down on fat and calories by trying the reduced–fat or lighter versions of favourite foods—sometimes you can't even taste the difference!

Embrace this philosophy when buying meats as well. Trim the fat off your meat before cooking. Use leaner cuts, poultry without skin and white meat instead of dark. Choose deli meats less often—but when you do, choose leaner meats with less sodium.

Taking it a step further

So, now that you've got the right ingredients and the right recipes, are there any other ways you can make your cooking healthier? You bet! Just follow some of the tips below and apply them in your cooking whenever possible.

- To retain more nutrients, steam or microwave vegetables instead of boiling them.

- Use non-stick cookware to minimize your use of oil or margarine.

- Use whole wheat pasta, bread and tortillas and brown or wild rice in your meals.

- If you're concerned about sodium, don't add salt in the preparation stages of cooking. Many ingredients already have salt added to them including condiments, canned and dried soups and seasonings. Make healthier meals by using reduced–sodium products or substitutes.

Making it faster with freezer fare

Your freezer can be your best friend when trying to plan and serve healthy meals—because, really, all you have to do is reheat. Stackable plastic containers and sealable freezer bags are your best options when freezing food. Remove as much air as possible from freezer bags to keep your food at its optimum freshness, but leave some space in rigid plastic containers to allow for expansion. Be sure to label each container with the contents and the date you froze it. No one wants to eat the "mystery meat" or the "dinner surprise!"

Blast O' Berry Smoothie

Get your morning blast o' energy from this creamy, purple smoothie full of refreshing tropical flavours.

Chopped papaya	2 cups	500 mL
Frozen (or fresh) blueberries	2 cups	500 mL
Peach mango dessert tofu	10 2/3 oz.	300 g
Pineapple juice	1 cup	250 mL
Low-fat plain yogurt	1/2 cup	125 mL

Process all 5 ingredients in blender or food processor until smooth. Makes about 6 cups (1.5 L). Serves 4.

1 serving: 164 Calories; 2.3 g Total Fat (0.2 g Mono, trace Poly, 0.5 g Sat); 2 mg Cholesterol; 35 g Carbohydrate; 4 g Fibre; 5 g Protein; 30 mg Sodium

Mango Tango

Get your morning energy boost in a convenient beverage! Using frozen fruit helps to thicken and chill smoothies. For a more intense mango flavour use mango nectar or mango-peach fruit cocktail instead of orange juice.

Frozen mango pieces	2 cups	500 mL
Milk (or soy milk)	1 cup	250 mL
Peach (or peach-mango) dessert tofu	5 1/3 oz.	150 g
Orange juice	1/2 cup	125 mL
Wheat germ, toasted (see Tip, below)	1 tbsp.	15 mL

Process all 5 ingredients in blender until smooth. Makes 3 1/2 cups (875 mL). Serves 2.

1 serving: 254 Calories; 3.5 g Total Fat (0.7 g Mono, 0.3 g Poly, 1.1 g Sat); 8 mg Cholesterol; 52 g Carbohydrate; 4 g Fibre; 9 g Protein; 74 mg Sodium

To toast wheat germ, spread evenly in an ungreased shallow frying pan. Heat and stir on medium until golden. To bake, spread evenly in an ungreased shallow pan. Bake in a 350°F (175°C) oven for 3 minutes, stirring or shaking often, until golden. Cool before adding to recipe.

Cranberry Oatmeal

Oatmeal doesn't have to be boring! We've jazzed up this version with the tangy taste of cranberry. Just add milk or sprinkle a few toasted almonds over the top for a delicious breakfast that's also a good source of fibre.

Cranberry cocktail	2 cups	500 mL
Water	1 cup	250 mL
Salt	1/4 tsp.	1 mL
Quick-cooking rolled oats	1 1/3 cups	325 mL
Dried cranberries	1/2 cup	125 mL

Combine first 3 ingredients in medium saucepan. Bring to a boil.

Add oats and cranberries. Stir. Cook on medium for 3 to 5 minutes, stirring occasionally, until thickened. Remove from heat. Cover. Let stand for 5 minutes. Makes about 3 cups (750 mL).

1 cup (250 mL): 306 Calories; 3.2 g Total Fat (0.1 g Mono, 0.2 g Poly, trace Sat); 0 mg Cholesterol; 66 g Carbohydrate; 5 g Fibre; 6 g Protein; 199 mg Sodium

Variation: Instead of cranberry cocktail and dried cranberries, use the same amounts of your favourite fruit juice blend and a dried fruit to complement. Peach-mango cocktail with chopped dried apricot makes a great combination.

Paradise Smoothie

Jump-start your morning with a taste of paradise—beverage style! Tasty and tropical flavours of coconut, pineapple and banana are sure to get you on your way. Chill the can of crushed pineapple to make it even more refreshing.

Frozen overripe medium banana (see Tip, page 13)	1	1
Can of crushed pineapple (with juice)	14 oz.	398 mL
Vanilla frozen yogurt	1 cup	250 mL
Light silken tofu (about 3/4 cup, 175 mL)	6 oz.	170 g
Sliced natural almonds	1 tbsp.	15 mL
Medium unsweetened coconut	1 tbsp.	15 mL

Combine all 6 ingredients in blender. Process with on/off motion until almonds are broken up. Blend until smooth. Makes about 3 1/4 cups (800 mL). Serves 2.

1 serving: 375 Calories; 8.4 g Total Fat (1.1 g Mono, 0.8 g Poly, 4.6 g Sat); 15 mg Cholesterol; 65 g Carbohydrate; 4 g Fibre; 10 g Protein; 136 mg Sodium

Potato Kale Frittata

Who doesn't love a one-dish meal? This hearty frittata has just enough spicy heat to put some pep in your early-morning step. This recipe can be easily halved and prepared in a medium-sized frying pan.

Canola oil	1 tbsp.	15 mL
Diced peeled potato	1 1/2 cups	375 mL
Finely chopped onion	2/3 cup	150 mL
Garlic cloves, minced (or 1/2 tsp., 2 mL, powder)	2	2
Dried crushed chilies	1/2 tsp.	2 mL
Finely chopped kale leaves, lightly packed (see Tip, page 110)	3 cups	750 mL
Sun-dried tomato pesto	1 tbsp.	15 mL
Packages of low-cholesterol egg product (8 oz., 227 mL, each), see Note	2	2
Grated Parmesan cheese	1/4 cup	60 mL

Preheat broiler. Heat canola oil in large frying pan on medium. Add next 4 ingredients. Cook, covered, for about 8 minutes, stirring occasionally, until potato is browned and tender-crisp.

Add kale and pesto. Stir well. Cook, covered, for about 5 minutes, stirring occasionally, until kale is softened.

Pour egg product over kale mixture. Reduce heat to medium-low. Cook, covered, for 3 to 5 minutes until bottom is golden and top is almost set. Remove from heat. Sprinkle with Parmesan cheese. Broil on centre rack in oven for 3 to 5 minutes until golden and set (See Tip, page 15). Serves 4.

1 serving: 224 Calories; 8.7 g Total Fat (4.0 g Mono, 1.5 g Poly, 2.3 g Sat); 100 mg Cholesterol; 18 g Carbohydrate; 2 g Fibre; 16 g Protein; 147 mg Sodium

Note: Instead of using low-cholesterol egg product, use 8 large eggs, fork-beaten.

When your bananas get too ripe to enjoy fresh, peel and freeze them on a baking sheet. Once frozen, transfer to freezer bag for use in any blended beverage. Overripe bananas have superior flavour for beverages.

Double Strawberry Toast

Strawberries as far as the eye can see! These French toast sandwiches have strawberries inside and out! The honey and lime strawberry topping adds that extra bit of delightful decadence.

Liquid honey	**1/4 cup**	**60 mL**
Lime juice	**2 tbsp.**	**30 mL**
Grated lime zest	**1 tsp.**	**5 mL**
Sliced fresh strawberries	**3 cups**	**750 mL**
Package of low-cholesterol egg product (see Note)	**8 oz.**	**227 mL**
Vanilla soy milk	**1 cup**	**250 mL**
Coconut (or vanilla) extract	**1/2 tsp.**	**2 mL**
Strawberry jam	**2/3 cup**	**150 mL**
Whole grain bread slices	**12**	**12**
Canola oil	**2 tbsp.**	**30 mL**

Combine first 3 ingredients in medium bowl. Add strawberries. Stir well. Set aside.

Beat next 3 ingredients in large shallow bowl with a whisk until frothy. Set aside.

Spread about 1 1/2 tbsp. (25 mL) jam on 1 bread slice. Cover with second bread slice. Repeat with remaining jam and bread slices, making 6 sandwiches.

Heat 1 tbsp. (15 mL) canola oil in large frying pan on medium-low. Press one sandwich into egg mixture. Turn over to coat both sides. Transfer to frying pan. Repeat with 2 more sandwiches. Cook for about 4 minutes per side until golden. Transfer to serving platter. Keep warm in 200°F (95°C) oven. Repeat with remaining oil, sandwiches and egg mixture. Spoon 1/2 cup (125 mL) strawberry mixture over each sandwich. Serves 6.

1 serving: 399 Calories; 8.6 g Total Fat (4.0 g Mono, 2.1 g Poly, 1.2 g Sat); 32 mg Cholesterol; 71 g Carbohydrate; 6 g Fibre; 12 g Protein; 336 mg Sodium

Pictured on page 17.

Note: Instead of using low-cholesterol egg product, use 4 large eggs, fork-beaten.

Sunny Tuscan Eggwiches

Try the sunny side of Italy! Sun-dried tomato and balsamic flavours are a unique addition to a breakfast classic. The hand-held sandwich variation is easy to eat on the go. Excellent with a serving of fresh fruit.

Whole wheat English muffins, split	2	2
Sun-dried tomato pesto	1/4 cup	60 mL
Balsamic vinegar	1 tbsp.	15 mL
Dried crushed chilies	1/4 tsp.	1 mL
Olive (or canola) oil	1 tsp.	5 mL
Large eggs	4	4
Chopped fresh chives	2 tbsp.	30 mL
Grated Parmesan cheese	1 tbsp.	15 mL

Toast English muffin halves in toaster until golden. Transfer to plate.

Meanwhile, combine next 3 ingredients in small bowl. Spoon mixture onto muffin halves. Set aside.

Heat olive oil in small frying pan on medium. Break eggs into pan. Cook, covered, for about 2 minutes until egg whites are just set and form a light film over yolk. Carefully place 1 egg over pesto mixture on each muffin half.

Sprinkle chives and Parmesan cheese over eggs. Makes 4 eggwiches.

1 eggwich: 209 Calories; 10.5 g Total Fat (5.3 g Mono, 1.6 g Poly, 2.5 g Sat); 187 mg Cholesterol; 20 g Carbohydrate; 4 g Fibre; 11 g Protein; 363 mg Sodium

Pictured on page 17.

Variation: To make these into hand-held sandwiches, cook the eggs until fully set and toast 2 additional split English muffins for eggwich tops.

When baking or broiling food in a frying pan and the handle is not ovenproof, wrap the handle in tin foil and keep it to the front of the oven, away from the element.

Cinnamon Apple Grits

You may not want to kiss these grits, but you'll probably want to kiss the cook who made them! This sunny yellow cornmeal mixture with an apple, raisin and walnut topping provides sweet relief from everyday oatmeal.

Chopped, peeled cooking apple (such as McIntosh)	**1 1/2 cups**	**375 mL**
Frozen concentrated apple juice, thawed	**1 cup**	**250 mL**
Water	**1/2 cup**	**125 mL**
Golden raisins	**1/2 cup**	**125 mL**
Liquid honey	**2 tbsp.**	**30 mL**
Ground cinnamon	**1 tsp.**	**5 mL**
Water	**3 1/2 cups**	**875 mL**
Frozen concentrated apple juice, thawed	**1/2 cup**	**125 mL**
Salt	**1/2 tsp.**	**2 mL**
Yellow cornmeal	**1 cup**	**250 mL**
Coarsely chopped walnuts	**1/2 cup**	**125 mL**

Combine first 6 ingredients in medium saucepan. Bring to a boil. Reduce heat to medium. Boil gently, uncovered, for 10 minutes.

Meanwhile, combine next 3 ingredients in large saucepan. Bring to a boil. Slowly add cornmeal, stirring constantly. Reduce heat to low. Cook for 3 to 5 minutes, stirring often, until thickened to consistency of soft porridge.

Add walnuts to apple mixture. Stir. Spoon cornmeal mixture into 4 individual serving bowls. Spoon apple mixture over top. Serves 4.

1 serving: 517 Calories; 10.9 g Total Fat (1.5 g Mono, 7.5 g Poly, 1.1 g Sat); 0 mg Cholesterol; 103 g Carbohydrate; 5 g Fibre; 7 g Protein; 323 mg Sodium

Pictured at right.

1. Double Strawberry Toast, page 14
2. Cinnamon Apple Grits, above
3. Sunny Tuscan Eggwiches, page 15

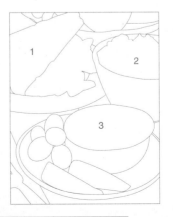

Cottage Apple Pancakes

Enjoy the positively pleasing taste of apples and cinnamon in these moist pancakes. Lots of cottage cheese and milk make these a great source of calcium.

All-purpose flour	3/4 cup	175 mL
Granulated sugar	1 tbsp.	15 mL
Baking powder	2 tsp.	10 mL
Salt	1/2 tsp.	2 mL
Ground cinnamon	1/8 tsp.	0.5 mL
Large egg	1	1
1% cottage cheese	3/4 cup	175 mL
Milk	1/3 cup	75 mL
Melted butter (or hard margarine)	1 tbsp.	15 mL
Coarsely grated peeled cooking apple (such as McIntosh)	3/4 cup	175 mL
Canola oil	1/2 tsp.	2 mL

Combine first 5 ingredients in medium bowl. Make a well in centre.

Measure next 4 ingredients into blender. Process until cottage cheese is almost smooth. Add to well.

Add apple. Stir until just moistened. Batter will be lumpy.

Preheat griddle to 375°F (190°C) or large frying pan on medium. Add canola oil. Pour batter onto griddle, using about 1/4 cup (60 mL) for each pancake. Cook for about 3 minutes until bubbles form on top and edges appear dry. Turn pancake over. Cook for about 3 minutes until golden. Remove to large plate. Cover to keep warm. Repeat with remaining batter, adding more canola oil if necessary to prevent sticking. Makes about 8 pancakes.

1 pancake: 111 Calories; 2.8 g Total Fat (0.9 g Mono, 0.3 g Poly, 1.3 g Sat); 28 mg Cholesterol; 16 g Carbohydrate; 1 g Fibre; 5 g Protein; 323 mg Sodium

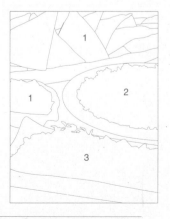

1. Tofu Bean Dip And Crisps, page 25
2. Apricot Jalapeño Pork, page 123
3. Black Bean And Corn Skillet, page 137

Peppered Egg Quesadilla

Quesadillas aren't just for dinner anymore! A nutritious and delicious hand-held breakfast that's sure to please the kids.

Whole wheat flour tortillas (9 inch, 22 cm, diameter)	2	2
Grated jalapeño Monterey Jack cheese	2 tbsp.	30 mL
Canola oil	1/2 tsp.	2 mL
Sliced fresh white mushrooms	1/2 cup	125 mL
Chopped red pepper	1/4 cup	60 mL
Large eggs, fork-beaten	2	2
Chopped green onion	2 tbsp.	30 mL
Pepper	1/8 tsp.	0.5 mL
Grated jalapeño Monterey Jack cheese	2 tbsp.	30 mL

Preheat oven to 400°F (205°C). Place 1 tortilla on ungreased baking sheet. Sprinkle with first amount of cheese. Set aside.

Heat canola oil in medium non-stick frying pan on medium. Add mushrooms and red pepper. Cook for about 3 minutes, stirring occasionally, until red pepper is softened.

Add eggs. Sprinkle with green onion and pepper. Reduce heat to medium-low. Cook, covered, for about 2 minutes, without stirring, until eggs are set. Slide egg mixture onto tortilla on baking sheet.

Sprinkle with second amount of cheese. Place remaining tortilla on top. Bake in oven for about 3 minutes until cheese is melted. Cut into wedges. Serves 2.

1 serving: 274 Calories; 11.2 g Total Fat (4.2 g Mono, 1.6 g Poly, 4.5 g Sat); 199 mg Cholesterol; 37 g Carbohydrate; 4 g Fibre; 15 g Protein; 439 mg Sodium

Breakfast Bites

Cookies for breakfast? Not quite, but these bites are quick and easy to make. Healthy whether eaten as a breakfast, a dessert or a snack.

Large egg, fork-beaten	1	1
Overripe medium banana, mashed	1	1
Grated carrot	1 cup	250 mL
Sliced natural almonds, toasted (see Tip, below)	1/2 cup	125 mL
Brown sugar, packed	1/2 cup	125 mL
Unsweetened applesauce	1/4 cup	60 mL
Vanilla extract	1/4 tsp.	1 mL
Whole wheat flour	1 cup	250 mL
Quick-cooking rolled oats	1/2 cup	125 mL
Flaxseed	1/4 cup	60 mL
Baking soda	1/2 tsp.	2 mL
Salt	1/2 tsp.	2 mL
Ground cinnamon	1/4 tsp.	1 mL

Combine first 7 ingredients in large bowl.

Add remaining 6 ingredients. Stir until no dry flour remains. Drop by rounded tablespoonfuls about 1 inch (2.5 cm) apart onto greased cookie sheet. Bake in 350°F (175°C) oven for about 12 minutes until set and bottoms are browned. Remove bites from cookie sheet and place on wire rack to cool. Makes 24 bites.

1 bite: 74 Calories; 2.2 g Total Fat (0.9 g Mono, 0.9 g Poly, 0.2 g Sat); 8 mg Cholesterol; 12 g Carbohydrate; 2 g Fibre; 2 g Protein; 84 mg Sodium

To toast nuts, seeds or coconut, place them in an ungreased shallow frying pan. Heat on medium for 3 to 5 minutes, stirring often, until golden. To bake, spread them evenly in an ungreased shallow pan. Bake in a 350°F (175°C) oven for 5 to 10 minutes, stirring or shaking often, until golden.

Curry Egg Pockets

A great breakfast to eat on the run. A convenient pocket stuffed with curried scrambled eggs, tomato, onion and cheese. Very quick and easy to prepare. If you love curry, just add a touch more.

Canola oil	1 tbsp.	15 mL
Chopped tomato	1/2 cup	125 mL
Chopped green onion	1/4 cup	60 mL
Curry powder	1 tsp.	5 mL
Large eggs, fork-beaten	6	6
Salt, sprinkle		
Pepper, sprinkle		
Whole wheat pita bread (7 inch, 18 cm, diameter), halved and opened	2	2
Grated medium Cheddar cheese	1/2 cup	125 mL
Chopped fresh cilantro or parsley	1 tbsp.	15 mL

Heat canola oil in medium frying pan on medium. Add tomato and green onion. Cook for 2 to 3 minutes, stirring occasionally, until softened. Add curry powder. Stir. Cook for 1 minute to blend flavours.

Add eggs. Sprinkle with salt and pepper. Cook and stir until eggs are set.

Warm pita bread in microwave on high (100%) for 10 seconds. Spoon egg mixture into pita pockets. Sprinkle cheese and cilantro into pita pockets. Makes 4 pockets.

1 pocket: 258 Calories; 14.5 g Total Fat (5.4 g Mono, 2.5 g Poly, 4.6 g Sat); 289 mg Cholesterol; 18 g Carbohydrate; 3 g Fibre; 15 g Protein; 304 mg Sodium

Yam And Eggs

An all-in-one breakfast. Eggs, bagel, yam and cheese—this is a dish that's sure to please! Add variety by using different types of cheese or by adding meat, vegetables or herbs. Comfort food at its best!

Large unpeeled yam (or sweet potato), quartered (about 1 lb., 454 g)	1	1
Olive oil	1 tbsp.	15 mL
Sliced onion	2 cups	500 mL
Whole wheat bagel, chopped	1	1
Grated Swiss cheese	1/2 cup	125 mL
Seasoned salt	1/2 tsp.	2 mL
Large eggs	8	8

(continued on next page)

Preheat broiler. Place yam in medium microwave-safe bowl. Microwave, covered, on high (100%) for about 7 minutes until softened. Let stand for about 5 minutes until cool enough to handle. Remove and discard skin. Cut yam into 1/2 inch (12 mm) pieces.

Meanwhile, heat olive oil in large frying pan on medium. Add onion. Cook for 8 to 10 minutes, stirring occasionally, until softened and starting to brown. Add yam. Spread evenly in pan.

Process bagel in blender until crumbs form. Transfer to small bowl. Add cheese and seasoned salt. Stir. Sprinkle half of crumb mixture over yam and onion.

Break eggs over crumb mixture in frying pan. Cook, covered, for 1 minute. Sprinkle remaining crumb mixture over eggs. Broil on centre rack in oven (see Tip, page 15) for about 4 minutes until crumb mixture is golden and eggs are set to desired doneness. Serves 4.

1 serving: 416 Calories; 17.8 g Total Fat (7.9 g Mono, 2.2 g Poly, 6.2 g Sat); 385 mg Cholesterol; 43 g Carbohydrate; 7 g Fibre; 22 g Protein; 520 mg Sodium

Salmon Feta Frittata

Easier than omelettes! Wow your nearest and dearest at your next brunch with this delicious salmon and onion egg dish—complemented with Dijon mustard and feta cheese.

Canola oil	**1 tbsp.**	**15 mL**
Large eggs	**6**	**6**
Milk	**1 1/3 cups**	**325 mL**
Dijon mustard	**1 tbsp.**	**15 mL**
Lemon pepper	**1/4 tsp.**	**1 mL**
Can of pink salmon, drained, skin and round bones removed	**6 1/2 oz.**	**184 g**
Crumbled light feta cheese	**1/4 cup**	**60 mL**
Chopped green onion	**2 tbsp.**	**30 mL**

Preheat broiler. Heat canola oil in large frying pan on medium.

Meanwhile, whisk next 4 ingredients in medium bowl until combined. Pour into frying pan. Cook, uncovered, without stirring, for 5 minutes.

Sprinkle with remaining 3 ingredients. Cook, covered, for about 5 minutes until bottom is golden and top is almost set. Remove from heat. Broil on centre rack in oven for about 2 minutes until golden and set (see Tip, page 15). Serves 4.

1 serving: 244 Calories; 14.2 g Total Fat (5.4 g Mono, 2.2 g Poly, 3.7 g Sat); 316 mg Cholesterol; 5 g Carbohydrate; trace Fibre; 24 g Protein; 471 mg Sodium

Red Pepper Hummus And Chips

Roasted red peppers give hummus a sultry Mediterranean interpretation. Perfect as a dip for fresh vegetables. This hummus is also used as the spread for Greek Chicken Pockets, page 28.

PITA CHIPS

Whole wheat pita bread (7 inch, 18 cm, diameter)	3	3
Olive oil	1 tbsp.	15 mL

HUMMUS

Can of chickpeas (garbanzo beans), rinsed and drained	19 oz.	540 mL
Roasted red peppers, drained and blotted dry	1/2 cup	125 mL
Tahini (sesame paste)	2 tbsp.	30 mL
Lemon juice	2 tbsp.	30 mL
Olive oil	1 tbsp.	15 mL
Garlic clove, minced (or 1/4 tsp., 1 mL, powder)	1	1
Dried oregano	1 tsp.	5 mL
Ground cumin	1 tsp.	5 mL
Salt, sprinkle (optional)		

Pita Chips: Preheat oven to 350°F (175°C). Carefully split pita bread in half horizontally to make 6 rounds. Brush first amount of olive oil on one side of each round. Stack rounds on top of each other. Cut into 8 wedges. Arrange wedges, oil side up, in single layer on 2 ungreased baking sheets with sides. Bake on separate racks in oven for about 10 minutes, switching position of baking sheets at halftime, until lightly browned. Let stand on baking sheets to cool.

Hummus: Meanwhile, process remaining 9 ingredients in blender or food processor until smooth. Serve with pita chips. Serves 4.

1 serving: 453 Calories; 15.5 g Total Fat (7.4 g Mono, 4.4 g Poly, 2.0 g Sat); 0 mg Cholesterol; 65 g Carbohydrate; 10 g Fibre; 18 g Protein; 633 mg Sodium

Our hummus is a real humdinger when it comes to healthy eating. Chickpeas are full of fibre, B vitamins and minerals, including iron. Tahini is made from sesame seeds and is rich in fibre, B vitamins and many minerals.

Tofu Bean Dip And Crisps

We're not trying tofu'll you, but no one's going to believe this hummus-like dip is made with tofu. With beans and a hint of salsa flavour you'll be able to aptly usher in any fiesta.

WHEAT POINT CRISPS		
Russian dressing	**2 tsp.**	**10 mL**
Ground cumin	**1/4 tsp.**	**1 mL**
Cayenne pepper, sprinkle		
Whole wheat flour tortillas (9 inch, 22 cm, diameter)	**2**	**2**
DIP		
Can of white kidney beans, rinsed and drained	**19 oz.**	**540 mL**
Soft tofu	**1/2 cup**	**125 mL**
Chili powder	**2 tsp.**	**10 mL**
Ground cumin	**1/2 tsp.**	**2 mL**
Garlic salt	**1/4 tsp.**	**1 mL**
Chopped tomato	**1/2 cup**	**125 mL**
Sliced green onion	**1/4 cup**	**60 mL**

Wheat Point Crisps: Preheat oven to 425°F (220°C). Combine first 3 ingredients in small cup. Spread on tortillas. Cut each tortilla into 8 wedges. Arrange in single layer on ungreased baking sheet with sides. Bake in oven for about 5 minutes until edges are golden. Makes 16 wheat points.

Dip: Process first 5 ingredients in blender or food processor until smooth. Transfer to medium bowl.

Add tomato and green onion. Stir. Makes about 2 cups (500 mL) dip. Serve with Wheat Point Crisps. Serves 2.

1 serving: 422 Calories; 8.5 g Total Fat (2.2 g Mono, 2.7 g Poly, 0.8 g Sat); 1 mg Cholesterol; 76 g Carbohydrate; 16 g Fibre; 23 g Protein; 586 mg Sodium

Pictured on page 18.

Tuna Mango Wraps

This fresh, light sandwich alternative is a unique diversion from everyday luncheon fare. Line the wrap with spinach first to keep it from getting soggy. Try with fresh mango when it's in season.

Frozen (or fresh) mango pieces, thawed, drained and chopped	**1 cup**	**250 mL**
Can of flaked white tuna in water, drained	**6 oz.**	**170 g**
Light mayonnaise	**2 tbsp.**	**30 mL**
Chopped green onion	**1 tbsp.**	**15 mL**
Low-sodium soy sauce	**1 1/2 tsp.**	**7 mL**
Lime juice	**1 tsp.**	**5 mL**
Fresh spinach leaves, lightly packed	**1/2 cup**	**125 mL**
Whole wheat flour tortillas (9 inch, 22 cm, diameter)	**2**	**2**

Combine first 6 ingredients in small bowl.

Arrange spinach along centre of tortillas. Spoon tuna mixture over spinach. Fold bottom ends of tortillas over filling. Fold in sides, leaving top ends open. Makes 2 wraps.

1 wrap: 347 Calories; 8.5 g Total Fat (0.9 g Mono, 1.3 g Poly, 1.6 g Sat); 41 mg Cholesterol; 51 g Carbohydrate; 5 g Fibre; 26 g Protein; 601 mg Sodium

Modern Caesar Pitas

Don't get your toga in a tangle, this update on an old favourite is sure to please. What makes these pitas so pleasingly different? The added flavours of tahini and walnuts. All hail Caesar!

Chopped or torn romaine lettuce, lightly packed	**3 cups**	**750 mL**
Diced cooked chicken	**1 cup**	**250 mL**
Chopped walnuts	**1/4 cup**	**60 mL**
GARLIC SESAME DRESSING		
Olive oil	**1 tbsp.**	**15 mL**
Lemon juice	**1 tbsp.**	**15 mL**
White wine vinegar	**1 tbsp.**	**15 mL**
Tahini (sesame paste)	**1 tbsp.**	**15 mL**
Anchovy paste (optional)	**1/4 tsp.**	**1 mL**
Garlic clove, minced (or 1/4 tsp., 1 mL, powder)	**1**	**1**
Pepper	**1/8 tsp.**	**0.5 mL**
Whole wheat pita bread (7 inch, 18 cm, diameter), halved and opened	**2**	**2**

(continued on next page)

Put first 3 ingredients into medium bowl.

Garlic Sesame Dressing: Beat first 7 ingredients with fork in small cup. Makes about 1/4 cup (60 mL) dressing. Pour over lettuce mixture. Toss well.

Spoon lettuce mixture into pita pockets. Makes 4 pitas.

1 pita: 243 Calories; 13.4 g Total Fat (4.9 g Mono, 5.6 g Poly, 2.0 g Sat); 26 mg Cholesterol; 19 g Carbohydrate; 4 g Fibre; 14 g Protein; 182 mg Sodium

Turkey Pear Sandwich

A gourmet sandwich shop couldn't do any better! This tasty treat is similar to a clubhouse but uses pear instead of bacon.

Light mayonnaise	4 tsp.	20 mL
Whole wheat bread slices	4	4
Chopped pecans, toasted (see Tip, page 21)	1 tbsp.	15 mL
Fresh small pear, sliced (see Note)	1	1
Lean deli smoked turkey breast slices (about 4 oz., 113 g)	4	4
Salt, sprinkle		
Pepper, sprinkle		
Thin slices of light Havarti cheese	2	2
Small Roma (plum) tomato, thinly sliced	1	1
Butter lettuce leaves	6 – 8	6 – 8

Spread mayonnaise on bread slices. Sprinkle pecans over mayonnaise on 2 bread slices.

Arrange pear slices over pecans.

Loosely roll turkey slices and place over pear. Sprinkle with salt and pepper.

Arrange next 3 ingredients, in order given, over turkey. Top with remaining bread slices, mayonnaise-side down. Cut sandwiches in half. Makes 2 sandwiches.

1 sandwich: 436 Calories; 19.9 g Total Fat (2.5 g Mono, 1.5 g Poly, 7.4 g Sat); 64 mg Cholesterol; 42 g Carbohydrate; 7 g Fibre; 27 g Protein; 1065 mg Sodium

Note: If not eating sandwich right away, dip pear in acidulated water (about 1 tsp., 5 mL, lemon juice and 1/2 cup, 125 mL, water) and drain on paper towel before adding to sandwich.

Greek Chicken Pockets

You don't have to be Zorba to enjoy these tzatziki-inspired (pronounced dzah-DZEE-kee) pita pockets. Red Pepper Hummus, page 24, is used as a spread for this recipe but you may want to substitute with a family favourite spread instead.

Red Pepper Hummus, page 24	1/4 cup	60 mL
Whole wheat pita bread (7 inch, 18 cm, diameter), halved and opened	2	2
Chopped cooked chicken	1 cup	250 mL
Thinly sliced red pepper	1/2 cup	125 mL
Plain yogurt	1/3 cup	75 mL
Chopped tomato	1/4 cup	60 mL
Chopped pitted kalamata (or black) olives	1/4 cup	60 mL
Finely chopped English cucumber	1/4 cup	60 mL
Chopped red onion	2 tbsp.	30 mL
Chopped fresh oregano (or 3/4 tsp., 4 mL, dried)	1 tbsp.	15 mL
Pepper	1/4 tsp.	1 mL

Spread hummus inside pita pockets.

Combine remaining 9 ingredients in medium bowl. Spoon into pita pockets. Makes 4 pockets.

1 pocket: 193 Calories; 5.5 g Total Fat (2.2 g Mono, 1.3 g Poly, 1.3 g Sat); 29 mg Cholesterol; 23 g Carbohydrate; 4 g Fibre; 14 g Protein; 318 mg Sodium

Pumpernickel Deli Delight

Fit for a very fashionable king or queen, this delight represents the most noble of flavours—blue cheese, roasted peppers and pumpernickel. If you think cheese reigns supreme, add a slice of light havarti.

Blue cheese dressing	2 tbsp.	30 mL
Pumpernickel bread slices, toasted	4	4
Thinly sliced lean deli smoked turkey breast	4 oz.	113 g
Roasted red peppers, drained and blotted dry (do not slice)	1/2 cup	125 mL
Fresh spinach leaves, lightly packed	1/2 cup	125 mL

(continued on next page)

Spread dressing on toast.

Layer next 3 ingredients, in order given, over dressing on 2 toast slices. Top with remaining toast slices, dressing-side down. Makes 2 sandwiches.

1 sandwich: 313 Calories; 11.2 g Total Fat (4.8 g Mono, 3.4 g Poly, 1.4 g Sat); 27.9 mg Cholesterol; 38 g Carbohydrate; 5 g Fibre; 16 g Protein; 1451 mg Sodium

Asian Chicken Wraps

An Asian-influenced wrap with a great coleslaw crunch similar to that of bean sprouts. Don't shy away from adding your own special touches, such as sliced mushrooms, shredded carrot or chopped pepper.

Coleslaw mix	1 1/2 cups	375 mL
Chopped cooked chicken	1 cup	250 mL
Chopped green onion	1/4 cup	60 mL
Sesame seeds, toasted (see Tip, page 21)	1 tbsp.	15 mL
HONEY SOY DRESSING		
Rice vinegar	1 tbsp.	15 mL
Liquid honey	1 tbsp.	15 mL
Olive oil	2 tsp.	10 mL
Low-sodium soy sauce	2 tsp.	10 mL
Cayenne pepper, just a pinch		
Green leaf lettuce leaves, centre ribs removed (see Tip, page 110)	4	4
Whole wheat flour tortillas (9 inch, 22 cm, diameter)	2	2

Combine first 4 ingredients in medium bowl.

Honey Soy Dressing: Combine first 5 ingredients in small cup. Makes about 3 tbsp. (50 mL) dressing. Drizzle over coleslaw mixture. Toss well.

Place 2 lettuce leaves on each tortilla. Spoon coleslaw mixture over lettuce down centre of tortillas. Fold bottom ends of tortillas over filling. Fold in sides, leaving top ends open. Makes 2 wraps.

1 wrap: 366 Calories; 12.2 g Total Fat (6.0 g Mono, 2.8 g Poly, 2.3 g Sat); 53 mg Cholesterol; 49 g Carbohydrate; 5 g Fibre; 24 g Protein; 533 mg Sodium

Summer Cucumber Sandwiches

For those who like to crunch, this sandwich is for you. A garden-inspired spread that tastes great on all your favourite breads.

Light vegetable cream cheese	1/4 cup	60 mL
Minced radish	1/4 cup	60 mL
Light rye bread slices	4	4
Raw sunflower seeds	1 tsp.	5 mL
Salt, sprinkle		
Pepper, sprinkle		
Slices of English cucumber (with peel)	12	12
Alfalfa sprouts, lightly packed	1/3 cup	75 mL

Mix cream cheese and radish in small bowl. Spread mixture on 4 bread slices.

Sprinkle next 3 ingredients over cream cheese mixture on 2 bread slices.

Arrange cucumber slices and alfalfa sprouts over sunflower seeds. Top with remaining bread slices, cream cheese-side down. Cut sandwiches in half. Serves 2.

1 serving: 242 Calories; 7.2 g Total Fat (0.9 g Mono, 0.6 g Poly, 3.6 g Sat); 20 mg Cholesterol; 35 g Carbohydrate; 4 g Fibre; 8 g Protein; 591 mg Sodium

Variation: Use goat (chèvre) cheese instead of cream cheese.

Cottage Fruit Salad

Just call it fruit salad deluxe! Serve with rye toast or stuff into a lettuce-lined pita pocket to make a tasty fruit sandwich.

1% cottage cheese	1 1/2 cups	375 mL
Small tart apple (such as Granny Smith), diced	1	1
Chopped celery	1/4 cup	60 mL
Dried cranberries	1/4 cup	60 mL
Raisins	2 tbsp.	30 mL
Pecan pieces, toasted (see Tip, page 21)	2 tbsp.	30 mL
Walnut pieces, toasted (see Tip, page 21)	2 tbsp.	30 mL
Liquid honey	1 tbsp.	15 mL
Ground cinnamon	1/2 tsp.	2 mL

Combine all 9 ingredients in medium bowl. Mix well. Makes about 2 1/2 cups (625 mL).

1 cup (250 mL): 301 Calories; 10.0 g Total Fat (3.4 g Mono, 4.3 g Poly, 1.7 g Sat); 6 mg Cholesterol; 37 g Carbohydrate; 4 g Fibre; 19 g Protein; 580 mg Sodium

Beef And Onion Foccacia

Great flavour and texture in this hearty roast beef sandwich. It's sure to become a lunchtime, or anytime, favourite.

Canola oil	2 tsp.	10 mL
Thinly sliced onion	1 1/2 cups	375 mL
Salt, sprinkle		
Pepper, sprinkle		
Focaccia bread (10 inch, 25 cm, diameter)	1	1
Canola oil	1 tsp.	5 mL
Sun-dried tomato pesto	2 tbsp.	30 mL
Salad dressing (or mayonnaise)	2 tbsp.	30 mL
Creamed horseradish	1 tbsp.	15 mL
Balsamic vinegar	1 tsp.	5 mL
Thinly sliced deli roast beef	3/4 lb.	340 g
Thinly sliced Asiago cheese	7 oz.	200 g

Heat first amount of canola oil in large frying pan on medium-high. Add next 3 ingredients. Cook for 5 to 10 minutes, stirring often, until onion is softened.

Meanwhile, cut bread in half horizontally. Brush second amount of canola oil on uncut sides of each half.

Combine next 3 ingredients in small bowl. Spread on cut sides of bread.

Add vinegar to onion mixture. Stir well. Remove from heat.

Layer beef slices, onion mixture and cheese slices, in order given, on bottom half of bread. Cover with top half. Place in same large frying pan. Cook, covered, on medium-low for about 6 minutes until bottom is golden. Turn over. Cook, covered, for about 6 minutes until golden and cheese is melted. Cut into wedges. Serves 4.

1 wedge: 629 Calories; 29.1 g Total Fat (3.7 g Mono, 2.7 g Poly, 10.7 g Sat); 94 mg Cholesterol; 61 g Carbohydrate; 3 g Fibre; 37 g Protein; 1933 mg Sodium

Chipotle Lime Dip

Use this multipurpose dip whenever you want some southwestern zing. Serve with veggies or the chips from Red Pepper Hummus and Chips, page 24. Also try as a spread on Pepper Lime Burgers, page 82, or Polenta Vegetable Stacks, page 109.

Light sour cream	1/2 cup	125 mL
Light mayonnaise	1/2 cup	125 mL
Lime juice	1/4 cup	60 mL
Chopped fresh cilantro or parsley	1/4 cup	60 mL
Minced chipotle peppers in adobo sauce (see Tip, page 76)	1 tbsp.	15 mL
Grated lime zest	2 tsp.	10 mL

Combine all 6 ingredients in small bowl. Makes about 1 1/3 cups (325 mL).

1/4 cup (60 mL): 116 Calories; 9.7 g Total Fat (trace Mono, trace Poly, 2.3 g Sat); 16 mg Cholesterol; 5 g Carbohydrate; trace Fibre; 2 g Protein; 204 mg Sodium

Salmon Salad Bagels

A multi-flavoured filling in a multi-grain bagel—with a little pepper sauce to put a kick in your step. Very nutritious.

Thinly sliced celery	1/4 cup	60 mL
Plain yogurt	2 1/2 tbsp.	37 mL
Raw sunflower seeds	2 tbsp.	30 mL
Green onion, thinly sliced	1	1
Grated lemon zest	1/2 tsp.	2 mL
Dried dillweed	1/2 tsp.	2 mL
Drops of hot pepper sauce	3	3
Can of pink (or red) salmon, drained, skin and round bones removed (see Note)	6 1/2 oz.	184 g
Romaine lettuce leaves, halved	2	2
Multi-grain bagels, split	2	2

Combine first 7 ingredients in small bowl. Add salmon. Mix well.

Place lettuce on bottom halves of bagels. Spoon salmon mixture over lettuce. Place top halves of bagels over salmon mixture. Cut bagels in half. Serves 2.

1 serving: 475 Calories; 8 g Total Fat (0.4 g Mono, 0.7 g Poly, 1.2 g Sat); 68 mg Cholesterol; 69 g Carbohydrate; 12 g Fibre; 38 g Protein; 1000 mg Sodium

Note: Substitute 1 cup (250 mL) of flaked cooked salmon for canned salmon, if you happen to have some left over from a previous meal.

Ham And Chicken Stack

One giant sandwich stacked with enough ham, chicken and vegetables to serve 6! For easier cutting, secure sandwich in 6 places with long picks before cutting into wedges. Looks colossal, tastes colossal!

Herb focaccia bread (10 inch, 25 cm, diameter)	1	1
Olive oil	2 tsp.	10 mL
SWEET MUSTARD MAYO		
Dijon mustard	3 tbsp.	50 mL
Liquid honey	2 tbsp.	30 mL
Light mayonnaise	1 tbsp.	15 mL
Finely chopped fresh rosemary (or 1/8 tsp., 0.5 mL, dried, crushed)	1/2 tsp.	2 mL
FILLING		
Romaine lettuce leaves	4	4
Thin slices of yellow pepper	8	8
Thin slices of tomato	6	6
No-fat deli ham slices (about 4 1/2 oz., 125 g)	5	5
Sliced cooked chicken breast (about 2 small chicken breast halves, cooked)	1 1/4 cups	300 mL

Preheat broiler. Cut focaccia bread in half horizontally. Brush cut sides with olive oil. Place, cut side up, on ungreased baking sheet. Broil on top rack in oven for about 2 minutes until golden. Transfer to cutting surface.

Sweet Mustard Mayo: Combine all 4 ingredients in small bowl. Makes about 6 tbsp. (100 mL) mayo. Spread on toasted focaccia.

Filling: Place lettuce leaves on bottom half of focaccia. Layer remaining 4 ingredients, in order given, over lettuce. Cover with top half of focaccia. Cut into 6 wedges. Serves 6.

1 wedge: 241 Calories; 5.2 g Total Fat (1.6 g Mono, 0.4 g Poly, 0.7 g Sat); 28 mg Cholesterol; 35 g Carbohydrate; 1 g Fibre; 14 g Protein; 596 mg Sodium

Pictured on page 35.

Veggie Clubhouse

With cream cheese, soft whole wheat bread and veggies galore, this triple decker is a triple treat.
To add that deli touch, secure these sandwiches with long, decorative picks.

Light vegetable cream cheese	1 tbsp.	15 mL
Whole wheat bread slice	1	1
Fresh spinach leaves, lightly packed	1/4 cup	60 mL
Tomato slices	3	3
Thin red onion slice, rings separated	1	1
Pepper, sprinkle		
Light vegetable cream cheese	1 tbsp.	15 mL
Whole wheat bread slice	1	1
English cucumber slices	8	8
Yellow (or red) pepper rings	3	3
Avocado slices (about 1/2 avocado)	6	6
Pepper, sprinkle		
Light vegetable cream cheese	1 tbsp.	15 mL
Whole wheat bread slice	1	1

Spread first amount of cream cheese on 1 side of first bread slice. Layer next
3 ingredients, in order given, over cream cheese. Sprinkle with pepper.

Spread second amount of cream cheese on both sides of second bread slice. Place
on top of onion. Layer next 3 ingredients, in order given, over cream cheese. Sprinkle
with pepper.

Spread third amount of cream cheese on 1 side of third bread slice. Place cream
cheese-side down, on top of sandwich. Cut sandwich diagonally into 4 small triangles.
Makes 1 sandwich.

1 sandwich: 452 Calories; 25.6 g Total Fat (1.4 g Mono, 1 g Poly, 6.6 g Sat);
30 mg Cholesterol; 54 g Carbohydrate; 10 g Fibre; 15 g Protein; 698 mg Sodium

Pictured at right.

1. Veggie Clubhouse, above
2. Ham And Chicken Stack, page 33

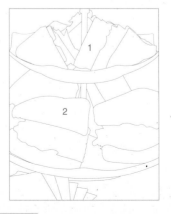

Tomato Bagel Melts

This quick and hearty sandwich is made special with the clever addition of Asiago cheese and olives. For a milder flavour, try the Bocconcini Salad Melts variation.

Whole wheat bagels, split	4	4
Chopped fresh basil	1/4 cup	60 mL
Sliced black olives	1/4 cup	60 mL
Thinly sliced medium tomatoes	2	2
Pepper	1/4 tsp.	1 mL
Grated Asiago cheese	1/2 cup	125 mL

Preheat broiler. Arrange bagel halves, cut side up, on ungreased baking sheet. Broil on top rack in oven for about 2 minutes until lightly golden and toasted. Cover top halves of bagels to keep warm.

Arrange next 3 ingredients on bottom halves of bagels. Sprinkle with pepper.

Sprinkle with cheese. Broil on top rack in oven for 2 to 3 minutes until cheese is melted. Top with remaining bagel halves. Let stand for 1 minute. Press down lightly to squeeze cheese between layers. Cut bagels in half. Makes 4 sandwiches.

1 sandwich: 493 Calories; 16.4 g Total Fat (1.0 g Mono, 0.8 g Poly, 8.0 g Sat); 38 mg Cholesterol; 69 g Carbohydrate; 13 g Fibre; 22 g Protein; 1097 mg Sodium

BOCCONCINI SALAD MELTS Use slices of bocconcini cheese instead of Asiago and sprinkle with a bit more pepper.

1. Balsamic Slaw, page 39
2. Broccoli Orange Salad, page 41
3. Nutty Quinoa Salad, page 38

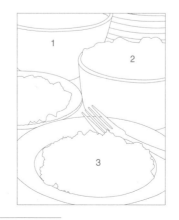

Nutty Quinoa Salad

You'll be nutty about this vegetable-packed salad with a zippy dressing. Quinoa (pronounced KEEN–wah) is a tasty alternative in salads that usually use couscous or bulgur. Find it in the bulk or health food sections of most grocery stores.

SALAD

Water	1 1/2 cups	375 mL
Quinoa, rinsed and drained	3/4 cup	175 mL
Chopped red pepper	1/2 cup	125 mL
Chopped celery	1/2 cup	125 mL
Diced English cucumber	1/2 cup	125 mL
Finely chopped green onion	1/4 cup	60 mL
Chopped fresh cilantro or parsley	2 tbsp.	30 mL
Salt, sprinkle		

NUTTY LIME DRESSING

Chunky peanut butter	3 tbsp.	50 mL
Lime juice	2 tbsp.	30 mL
Rice vinegar	2 tbsp.	30 mL
Low-sodium soy sauce	2 tsp.	10 mL
Garlic clove, minced (or 1/4 tsp., 1 mL, powder)	1	1
Finely grated gingerroot (or 1/2 tsp., 2 mL, ground ginger)	2 tsp.	10 mL
Cayenne pepper	1/8 tsp.	0.5 mL

TOPPING

Chopped salted peanuts	1/3 cup	75 mL

Salad: Combine water and quinoa in medium saucepan. Bring to a boil. Reduce heat to medium-low. Simmer, covered, for about 15 minutes until water is absorbed. Transfer to baking sheet with sides. Spread in thin layer. Chill for 5 to 10 minutes until cool.

Meanwhile, combine next 6 ingredients in medium bowl.

Nutty Lime Dressing: Whisk all 7 ingredients in small bowl until combined. Makes about 1/2 cup (125 mL) dressing. Drizzle over salad. Add quinoa. Mix well.

Topping: Sprinkle with peanuts. Serves 4.

1 serving: 273 Calories; 13.7 g Total Fat (6.3 g Mono, 4.4 g Poly, 2.0 g Sat); 0 mg Cholesterol; 31 g Carbohydrate; 5 g Fibre; 10 g Protein; 256 mg Sodium

Pictured on page 36.

TAHINI LIME DRESSING: Use the same amount of tahini (sesame paste) instead of peanut butter.

Balsamic Slaw

Slaw down and take the time to enjoy this tangy treat. The unique shades of this purple and orange salad will add colour to any entree.

Shredded red cabbage, lightly packed	4 cups	1 L
Can of whole baby beets, drained and grated (see Tip, page 47)	14 oz.	398 mL
Grated carrot	1 1/2 cups	375 mL
Thinly sliced red onion	1/4 cup	60 mL
BALSAMIC DRESSING		
Balsamic vinegar	1/4 cup	60 mL
Olive oil	1/4 cup	60 mL
Chili sauce	2 tbsp.	30 mL
Lemon juice	1 tbsp.	15 mL
Granulated sugar	1 tbsp.	15 mL
Salt	1/8 tsp.	0.5 mL
Pepper	1/8 tsp.	0.5 mL

Put first 4 ingredients into large bowl.

Balsamic Dressing: Whisk all 7 ingredients in small bowl until combined. Makes about 3/4 cup (175 mL) dressing. Drizzle over salad. Toss well. Serves 6.

1 serving: 150 Calories; 9.4 g Total Fat (6.7 g Mono, 0.9 g Poly, 1.3 g Sat); 0 mg Cholesterol; 16 g Carbohydrate; 3 g Fibre; 2 g Protein; 356 mg Sodium

Pictured on page 36.

It's time to get keen on quinoa. It cooks quickly and contains all of the 9 essential amino acids your body needs to build new cells. After cooking, remember to give it a quick rinse to remove any residue that may impart a bitter taste.

Portobellos And Greens

Fresh and summery—both in flavour and appearance. Make this salad a meal by bulking it up with cooked chickpeas or other beans. Grilling the asparagus will enhance its natural flavour.

Portobello mushrooms, stems removed	2	2
Fresh asparagus, trimmed of tough ends	1/2 lb.	225 g
Olive oil	1 1/2 tbsp.	25 mL
Salt, sprinkle		
Pepper, sprinkle		
SUN-DRIED TOMATO DRESSING		
Red wine vinegar	2 tbsp.	30 mL
Sun-dried tomato pesto	1 tbsp.	15 mL
Olive oil	1 tbsp.	15 mL
Balsamic vinegar	1 tbsp.	15 mL
Chopped or torn romaine lettuce, lightly packed	6 cups	1.5 L
Crumbled light feta cheese	1/2 cup	125 mL

Preheat gas barbecue to medium (see Note). Arrange mushrooms and asparagus on large plate. Brush with olive oil. Sprinkle with salt and pepper. Grill mushrooms for about 5 minutes per side until tender. Grill asparagus for 3 to 4 minutes, turning several times, until tender-crisp. Cut mushrooms into bite-size slices. Cut asparagus crosswise into 3 pieces each. Transfer to extra-large bowl. Set aside.

Sun-Dried Tomato Dressing: Whisk all 4 ingredients in small bowl until combined. Makes about 1/3 cup (75 mL) dressing.

Add lettuce and feta cheese to mushroom mixture. Drizzle with dressing. Toss well. Serves 4.

1 serving: 171 Calories; 12.5 g Total Fat (7.2 g Mono, 1.0 g Poly, 2.9 g Sat); 8 mg Cholesterol; 9 g Carbohydrate; 3 g Fibre; 8 g Protein; 305 mg Sodium

Pictured on page 125.

Note: Too cold to barbecue? Mushrooms and asparagus can be placed on a greased broiling pan and broiled on top rack in oven. Broil mushrooms for about 5 minutes per side until tender. Broil asparagus for 3 to 4 minutes, turning several times, until tender-crisp.

Broccoli Orange Salad

The perfect busy-day salad! Easy to make ahead of time because ingredients will stay fresh without dressing for an hour or more. Toss with dressing just before serving.

TANGY ORANGE DRESSING

Frozen concentrated orange juice, thawed	1/4 cup	60 mL
Sesame (or canola) oil	2 tbsp.	30 mL
Rice vinegar	2 tbsp.	30 mL
Dry mustard	1/2 tsp.	2 mL
Salt	1/4 tsp.	1 mL

SALAD

Broccoli florets	4 cups	1 L
Water	1 tbsp.	15 mL
Medium oranges, peeled and cut into 1 inch (2.5 cm) pieces	3	3
Sliced fresh white mushrooms	1 cup	250 mL
Sliced red onion	1/4 cup	60 mL

Tangy Orange Dressing: Whisk first 5 ingredients in small bowl until combined. Makes about 1/2 cup (125 mL) dressing. Set aside.

Salad: Arrange broccoli on large microwave-safe plate. Sprinkle with water. Microwave, covered, on high (100%) for about 2 minutes until broccoli begins to soften and turn bright green. Transfer to large bowl.

Add remaining 3 ingredients. Drizzle with dressing. Toss. Serves 4.

1 serving: 170 Calories; 7.1 g Total Fat (2.7 g Mono, 2.9 g Poly, 1 g Sat); 0 mg Cholesterol; 28 g Carbohydrate; 8 g Fibre; 4 g Protein; 139 mg Sodium

Pictured on page 36.

Instead of an orange, why not go for a mango? Mango is rich in Vitamin C, which is very important in maintaining a healthy immune system. It is also high in dietary fibre and low in calories. When selecting a mango, choose one with a firm, unblemished skin and a sweet, tropical scent at the stem end. A ripe mango will also have a little bit of give when you squeeze it gently.

Apple Carrot Slaw

I'm sure you slaw this coming—an apple coleslaw with a spicy heat. The addition of figs adds a pleasant, chewy sweetness. Best served immediately.

Grated carrot	2 cups	500 mL
Medium tart apples (such as Granny Smith), peeled and grated	2	2
Chopped dried figs	1/4 cup	60 mL
Chopped fresh parsley	1/4 cup	60 mL
Chopped pecans	1/4 cup	60 mL
SPICY ORANGE DRESSING		
Orange juice	1/2 cup	125 mL
Flax (or olive) oil	2 tbsp.	30 mL
Granulated sugar	2 tsp.	10 mL
Ground cinnamon	1/4 tsp.	1 mL
Ground cumin	1/4 tsp.	1 mL
Cayenne pepper	1/8 tsp.	0.5 mL

Combine first 5 ingredients in medium bowl. Toss.

Spicy Orange Dressing: Whisk all 6 ingredients in small bowl until combined. Makes about 2/3 cup (150 mL) dressing. Drizzle over salad. Toss well. Serves 4.

1 serving: 220 Calories; 12.6 g Total Fat (4.4 g Mono, 6.3 g Poly, 1.2 g Sat); 0 mg Cholesterol; 28 g Carbohydrate; 5 g Fibre; 2 g Protein; 42 mg Sodium

Pictured on page 71 and on back cover.

Summer Salad

"In the summertime when the weather is fine…" use fresh raspberries, but when the weather is less than fine frozen will do, too. The goat cheese and raspberries are a heavenly combination.

Spring mix lettuce, lightly packed	6 cups	1.5 L
Fresh (or frozen) raspberries	1 cup	250 mL
Goat (chèvre) cheese, crumbled (see Tip, page 43)	2 1/2 oz.	70 g
Sliced natural almonds, toasted (see Tip, page 21)	1/4 cup	60 mL
SWEET VINAIGRETTE		
Olive (or canola) oil	3 tbsp.	50 mL
White vinegar	2 tbsp.	30 mL
Granulated sugar	2 tbsp.	30 mL
Dry mustard	1 tsp.	5 mL
Salt, sprinkle		
Pepper, sprinkle		

(continued on next page)

Put first 4 ingredients into large bowl.

Sweet Vinaigrette: Whisk all 6 ingredients in small bowl until combined. Makes about 1/3 cup (75 mL) dressing. Drizzle over salad. Toss. Serves 4.

1 serving: 230 Calories; 18.1 g Total Fat (10.2 g Mono, 1.8 g Poly, 4.6 g Sat); 10 mg Cholesterol; 12 g Carbohydrate; 3 g Fibre; 6 g Protein; 83 mg Sodium

Pictured on page 143.

Cool Beets And Beans

Up your dinner's cool factor with this colourful, multi-textured salad tossed with a refreshing orange dressing. Serve with whole grain bread.

Olive (or canola) oil	3 tbsp.	50 mL
Frozen concentrated orange juice, thawed	2 tbsp.	30 mL
Red wine vinegar	1 tbsp.	15 mL
Chopped fresh dill (or 1/2 tsp., 2 mL, dried)	2 tsp.	10 mL
Salt	1/8 tsp.	0.5 mL
Pepper	1/8 tsp.	0.5 mL
Chopped or torn romaine lettuce, lightly packed	3 cups	750 mL
Can of chickpeas (garbanzo beans), rinsed and drained	19 oz.	540 mL
Can of whole baby beets, drained and chopped (see Tip, page 47)	14 oz.	398 mL
Grated carrot	1 cup	250 mL
Salted, roasted shelled pumpkin seeds	1/4 cup	60 mL

Whisk first 6 ingredients in large bowl until combined.

Add remaining 5 ingredients. Toss well. Serves 4.

1 serving: 448 Calories; 20.0 g Total Fat (10.2 g Mono, 5.3 g Poly, 2.9 g Sat); 0 mg Cholesterol; 53 g Carbohydrate; 10 g Fibre; 19 g Protein; 684 mg Sodium

To grate or crumble soft cheese easily, place in the freezer for 15 to 20 minutes until very firm.

Creamy Pasta Salad

Not your ordinary pasta salad! Packed with personality, this twist on a sometimes lacklustre staple is an excellent way to sneak some tofu into your diet. See the variation below for a spicier dressing that is also great as a vegetable dip.

Whole wheat rotini	**2 cups**	**500 mL**
CREAMY TOFU DRESSING		
Soft tofu	1/2 cup	125 mL
Italian seasoning	1 tsp.	5 mL
Dijon mustard	1 tbsp.	15 mL
Lemon juice	1 tbsp.	15 mL
Garlic cloves, minced	1 – 2	1 – 2
Pepper	1/4 tsp.	1 mL
Can of artichoke hearts, drained and chopped	14 oz.	398 mL
Chopped red pepper	3/4 cup	175 mL
Chopped green onion	1/4 cup	60 mL
Pine nuts	1/4 cup	60 mL

Cook pasta in boiling salted water in large uncovered saucepan or Dutch oven for about 10 minutes until tender but firm. Drain. Rinse with cold water. Drain. Transfer to large bowl.

Creamy Tofu Dressing: Meanwhile, combine all 6 ingredients in small bowl. Process with hand blender until smooth. Makes about 3/4 cup (175 mL) dressing.

Add remaining 4 ingredients to pasta. Add dressing. Toss well. Serves 4.

1 serving: 279 Calories; 7.2 g Total Fat (2.3 g Mono, 3.1 g Poly, 1.1 g Sat); 0 mg Cholesterol; 46 g Carbohydrate; 11 g Fibre; 15 g Protein; 209 mg Sodium

Pictured on page 71 and on back cover.

CREAMY CHIPOTLE DRESSING: Add 1 minced chipotle pepper (see Tip, page 76) to Creamy Tofu Dressing.

Bulgur Chicken Salad

The perfect blend of fresh and tangy, this little taste treat does double duty—serve it warm or chilled.

Prepared chicken broth	2 cups	500 mL
Frozen cut green beans	2 cups	500 mL
Bulgur, fine grind	1 cup	250 mL
Chopped cooked chicken	3 cups	750 mL
Chopped red onion	1/2 cup	125 mL
Dried cranberries (or raisins)	1/2 cup	125 mL
Chopped fresh mint (or basil)	1/3 cup	75 mL
Olive oil	1/4 cup	60 mL
Plain yogurt	3 tbsp.	50 mL
Lemon juice	3 tbsp.	50 mL
Salt	1/2 tsp.	2 mL
Pepper	1/4 tsp.	1 mL
Red leaf lettuce leaves	12	12

Measure broth and green beans into medium saucepan. Bring to a boil. Remove from heat.

Add bulgur. Stir. Cover. Let stand for about 20 minutes until broth is absorbed.

Add next 4 ingredients. Stir.

Whisk next 5 ingredients in small bowl until combined. Pour over chicken mixture. Toss.

Arrange lettuce leaves on 6 salad plates. Spoon chicken mixture over lettuce. Serves 6.

1 serving: 355 Calories; 14.9 g Total Fat (8.8 g Mono, 2.1 g Poly, 2.9 g Sat); 54 mg Cholesterol; 32 g Carbohydrate; 5 g Fibre; 23 g Protein; 534 mg Sodium

Instead of adding cooked chicken or beef to a salad, add a juicy grilled portobello mushroom instead. It will give you a satisfying meaty texture without the meat!

Beet And Walnut Salad

This tempting salad beets all others! An uncomplicated salad perfectly enhanced by creamy dressing and a generous amount of walnuts.

CREAMY GOAT CHEESE DRESSING

Light mayonnaise	2 tbsp.	30 mL
Goat (chèvre) cheese, softened	2 tbsp.	30 mL
Orange juice	2 tbsp.	30 mL
Dried dillweed	1/8 tsp.	0.5 mL

SALAD

Mixed salad greens, lightly packed	6 cups	1.5 L
Can of sliced beets, drained and quartered (see Tip, page 47)	14 oz.	398 mL
Walnut halves, toasted (see Tip, page 21)	1 cup	250 mL

Creamy Goat Cheese Dressing: Combine first 4 ingredients in small bowl. Makes about 1/3 cup (75 mL) dressing.

Salad: Combine remaining 3 ingredients in large bowl. Add dressing. Toss well. Serves 4.

1 serving: 249 Calories; 20.1 g Total Fat (2.5 g Mono, 12.0 g Poly, 2.7 g Sat); 5 mg Cholesterol; 15 g Carbohydrate; 6 g Fibre; 7 g Protein; 291 mg Sodium

Lemony White Bean Salad

Crisp romaine all dressed up with juicy tomatoes and soft beans. Use spinach instead of romaine for an extra iron boost.

Can of white kidney beans, rinsed and drained	19 oz.	540 mL
Ranch dressing	1/4 cup	60 mL
Lemon juice	1 tbsp.	15 mL
Grated lemon zest	1 tsp.	5 mL
Chopped or torn romaine lettuce, lightly packed	8 cups	2 L
Grape tomatoes, halved	2/3 cup	150 mL
Thinly sliced red onion	1/4 cup	60 mL

Combine first 4 ingredients in large bowl.

Add remaining 3 ingredients. Toss. Serves 6.

1 serving: 136 Calories; 6.1 g Total Fat (trace Mono, 0.1 g Poly, 0.8 g Sat); 3 mg Cholesterol; 16 g Carbohydrate; 5 g Fibre; 6 g Protein; 132 mg Sodium

Baby Potato Sage Toss

Earthy sage, sweet honey and tangy Dijon coat roasted potatoes and crisp sugar snap peas in this splendid summertime salad that perfectly complements grilled meats.

Baby red potatoes, quartered	1 lb.	454 g
Chopped fresh sage	2 tbsp.	30 mL
Olive oil	1 tbsp.	15 mL
HONEY DIJON DRESSING		
Olive oil	2 tbsp.	30 mL
White vinegar	2 tbsp.	30 mL
Liquid honey	2 tsp.	10 mL
Dijon (or prepared) mustard	1/2 tsp.	2 mL
Chopped or torn green leaf lettuce, lightly packed	4 cups	1 L
Sugar snap peas, trimmed and halved	1 cup	250 mL
Chopped green onion	1/3 cup	75 mL

Preheat oven to 400°F (205°C). Combine first 3 ingredients in large bowl. Toss well. Spread in single layer in ungreased 9 × 13 inch (22 × 33 cm) baking dish. Bake in oven for about 15 minutes until tender.

Honey Dijon Dressing: Meanwhile, whisk all 4 ingredients in small bowl until combined. Makes about 1/4 cup (75 mL) dressing.

Combine remaining 3 ingredients in large bowl. Add potatoes and dressing. Toss well. Serves 4.

1 serving: 231 Calories; 10.5 g Total Fat (7.5 g Mono, 1.0 g Poly, 1.4 g Sat); 0 mg Cholesterol; 30 g Carbohydrate; 4 g Fibre; 4 g Protein; 28 mg Sodium

Pictured on page 54.

Don't get caught red-handed! Wear rubber gloves when handling beets.

Grilled Beef Salad

Daikon, a juicy, long, white Asian radish, has a peppery flavour and crunch that is well-matched with the spicy beef and sesame dressing in this exotic taste treat.

Beef strip loin steak	3/4 lb.	340 g
Chili paste (sambal oelek)	2 tsp.	10 mL
SESAME LIME DRESSING		
Lime juice	1/4 cup	60 mL
Sesame oil	2 tbsp.	30 mL
Low-sodium soy sauce	2 tbsp.	30 mL
Brown sugar, packed	2 tbsp.	30 mL
Garlic cloves, minced	1 – 2	1 – 2
Chopped or torn romaine lettuce, lightly packed	6 cups	1.5 L
Grated daikon radish	1 cup	250 mL
Grated carrot	1/2 cup	125 mL
Coarsely chopped fresh basil	1/2 cup	125 mL

Preheat barbecue to medium-high (see Note). Poke holes in steak with fork. Spread chili paste on each side of steak. Set aside.

Sesame Lime Dressing: Combine next 5 ingredients in small cup. Makes about 1/4 cup (60 mL) dressing.

Arrange remaining 4 ingredients on 4 salad plates. Cook steak on greased grill for 3 to 5 minutes per side until desired doneness. Transfer to cutting board. Let stand for 5 minutes. Cut steak into 1/8 inch (3 mm) wide strips. Arrange strips on each salad. Drizzle with dressing. Serves 4.

1 serving: 304 Calories; 20.1 g Total Fat (8.1 g Mono, 3.4 g Poly, 6.1 g Sat); 47 mg Cholesterol; 12 g Carbohydrate; 1 g Fibre; 19 g Protein; 301 mg Sodium

Pictured on page 53.

Note: Too cold to barbecue? Steak can be placed on a greased broiling pan and broiled on top rack in oven for 3 to 5 minutes per side until desired doneness.

Thai Cucumber Salad

Fresh-tasting with a touch of heat—you would expect nothing less from a Thai salad! Goes great with roasted meats.

English cucumber, peeled, quartered lengthwise and cut diagonally into 1/2 inch (12 mm) pieces	1	1
Medium tomatoes, cut into 8 wedges each and halved	2	2
Green onions, cut into 1/2 inch (12 mm) pieces	4	4
Chopped fresh cilantro	2 tbsp.	30 mL
PEPPY LIME DRESSING		
Lime juice	3 tbsp.	50 mL
Soy sauce	1 tbsp.	15 mL
Granulated sugar	1 tbsp.	15 mL
Cayenne pepper	1/8 tsp.	0.5 mL

Put first 4 ingredients into large bowl.

Peppy Lime Dressing: Whisk all 4 ingredients in small bowl until combined. Makes about 1/4 cup (60 mL) dressing. Drizzle over salad. Toss. Serves 4.

1 serving: 48 Calories; 0.4 g Total Fat (trace Mono, 0.1 g Poly, 0.1 g Sat); 0 mg Cholesterol; 11 g Carbohydrate; 2 g Fibre; 2 g Protein; 339 mg Sodium

Pictured on page 107.

Shrimp Avocado Salad

"Pretty in pink" shrimp top a bed of crisp greens. This attractive salad is sure to please!

Lime juice	1/3 cup	75 mL
Chopped fresh cilantro or parsley	1/4 cup	60 mL
Olive oil	1 tbsp.	15 mL
Jalapeño pepper, finely diced (see Tip, page 59)	1	1
Garlic and herb no-salt seasoning	1 tsp.	5 mL
Water	4 cups	1 L
Garlic and herb no-salt seasoning	1 tsp.	5 mL
Frozen uncooked medium shrimp (peeled and deveined), thawed	1 lb.	454 g
Chopped or torn romaine lettuce, lightly packed	4 cups	1 L
Diced fresh tomato	1 cup	250 mL
Medium avocados, cut into 8 slices each	2	2
Sliced green onion	1/4 cup	60 mL

Combine first 5 ingredients in medium bowl.

Combine water and seasoning in medium saucepan. Bring to a boil. Add shrimp. Cook for about 2 minutes until shrimp turn pink. Drain. Rinse with cold water. Drain. Add to lime juice mixture. Stir.

Arrange next 3 ingredients, in order given, on 4 individual serving plates. Spoon shrimp mixture over top.

Sprinkle with green onion. Serves 4.

1 serving: 301 Calories; 20.6 g Total Fat (2.8 g Mono, 1.2 g Poly, 2.1 g Sat); 172 mg Cholesterol; 12 g Carbohydrate; 4.5 g Fibre; 27 g Protein; 180 mg Sodium

Pictured on page 53.

Lean Chef's Salad

Eat enough of this salad and you'll be a lean chef too! Consider it a full meal deal with plenty of meat, cheese and eggs.

Chopped or torn romaine lettuce, lightly packed	4 cups	1 L
Green onion, sliced	1	1
Cherry tomatoes, halved	8	8
Fat-free Italian dressing	1/3 cup	75 mL
Pepper, sprinkle		
Diced light medium Cheddar cheese	1/2 cup	125 mL
No-fat deli ham slices, cut into thin strips	3 oz.	85 g
Lean deli smoked turkey breast slices, cut into thin strips	3 oz.	85 g
Large hard-cooked eggs, chopped (see Note)	2	2
Fat-free Italian dressing (optional)	2 tbsp.	30 mL

Put first 3 ingredients into large bowl. Drizzle with first amount of dressing. Sprinkle with pepper. Toss well. Arrange on two individual serving plates.

Arrange next 3 ingredients over lettuce mixture.

Sprinkle eggs over top.

Serve with second amount of dressing on the side. Serves 2.

1 serving: 328 Calories; 14.9 g Total Fat (2.2 g Mono, 1.0 g Poly, 7.3 g Sat); 277 mg Cholesterol; 16 g Carbohydrate; 3 g Fibre; 36 g Protein; 1878 mg Sodium

Pictured on page 53.

Note: Reserve 1 cooked egg yolk before chopping eggs. Use to garnish assembled salads by pressing egg yolk with a spoon through a sieve held over the salad.

Curried Tofu Spinach Salad

It's yellow—but it's sure not mellow! Bright yellow cubes of curried tofu are sure to stand out in this uniquely spicy and sweet flavour combination.

Curry powder	1 tbsp.	15 mL
Cornstarch	1 tbsp.	15 mL
Salt	1 tsp.	5 mL
Package of firm tofu, cut into 1/2 inch (12 mm) cubes	12 1/4 oz.	350 g
Olive oil	1 tbsp.	15 mL
MANGO DRESSING		
Mango chutney, larger pieces chopped	1/4 cup	60 mL
Lime juice	2 tbsp.	30 mL
Olive oil	1 tbsp.	15 mL
Fresh spinach leaves, lightly packed	5 cups	1.25 L
Sliced natural almonds, toasted (see Tip, page 21)	2 tbsp.	30 mL

Combine first 3 ingredients in shallow bowl.

Pat tofu dry with paper towel. Add to curry mixture. Toss until coated.

Heat olive oil in medium frying pan on medium. Add tofu. Cook for about 8 minutes, stirring occasionally, until golden and crisp on outside.

Mango Dressing: Meanwhile, whisk first 3 ingredients in large bowl until combined. Makes about 1/2 cup (125 mL) dressing.

Add spinach. Toss well. Arrange on 4 salad plates.

Sprinkle with almonds and tofu. Serves 4.

1 serving: 188 Calories; 11.2 g Total Fat (6.5 g Mono, 2.4 g Poly, 1.5 g Sat); 0 mg Cholesterol; 15 g Carbohydrate; 3 g Fibre; 9 g Protein; 676 mg Sodium

1. Grilled Beef Salad, page 48
2. Shrimp Avocado Salad, page 50
3. Lean Chef's Salad, page 51

Autumn Pumpkin Soup

The perfect blend of pumpkin and spices! This thick pumpkin and apple soup is just what you need on a chilly fall day. Serve with slices of whole wheat bread.

Olive (or canola) oil	2 tsp.	10 mL
Chopped onion	1 1/2 cups	375 mL
Low-sodium prepared chicken (or vegetable) broth	4 cups	1 L
Can of pure pumpkin (no spices)	14 oz.	398 mL
Unsweetened applesauce	1 cup	250 mL
Bay leaf	1	1
Chopped fresh thyme (or 1/2 tsp., 2 mL, dried)	2 tsp.	10 mL
Lemon pepper	1 tsp.	5 mL
Salt, sprinkle		

Heat olive oil in large saucepan on medium. Add onion. Cook for 5 to 10 minutes, stirring occasionally, until softened and starting to brown.

Add remaining 7 ingredients. Stir. Bring to a boil. Reduce heat to medium-low. Simmer, partially covered, for 10 minutes to blend flavours. Discard bay leaf. Makes about 7 cups (1.75 L).

1 cup (250 mL): 72 Calories; 1.9 g Total Fat (1.2 g Mono, 0.2 g Poly, 0.4 g Sat); 0 mg Cholesterol; 13 g Carbohydrate; 3 g Fibre; 2 g Protein; 42 mg Sodium

Pictured at left.

1. Autumn Pumpkin Soup, above
2. Baby Potato Sage Toss, page 47
3. Cranberry-Topped Chicken, page 92

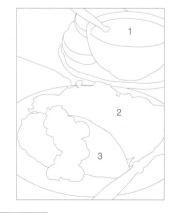

Potato Pear Soup

Nothing com-pears! Different and delicious—not your everyday potato soup. Leek and lemon enhance sweet pear to give this soup an interesting elegance.

Olive oil	2 tsp.	10 mL
Chopped peeled pear	3 cups	750 mL
Sliced leek (white part only)	1 cup	250 mL
Chopped peeled potato	3 cups	750 mL
Low-sodium prepared chicken broth	3 cups	750 mL
Pepper	1/8 tsp.	0.5 mL
Lemon juice	1 tbsp.	15 mL
Grated lemon zest	1/2 tsp.	2 mL

Heat olive oil in large saucepan on medium. Add pear and leek. Cook for about 5 minutes, stirring often, until leek is softened.

Add next 3 ingredients. Stir. Bring to a boil. Reduce heat to medium-low. Simmer, covered, for about 10 minutes until potato is soft. Carefully process with hand blender or in blender until smooth.

Stir in lemon juice and lemon zest. Makes about 6 cups (1.5 L).

1 cup (250 mL): 148 Calories; 2.1 g Total Fat (1.3 g Mono, 0.3 g Poly, 0.3 g Sat); 0 mg Cholesterol; 31 g Carbohydrate; 4 g Fibre; 3 g Protein; 26 mg Sodium

Avocado Gazpacho

The soup is chilled but the heat's still in the spicy broth that surrounds chunks of cool avocado. Chilled vegetable cocktail ensures soup is cold and ready to serve. Try it with chopped fresh cilantro.

Low-sodium vegetable cocktail juice, chilled	2 cups	500 mL
Coarsely chopped green pepper	1/2 cup	125 mL
Coarsely chopped English cucumber	1/2 cup	125 mL
Coarsely chopped green onion	2 tbsp.	30 mL
Lemon juice	2 tbsp.	30 mL
Red wine vinegar	2 tsp.	10 mL
Worcestershire sauce	1/2 tsp.	2 mL
Hot pepper sauce	1/4 tsp.	1 mL
Diced avocado	1 cup	250 mL

Process first 8 ingredients in blender or food processor until smooth. Pour into 2 serving bowls. Makes about 3 cups (750 mL) soup.

Spoon avocado into bowls. Stir. Serves 2.

1 serving: 189 Calories; 11.1 g Total Fat (7.4 g Mono, 1.4 g Poly, 1.6 g Sat); trace Cholesterol; 22 g Carbohydrate; 8 g Fibre; 3 g Protein; 174 mg Sodium

Curry Chicken Vegetable Soup

Perfect for a cold wintry day! A quick and warming soup filled with chicken and vegetables. Tastes just like mulligatawny without the rice. Curry lovers can add a smidgeon more to increase the heat level.

Canola oil	1 1/2 tsp.	7 mL
Finely chopped celery	3/4 cup	175 mL
Finely chopped onion	3/4 cup	175 mL
Medium cooking apple (such as McIntosh), peeled and grated	1	1
All-purpose flour	2 tbsp.	30 mL
Curry powder	1 tsp.	5 mL
Salt	1/4 tsp.	1 mL
Cayenne pepper	1/8 tsp.	0.5 mL
Low-sodium prepared chicken broth	5 cups	1.25 L
Chopped cooked chicken	1 1/2 cups	375 mL
Frozen mixed vegetables	1 1/2 cups	375 mL
Lemon juice	1 tbsp.	15 mL

Heat canola oil in large saucepan on medium. Add celery and onion. Cook for about 3 minutes, stirring occasionally, until starting to soften.

Add next 5 ingredients. Heat and stir for 1 minute.

Add 1 cup (250 mL) broth. Heat and stir until boiling and thickened. Add remaining broth, chicken and vegetables. Bring to a boil. Reduce heat to medium-low. Simmer, uncovered, for 8 minutes to blend flavours.

Add lemon juice. Stir. Makes about 7 1/2 cups (1.9 L).

1 cup (250 mL): 94 Calories; 2.7 g Total Fat (1.2 g Mono, 0.7 g Poly, 0.6 g Sat); 14 mg Cholesterol; 10 g Carbohydrate; 2 g Fibre; 7 g Protein; 149 mg Sodium

Sweet Pea Soup

Not to worry, we don't expect you to sup on your garden flora—it's the peas that impart a sweet flavour. Great on its own, but sensational with the creamy Minted Yogurt topping.

Olive (or canola) oil	2 tsp.	10 mL
Finely chopped green onion	1/2 cup	125 mL
Garlic clove, minced (or 1/4 tsp., 1 mL, powder)	1	1
Frozen peas	2 cups	500 mL
Chopped or torn green leaf lettuce, lightly packed	1 1/2 cups	375 mL
Low-sodium prepared chicken (or vegetable) broth	3 cups	750 mL
Pepper	1/4 tsp.	1 mL
Frozen peas	1/2 cup	125 mL
MINTED YOGURT		
Plain yogurt	1/3 cup	75 mL
Chopped fresh mint	2 tbsp.	30 mL

Heat olive oil in medium saucepan on medium. Add green onion and garlic. Cook for about 5 minutes, stirring occasionally, until green onion is softened.

Add first amount of peas and lettuce. Heat and stir for 1 minute. Add broth and pepper. Bring to a boil. Reduce heat to medium-low. Simmer for 3 to 5 minutes, stirring occasionally, until peas are tender. Carefully process with hand blender or in blender until smooth.

Add second amount of peas. Heat and stir on medium for about 2 minutes until peas are tender. Makes about 4 1/2 cups (1.1 L) soup.

Minted Yogurt: Combine yogurt and mint in small bowl. Makes about 6 tbsp. (100 mL) yogurt. Spoon onto individual servings. Serves 4.

1 serving: 126 Calories; 3.8 g Total Fat (2.1 g Mono, 0.5 g Poly, 0.9 g Sat); 3 mg Cholesterol; 16 g Carbohydrate; 5 g Fibre; 8 g Protein; 144 mg Sodium

Pictured on page 143.

Zucchini Dill Soup

Kitchen overflowing with a fall harvest of zucchini? Put that bounty to good use in this easy-to-make, creamy soup with a subtle flavouring of dill. Garnish with fresh dill sprigs.

Canola oil	2 tsp.	10 mL
Sliced zucchini	3 cups	750 mL
Chopped onion	3/4 cup	175 mL
Sliced celery	3/4 cup	175 mL
All-purpose flour	2 tbsp.	30 mL
Dried dillweed	1/2 tsp.	2 mL
Pepper	1/8 tsp.	0.5 mL
Low-sodium prepared chicken broth	2 cups	500 mL
Milk	1 1/2 cups	375 mL

Heat canola oil in large saucepan on medium-high. Add next 3 ingredients. Cook for about 8 minutes, stirring often, until onion and celery are softened and starting to brown.

Sprinkle next 3 ingredients over zucchini mixture. Heat and stir for 1 minute.

Add 1 cup (250 mL) broth. Heat and stir until boiling and thickened. Add remaining broth and milk. Bring to a boil. Reduce heat to medium-low. Simmer for 5 minutes to blend flavours. Carefully process with hand blender or in blender until smooth. Makes about 5 cups (1.25 L).

1 cup (250 mL): 93 Calories; 3.2 g Total Fat (1.5 g Mono, 0.7 g Poly, 0.8 g Sat); 3 mg Cholesterol; 12 g Carbohydrate; 1 g Fibre; 5 g Protein; 79 mg Sodium

Hot peppers contain capsaicin in the seeds and ribs. Removing the seeds and ribs will reduce the heat. Wear rubber gloves when handling hot peppers and avoid touching your eyes. Wash your hands well afterwards.

Pepper Power Soup

This tasty treat will give you all the "souper powers" you need to get through your day! Loaded with flavour and hearty vegetables.

Olive oil	2 tsp.	10 mL
Chopped red pepper	2 cups	500 mL
Chopped onion	1 cup	250 mL
Finely diced jalapeño pepper (see Tip, page 59)	1 tbsp.	15 mL
Garlic cloves, minced	2	2
Low-sodium prepared chicken broth	6 cups	1.5 L
Frozen kernel corn	2 cups	500 mL
Chopped kale leaves, lightly packed (see Tip, page 110)	2 cups	500 mL
Can of diced tomatoes (with juice)	14 oz.	398 mL
Lime juice	2 tbsp.	30 mL
Chopped fresh cilantro or parsley	3 tbsp.	50 mL

Heat olive oil in large saucepan or Dutch oven on medium. Add next 4 ingredients. Cook for about 5 minutes, stirring occasionally, until red pepper is softened.

Add next 5 ingredients. Stir. Bring to a boil. Reduce heat to medium-low. Simmer, partially covered, for about 15 minutes until kale is tender.

Add cilantro. Stir. Makes about 10 1/2 cups (2.6 L).

1 cup (250 mL): 75 Calories; 1.7 g Total Fat (0.9 g Mono, 0.4 g Poly, 0.3 g Sat); 0 mg Cholesterol; 14 g Carbohydrate; 2 g Fibre; 4 g Protein; 132 mg Sodium

Variation: Use same amount of chopped fresh spinach leaves instead of chopped kale. Reduce simmering time to 5 minutes.

Let's raise our glasses and make a toast to red wine. Drinking it in moderation actually improves cardiovascular health (how often can you say that about something many of us consider an indulgence?). If you choose not to imbibe alcohol, opt for a non-alcoholic red wine—it offers similar benefits.

Quick Carrot Soup

If carrots help your vision, then it's easy to see that this soup is an excellent choice! Orange juice and honey make this treat all the sweeter.

Canola (or olive) oil	2 tsp.	10 mL
Baby carrots, coarsely chopped	1 lb.	454 g
Chopped onion	1/2 cup	125 mL
Low-sodium prepared chicken broth	3 cups	750 mL
Chopped fresh dill (or 3/4 tsp., 4 mL, dried)	1 tbsp.	15 mL
No-salt seasoning	1 1/2 tsp.	7 mL
Orange juice	1/4 cup	60 mL
Chopped fresh dill (or 3/4 tsp., 4 mL, dried)	1 tbsp.	15 mL
Liquid honey	1 tbsp.	15 mL

Heat canola oil in large saucepan on medium. Add carrot and onion. Cook for about 10 minutes, stirring occasionally, until onion is softened.

Add next 3 ingredients. Bring to a boil. Reduce heat to medium-low. Simmer, uncovered, for about 5 minutes until carrot is tender. Carefully process with hand blender or in blender until smooth.

Add remaining 3 ingredients. Cook on medium for about 1 minute, stirring occasionally, until heated through. Makes about 4 1/2 cups (1.1 L).

1 cup (250 mL): 107 Calories; 2.5 g Total Fat (1.4 g Mono, 0.7 g Poly, 0.3 g Sat); 0 mg Cholesterol; 19 g Carbohydrate; 3 g Fibre; 3 g Protein; 78 mg Sodium

Chicken Yam Chowder

Your family will be yammering for more! Yams replace traditional potatoes in this chicken corn chowder with a southwestern twist.

Large unpeeled yam (or sweet potato) **(about 1 1/2 lbs., 680g), see Note**	1	1
Canola oil	2 tsp.	10 mL
Diced onion	1 cup	250 mL
Diced green pepper	1 cup	250 mL
Low-sodium prepared chicken broth	4 cups	1 L
Chopped cooked chicken	2 cups	500 mL
Frozen kernel corn	1 cup	250 mL
Chunky salsa	1/2 cup	125 mL
Chopped fresh oregano (or 1/4 tsp., 1 mL, dried)	1 tsp.	5 mL
No-salt seasoning	1 tsp.	5 mL
Can of evaporated milk	5 1/2 oz.	160 mL

Cut yam in half lengthwise. Microwave, covered, on high (100%), for about 8 minutes until tender. Remove pulp to medium bowl. Mash with fork. Discard peel.

Meanwhile, heat canola oil in large saucepan on medium. Add onion and green pepper. Cook for 5 to 10 minutes, stirring occasionally, until softened.

Add yam and next 6 ingredients. Bring to a boil. Reduce heat to medium. Boil gently, partially covered, for 5 minutes to blend flavours.

Add evaporated milk. Heat and stir until hot, but not boiling. Makes about 9 cups (2.25 L).

1 cup (250 mL): 201 Calories; 5.4 g Total Fat (2.1 g Mono, 1.1 g Poly, 1.8 g Sat); 32 mg Cholesterol; 26 g Carbohydrate; 4 g Fibre; 13 g Protein; 184 mg Sodium

Note: You can make this soup even more quickly by using 3 cups (750 mL) of mashed canned sweet potato. The microwave cooking time for the yam is then eliminated.

Turkey Minestrone

A hearty, meal-style soup. Not too spicy, but very flavourful. Freeze in individual portions and take for lunch.

Olive oil	2 tsp.	10 mL
Extra-lean ground turkey	3/4 lb.	340 g
Finely chopped onion	3/4 cup	175 mL
Finely chopped celery	3/4 cup	175 mL
Garlic cloves, minced (or 1/2 tsp., 2 mL, powder)	2	2
Italian seasoning	1 tsp.	5 mL
Low-sodium prepared chicken broth	6 cups	1.5 L
Can of white kidney beans, rinsed and drained	19 oz.	540 mL
Can of diced tomatoes (with juice)	14 oz.	398 mL
Whole wheat elbow macaroni	1/2 cup	125 mL
Frozen cut green beans	1 cup	250 mL
Chopped fresh oregano (or 3/4 tsp., 4 mL, dried)	1 tbsp.	15 mL
Chopped fresh sage (or 1/4 tsp., 1 mL, dried)	1 1/2 tsp.	7 mL

Heat olive oil in large saucepan or Dutch oven on medium-high. Add next 5 ingredients. Scramble-fry for 5 to 10 minutes until turkey is no longer pink and vegetables are tender.

Add next 4 ingredients. Bring to a boil. Reduce heat to medium. Boil gently, partially covered, for 8 to 10 minutes, stirring occasionally, until macaroni is tender but firm.

Add remaining 3 ingredients. Cook for about 2 minutes until beans are tender-crisp. Makes about 10 cups (2.5 L).

1 cup (250 mL): 143 Calories; 4.0 g Total Fat (0.9 g Mono, 0.2 g Poly, 0.9 g Sat); 19 mg Cholesterol; 16 g Carbohydrate; 3 g Fibre; 12 g Protein; 199 mg Sodium

 Tomatoes are a great source of lycopene, a powerful antioxidant. And believe it or not, lycopene is actually more potent when the tomatoes are cooked.

Curried Vegetable Soup

This is one curry that's ready in a hurry—and will disappear in a hurry, too! This thick puréed soup with a medium level of curry heat is nicely balanced with sweet vegetables.

Canola oil	2 tsp.	10 mL
Chopped onion	1 cup	250 mL
Chopped carrot	1 cup	250 mL
Chopped celery	1 cup	250 mL
Granulated sugar	4 tsp.	20 mL
Curry powder	2 tsp.	10 mL
Garlic cloves, minced (or 1/2 tsp., 2 mL, powder)	2	2
Prepared vegetable (or chicken) broth	4 cups	1 L
Grated zucchini	2 cups	500 mL
Grated peeled potato	1 cup	250 mL
Salt	1/4 tsp.	1 mL
Pepper	1/4 tsp.	1 mL
Plain yogurt	1/2 cup	125 mL

Sliced green onion, for garnish

Heat canola oil in large saucepan on medium-high. Add next 3 ingredients. Cook for about 3 minutes, stirring often, until vegetables start to soften.

Add next 3 ingredients. Heat and stir for about 1 minute until fragrant.

Add next 5 ingredients. Stir. Bring to a boil. Reduce heat to medium-low. Simmer, covered, for about 10 minutes until vegetables are soft. Carefully process with hand blender or in blender until smooth.

Add yogurt. Stir.

Garnish with green onion. Makes about 7 1/2 cups (1.9 L).

1 cup (250 mL): 75 Calories; 2.0 g Total Fat (0.9 g Mono, 0.5 g Poly, 0.5 g Sat); 2 mg Cholesterol; 13 g Carbohydrate; 2 g Fibre; 2 g Protein; 602 mg Sodium

Chicken Bean Soup

There's certainly nothing wrong with being full of beans—when you're talking about a soup! This veggie-packed chicken soup has just a hint of cayenne heat. Perfect when you're feeling under the weather.

Olive oil	**2 tsp.**	**10 mL**
Chopped onion	**1 cup**	**250 mL**
Chopped carrot	**2/3 cup**	**150 mL**
Chopped celery	**1/2 cup**	**125 mL**
Low-sodium prepared chicken broth	**8 cups**	**2 L**
Diced peeled potato	**1 1/2 cups**	**375 mL**
Paprika	**1 1/2 tsp.**	**7 mL**
Cayenne pepper, sprinkle		
Can of navy beans, rinsed and drained	**14 oz.**	**398 mL**
Chopped cooked chicken	**1 cup**	**250 mL**

Heat olive oil in large saucepan or Dutch oven on medium-high. Add next 3 ingredients. Cook for about 5 minutes, stirring often, until onion starts to brown.

Add next 4 ingredients. Stir. Bring to a boil. Reduce heat to medium. Boil gently, partially covered, for about 10 minutes until potato is softened.

Add beans and chicken. Stir. Cook for about 2 minutes until heated through. Makes about 10 cups (2.5 L).

1 cup (250 mL): 135 Calories; 2.7 g Total Fat (1.3 g Mono, 0.6 g Poly, 0.6 g Sat); 11 mg Cholesterol; 19 g Carbohydrate; 4 g Fibre; 10 g Protein; 145 mg Sodium

Speedy Beef Ragout

With just a little thyme, you'll have an attractive and appetizing stew! Serve with crusty rolls or slices of whole wheat French bread.

All-purpose flour	2 tbsp.	30 mL
Seasoned salt	1/2 tsp.	2 mL
Pepper	1 tsp.	5 mL
Beef stir-fry strips	1 lb.	454 g
Canola oil	1 tbsp.	15 mL
Canola oil	1 tsp.	5 mL
Sliced fresh white mushrooms	2 cups	500 mL
Chopped onion	1 cup	250 mL
Thinly sliced carrot	3/4 cup	175 mL
Garlic cloves, minced (or 1/2 tsp., 2 mL, powder)	2	2
Dried thyme	1 tsp.	5 mL
All-purpose flour	1 tsp.	5 mL
Prepared beef broth	1 1/2 cups	375 mL
Red wine vinegar	1 tbsp.	15 mL
Chopped fresh parsley	2 tbsp.	30 mL

Measure first 3 ingredients into large resealable freezer bag. Add beef. Seal bag. Toss until coated.

Heat first amount of canola oil in large frying pan on medium-high. Add beef. Cook for 3 to 4 minutes, stirring often, until browned. Transfer to medium bowl. Cover to keep warm.

Heat second amount of canola oil in same frying pan. Add next 5 ingredients. Cook for about 2 minutes, stirring occasionally, until vegetables start to soften.

Add second amount of flour. Heat and stir for 1 minute.

Add broth and vinegar. Stir. Bring to a boil. Reduce heat to medium. Boil gently, covered, for about 10 minutes until vegetables are tender. Add beef. Heat and stir for 1 to 2 minutes until heated through. Transfer to large serving dish.

Sprinkle with parsley. Makes about 4 cups (1 L).

1 cup (250 mL): 356 Calories; 22.1 g Total Fat (10.1 g Mono, 2.1 g Poly, 7.4 g Sat); 62 mg Cholesterol; 12 g Carbohydrate; 2 g Fibre; 27 g Protein; 515 mg Sodium

Ginger Beef

The usual deep-fried breading is eliminated in this unique version of the takeout staple—but fear not, it's just as tasty.

Water	2 1/4 cups	550 mL
Converted white rice	1 cup	250 mL
Salt (optional)	1/4 tsp.	1 mL
Prepared beef broth	1/4 cup	60 mL
Medium sherry	2 tbsp.	30 mL
Soy sauce	2 tbsp.	30 mL
Cornstarch	1 tbsp.	15 mL
Finely grated gingerroot	1 tbsp.	15 mL
Brown sugar, packed	1 tbsp.	15 mL
Garlic clove, minced	1	1
Dried crushed chilies	1/4 tsp.	1 mL
Canola oil	2 tsp.	10 mL
Beef stir-fry strips	1 lb.	454 g
Sliced onion	1/2 cup	125 mL
Bag of frozen California mixed vegetables, thawed (see Tip, below)	1 lb.	454 g

Sesame seeds, for garnish

Measure first 3 ingredients into medium saucepan. Bring to a boil. Reduce heat to medium-low. Simmer, covered, for about 20 minutes, without stirring, until water is absorbed and rice is tender.

Meanwhile, combine next 8 ingredients in small bowl. Set aside.

Heat wok or large frying pan on medium-high until very hot. Add canola oil. Add beef and onion. Stir-fry for 4 minutes.

Add vegetables and broth mixture. Stir-fry for about 3 minutes until vegetables are tender-crisp and sauce is boiling and thickened. Fluff rice with fork. Spoon into 4 individual serving bowls. Spoon beef mixture over rice.

Garnish with sesame seeds. Serves 4.

1 serving: 515 Calories; 19.8 g Total Fat (8.8 g Mono, 1.5 g Poly, 7.2 g Sat); 62 mg Cholesterol; 52 g Carbohydrate; 4 g Fibre; 30 g Protein; 597 mg Sodium

To quickly thaw frozen vegetables, rinse under cool water or defrost in the microwave.

Beef Bourguignon Patties

You're never bourgeois when you're eating bourguignon (pronounced boor-gee-NYON)! You'll feel simply aristocratic when you nosh on these patties in a delicious mushroom and wine sauce. Serve with egg noodles or mashed potatoes.

Egg white (large)	1	1
Fine dry bread crumbs	3/4 cup	175 mL
Natural wheat bran	1/4 cup	60 mL
Dijon mustard	2 tbsp.	30 mL
Pepper	1/4 tsp.	1 mL
Extra-lean (or lean) ground beef	1 lb.	454 g
Canola oil	2 tsp.	10 mL
Sliced fresh white mushrooms	1 cup	250 mL
Finely chopped onion	1/4 cup	60 mL
Dry (or alcohol-free) red wine	1/2 cup	125 mL
Low-sodium prepared beef broth	1 cup	250 mL
Tomato paste (see Tip, page 83)	1 tbsp.	15 mL
Sprig of fresh rosemary	1/2	1/2
Sprig of fresh thyme	1	1
Low-sodium prepared beef broth	2 tbsp.	30 mL
All-purpose flour	2 tsp.	10 mL

Preheat broiler. Combine first 5 ingredients in large bowl. Add beef. Mix well. Divide into 4 equal portions. Shape into 1/2 inch (12 mm) thick patties. Place on greased broiling pan. Broil on centre rack in oven for about 5 minutes per side until fully cooked, and internal temperature of beef reaches 160°F (71°C).

Meanwhile, heat canola oil in large frying pan on medium-high. Add mushrooms and onion. Cook for about 4 minutes, stirring occasionally, until starting to turn golden.

Add wine. Stir. Reduce heat to medium.

Stir in next 4 ingredients. Boil gently, uncovered, for 5 minutes to blend flavours.

Stir second amount of beef broth and flour in small cup until smooth. Add to mushroom mixture. Heat and stir for about 2 minutes until sauce is boiling and thickened. Add patties. Cook for 2 to 3 minutes until heated through. Discard sprigs of rosemary and thyme. Serves 4.

1 serving: 288 Calories; 8.1 g Total Fat (3.9 g Mono, 1.5 g Poly, 2.0 g Sat); 60 mg Cholesterol; 21 g Carbohydrate; 2.5 g Fibre; 28 g Protein; 363 mg Sodium

Mushroom Steak Sandwiches

You'll be strong to the finish when you sneak in your spinach (into this yummy deli-style sandwich).
A uniquely upscale take on an old favourite.

Sliced fresh white mushrooms	2 cups	500 mL
Garlic clove, minced (or 1/4 tsp., 1 mL, powder)	1	1
Montreal steak spice	1/4 tsp.	1 mL
Montreal steak spice	1/2 tsp.	2 mL
Beef strip loin steak	1 lb.	454 g
Light mayonnaise	2 tbsp.	30 mL
Sesame (or canola) oil	1 tbsp.	15 mL
Finely grated gingerroot (or 1/8 tsp., 0.5 mL, ground ginger)	1/2 tsp.	2 mL
Chopped fresh spinach leaves, lightly packed	2 cups	500 mL
Whole wheat kaiser rolls, split	4	4

Preheat gas barbecue to medium-high. Place mushrooms and garlic on 18 inch (45 cm) long sheet of heavy-duty (or double layer of regular) foil. Sprinkle with first amount of steak spice. Fold edges of foil together over mushrooms to enclose. Fold ends to seal completely. Place on grill.

Sprinkle second amount of steak spice on steak. Cook on greased grill for 4 to 5 minutes per side until desired doneness. Transfer to cutting board. Let stand for 5 minutes. Cut steak crosswise into 1/8 inch (3 mm) slices. Remove mushroom packet from grill.

Meanwhile, combine next 3 ingredients in small bowl. Add spinach. Toss.

Arrange spinach mixture on bottom halves of rolls. Arrange steak slices over spinach. Spoon mushrooms over steak. Cover with top halves of rolls. Makes 4 sandwiches.

1 sandwich: 494 Calories; 29.0 g Total Fat (10.8 g Mono, 3.4 g Poly, 9.6 g Sat); 79 mg Cholesterol; 32 g Carbohydrate; 5 g Fibre; 28 g Protein; 534 mg Sodium

Pictured on page 71 and on back cover.

Moroccan Steaks

Grilled steaks with an exotic flair. Cinnamon, cumin and olives make this dish de-lish!

Orange juice	3 tbsp.	50 mL
Tomato paste (see Tip, page 83)	1 tbsp.	15 mL
Olive oil	1 tbsp.	15 mL
Garlic powder	1/2 tsp.	2 mL
Ground cinnamon	1/2 tsp.	2 mL
Ground cumin	1/2 tsp.	2 mL
Beef strip loin steaks, halved crosswise (about 8 oz., 225 g, each)	2	2
Large red peppers, cut into 1/2 inch (12 mm) rings	2	2
Salt, sprinkle		
Pepper, sprinkle		
Can of sliced black olives, drained	4 1/2 oz.	125 mL

Preheat gas barbecue to medium-high (see Note). Combine first 6 ingredients in small cup.

Brush orange juice mixture on 1 side of steaks and both sides of red pepper. Sprinkle steaks with salt and pepper. Cook steaks and red pepper on greased grill for 4 to 6 minutes per side, brushing once with remaining orange juice mixture, until desired doneness. Transfer steaks to serving plate.

Chop red pepper. Add to olives in small bowl. Stir. Spoon over steaks. Serves 4.

1 serving: 352 Calories; 24.1 g Total Fat (12.3 g Mono, 1.4 g Poly, 7.8 g Sat); 62 mg Cholesterol; 10 g Carbohydrate; 3 g Fibre; 25 g Protein; 344 mg Sodium

Note: Too cold to barbecue? Steaks and red pepper can be placed on a greased broiling pan and broiled on top rack in oven for 4 to 6 minutes per side until steaks and red pepper reach desired doneness.

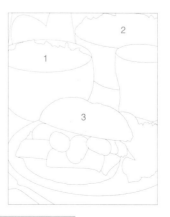

1. Apple Carrot Slaw, page 42
2. Creamy Pasta Salad, page 44
3. Mushroom Steak Sandwiches, page 69

Thai Beef Curry

Thai-up dinner in no time with this impressive curry. Long on taste and short on cooking time.

Canola oil	2 tsp.	10 mL
Thinly sliced beef top sirloin steak	1 lb.	454 g
Green onions, cut diagonally into 1 inch (2.5 cm) slices	3	3
Finely grated gingerroot	1 tbsp.	15 mL
Garlic cloves, minced (or 1/2 tsp., 2 mL, powder)	2	2
Cans of cut sweet potatoes (19 oz., 540 mL, each), drained	2	2
Can of diced tomatoes, drained	14 oz.	398 mL
Can of light coconut milk	14 oz.	398 mL
Brown sugar, packed	2 tbsp.	30 mL
Grated lime zest (see Tip, page 141)	1 tbsp.	15 mL
Red curry paste	1 tsp.	5 mL
Lime juice	1 tbsp.	15 mL

Heat canola oil in large frying pan on medium-high. Add next 4 ingredients. Stir-fry for 3 to 5 minutes until beef is starting to brown.

Add next 6 ingredients. Stir. Bring to a boil. Reduce heat to medium. Simmer, uncovered, for 10 minutes to blend flavours.

Add lime juice. Stir. Serves 4.

1 serving: 643 Calories; 27.1 g Total Fat (9.0 g Mono, 1.8 g Poly, 12.7 g Sat); 62 mg Cholesterol; 71 g Carbohydrate; 8 g Fibre; 28 g Protein; 397 mg Sodium

THAI CHICKEN CURRY: Use chicken instead of beef. Use about 4 cups (1 L) chopped fresh (or frozen) mango instead of sweet potato.

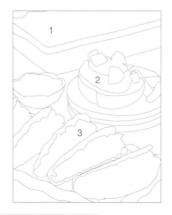

1. Enchilada Casserole, page 106
2. Open-Faced Burgers, page 74
3. Corn And Cod Tacos, page 94

Open-Faced Burgers

Top your burgers with all the flavours of a layered bean dip. Hearty and filling, with a colourful presentation.

Fine dry bread crumbs	2 tbsp.	30 mL
Chili powder	1 tbsp.	15 mL
Seasoned salt	1/2 tsp.	2 mL
Ground cumin	1/2 tsp.	2 mL
Extra-lean ground beef	1 lb.	454 g
Whole wheat French bread slices, about 1 inch (2.5 cm) thick	4	4
Refried beans	1/2 cup	125 mL
Thin avocado slices (about 1/2 avocado)	8	8
Small tomato, chopped	1	1
Green onion, sliced	1	1

Preheat gas barbecue to medium-high (see Note). Meanwhile, combine first 4 ingredients in large bowl. Add beef. Mix well. Shape into 4 oval patties to fit bread slices.

Toast bread slices on ungreased grill for about 1 minute per side until golden. Remove to plate. Cook patties on greased grill for about 5 minutes per side until fully cooked, and internal temperature of beef reaches 160°F (71°C).

Meanwhile, spread refried beans on toast. Place patties on top.

Top with avocado, tomato and green onion. Makes 4 burgers.

1 burger: 312 Calories; 10.7 g Total Fat (5.4 g Mono, 1.6 g Poly, 2.6 g Sat); 63 mg Cholesterol; 28 g Carbohydrate; 7 g Fibre; 29 g Protein; 539 mg Sodium

Pictured on page 72.

Note: Too cold to barbecue? Patties can be placed on a greased broiling pan and broiled on top rack in oven for about 5 minutes per side until fully cooked, and internal temperature of beef reaches 160°F (71°C). Bread slices can be placed on a baking sheet and broiled for about 1 minute per side until golden.

Simple Beef Broccoli

Don't let the name fool you—this dish's perfection is in its simplicity. Use precut beef stir-fry strips to fix this dish even faster. Serve with steamed rice for a complete meal.

Low-sodium prepared beef broth	3/4 cup	175 mL
Cornstarch	2 tbsp.	30 mL
Low-sodium soy sauce	2 tbsp.	30 mL
Sesame oil (optional)	1 tsp.	5 mL
Canola oil	1 tbsp.	15 mL
Beef top sirloin steak, thinly sliced	1 lb.	454 g
Dry sherry	2 tbsp.	30 mL
Garlic cloves, minced (or 1/2 tsp., 2 mL, powder)	2	2
Finely grated gingerroot (or 1/2 tsp., 2 mL, ground ginger)	2 tsp.	10 mL
Broccoli florets	4 cups	1 L
Sliced carrot, cut diagonally into 1/8 inch (3 mm) slices	1 1/4 cups	300 mL
Sliced green onion, cut diagonally into 1/2 inch (12 mm) slices	1/2 cup	125 mL

Combine first 4 ingredients in small bowl. Set aside.

Heat wok or large frying pan on medium-high until very hot. Add canola oil. Add beef. Stir-fry for 2 minutes.

Add next 3 ingredients. Stir-fry for 2 minutes.

Add broccoli and carrot. Stir-fry for about 3 minutes until vegetables are tender-crisp.

Add green onion. Stir broth mixture. Add to beef mixture. Heat and stir for about 2 minutes until boiling and thickened. Serves 4.

1 serving: 364 Calories; 22.1 g Total Fat (9.8 g Mono, 2.3 g Poly, 7.4 g Sat); 62 mg Cholesterol; 13 g Carbohydrate; 4 g Fibre; 27 g Protein; 357 mg Sodium

Don't just eat food, eat super food! Because of its many nutritional benefits, broccoli is considered a super food. It's high in antioxidants, high in fibre and high in vitamins A and C. Other super foods are: salmon, chili peppers, spinach, mangoes, beans and oats, to name just a few.

Chipotle Beef Skillet

Consider it chili extraordinaire! Spicy chipotles and dark raisins give this unique taste treat a smoky, yet sweet flavour.

Canola oil	**2 tsp.**	**10 mL**
Extra-lean ground beef	**1 lb.**	**454 g**
Chopped onion	**1/2 cup**	**125 mL**
All-purpose flour	**2 tbsp.**	**30 mL**
Garlic powder	**1/4 tsp.**	**1 mL**
Ground cumin	**1/4 tsp.**	**1 mL**
Pepper, sprinkle		
Low-sodium prepared beef broth	**2 cups**	**500 mL**
Can of red kidney beans, rinsed and drained	**14 oz.**	**398 mL**
Dark raisins	**1/2 cup**	**125 mL**
Tomato paste (see Tip, page 83)	**1 tbsp.**	**15 mL**
Chopped chipotle peppers in adobo sauce (see Tip, below)	**1 1/2 tsp.**	**7 mL**

Heat canola oil in large frying pan on medium-high. Add beef and onion. Scramble-fry for about 8 minutes until beef is no longer pink and onion is softened.

Add next 4 ingredients. Heat and stir for 1 minute.

Add 1 cup (250 mL) broth. Heat and stir until boiling and thickened. Reduce heat to medium. Add remaining broth and next 4 ingredients. Stir. Cook, uncovered, for 5 to 10 minutes, stirring occasionally. Serves 4.

1 serving: 359 Calories; 7.8 g Total Fat (3.5 g Mono, 1.3 g Poly, 1.8 g Sat); 60 mg Cholesterol; 42 g Carbohydrate; 10 g Fibre; 32 g Protein; 88 mg Sodium

Chipotle chili peppers are smoked jalapeno peppers. Be sure to wash your hands after handling. To store any leftover chipotle chili peppers, divide into recipe-friendly portions and freeze, with sauce, in airtight containers for up to one year.

Havana Beef Skillet

Hoppin' Havana, this sweet and savoury skillet will have you enjoying Cuban-inspired flavours in no time. Serve over rice or baked sweet potatoes.

Olive oil	**1 tsp.**	**5 mL**
Lean ground beef	**1 lb.**	**454 g**
Chopped onion	**1 1/4 cups**	**300 mL**
Chopped green pepper	**1 1/4 cups**	**300 mL**
Can of diced tomatoes (with juice)	**28 oz.**	**796 mL**
Can of black beans, rinsed and drained	**19 oz.**	**540 mL**
Large pitted green olives, sliced	**1/2 cup**	**125 mL**
Raisins	**1/2 cup**	**125 mL**
Balsamic vinegar	**2 tbsp.**	**30 mL**
Chili powder	**1 tbsp.**	**15 mL**
Brown sugar, packed	**1 tbsp.**	**15 mL**
Ground cinnamon	**1 tsp.**	**5 mL**
Ground ginger	**1/4 tsp.**	**1 mL**
Ground cloves	**1/8 tsp.**	**0.5 mL**

Heat olive oil in large frying pan on medium-high. Add next 3 ingredients. Cook, stirring occasionally, for 5 to 10 minutes until beef is no longer pink and onion is softened.

Add next 10 ingredients. Stir. Bring to a boil. Reduce heat to medium-low. Simmer, partially covered, for 10 minutes to blend flavours. Serves 4.

1 serving: 541 Calories; 21.5 g Total Fat (10.3 g Mono, 2.1 g Poly, 6.9 g Sat); 68 mg Cholesterol; 56 g Carbohydrate; 11 g Fibre; 33 g Protein; 1388 mg Sodium

Quick Beef Wraps

That's a wrap! All your bases are covered with this mix of fresh veggies, cheese, meat, beans and fresh dill yogurt. Good food for when you're on the go!

Ingredient	Imperial	Metric
Canola oil	2 tsp.	10 mL
Extra-lean ground beef	1 lb.	454 g
Finely chopped onion	1/2 cup	125 mL
Garlic clove, minced (or 1/4 tsp., 1 mL, powder)	1	1
Can of red kidney beans, rinsed and drained	14 oz.	398 mL
Low-sodium prepared beef broth	1/4 cup	60 mL
Plain yogurt	1/2 cup	125 mL
Chopped fresh dill (or 3/4 tsp., 4 mL, dried)	1 tbsp.	15 mL
Whole wheat flour tortillas (9 inch, 22 cm, diameter)	4	4
Chopped English cucumber	3/4 cup	175 mL
Chopped tomato	3/4 cup	175 mL
Crumbled light feta cheese (optional)	1/4 cup	60 mL

Heat canola oil in large frying pan on medium-high. Add next 3 ingredients. Scramble-fry for about 8 minutes until beef is no longer pink and onion is softened.

Mash half of beans with fork on small plate. Add to beef mixture. Add remaining beans and broth. Heat and stir until hot. Remove from heat.

Combine yogurt and dill in small bowl. Spread on tortillas, almost to edge. Spoon beef mixture down centre of tortillas.

Sprinkle with remaining 3 ingredients. Fold bottom ends of tortillas over filling. Fold in sides, leaving top ends open. Makes 4 wraps.

1 wrap: 462 Calories; 10.4 g Total Fat (3.8 g Mono, 1.6 g Poly, 3.2 g Sat); 68 mg Cholesterol; 64 g Carbohydrate; 14 g Fibre; 39 g Protein; 521 mg Sodium

Orange Chicken Stir-Fry

Orange you glad we came up with this recipe? One bite and you will be! Sweet orange and tangy mustard combine in this citrusy stir-fry. Serve over brown rice.

Low-sodium prepared chicken broth	3/4 cup	175 mL
Liquid honey	2 tbsp.	30 mL
Dijon mustard	2 tbsp.	30 mL
Cornstarch	2 tsp.	10 mL
White vinegar	1 tsp.	5 mL
Grated orange zest	1/2 tsp.	2 mL
Canola oil	1 tsp.	5 mL
Boneless, skinless chicken breast halves, sliced 1/4 inch (6 mm) thick	3/4 lb.	340 g
Canola oil	1 tsp.	5 mL
Thinly sliced onion	1/2 cup	125 mL
Broccoli slaw (or shredded cabbage with carrot)	4 1/2 cups	1.1 L
Chopped broccoli	2 cups	500 mL
Can of mandarin orange segments, drained	10 oz.	284 mL

Combine first 6 ingredients in small bowl. Set aside.

Heat wok or large frying pan on medium-high until very hot. Add first amount of canola oil. Add chicken. Stir-fry for about 3 minutes until no longer pink inside. Remove to plate. Set aside.

Add second amount of canola oil to hot wok. Add onion. Stir-fry for 1 to 2 minutes until onion is tender-crisp.

Add broccoli slaw, broccoli and chicken. Stir-fry for 3 to 4 minutes until broccoli is tender-crisp. Stir broth mixture. Add to wok. Heat and stir for 1 to 2 minutes until sauce is boiling and thickened. Remove from heat.

Add mandarin oranges. Toss gently. Serves 4.

1 serving: 224 Calories; 4.2 g Total Fat (1.8 g Mono, 1.2 g Poly, 0.6 g Sat); 49 mg Cholesterol; 25 g Carbohydrate; 4.3 g Fibre; 23 g Protein; 197 mg Sodium

Pictured on page 90.

Dill Turkey Burgers

So, you say you're a dill pickle lover? Don't just garnish your burger with pickles, cook them right in for a more intense flavour. Garnish with your favourite fixings.

Large egg, fork-beaten	1	1
Whole wheat bread slices, processed into crumbs (about 3/4 cup, 175 mL)	2	2
Finely chopped dill pickle	1/4 cup	60 mL
Chopped fresh dill (or 1/2 tsp., 2 mL, dried)	2 tsp.	10 mL
Lemon pepper	1 tsp.	5 mL
Extra-lean ground turkey	1 lb.	454 g
Olive oil	1 tbsp.	15 mL
Prepared mustard	2 tsp.	10 mL
Whole wheat hamburger buns, split	4	4
Large tomato, thinly sliced	1	1

Combine first 5 ingredients in medium bowl. Add turkey. Mix well. Divide into 4 equal portions. Shape into 1/2 inch (12 mm) thick patties.

Heat olive oil in large frying pan on medium. Add patties. Cook for about 7 minutes per side until fully cooked, and internal temperature of turkey reaches 175°F (80°C).

Spread mustard on bottom halves of buns. Serve patties, topped with tomato slices, in buns. Makes 4 burgers.

1 burger: 327 Calories; 8.9 g Total Fat (3.8 g Mono, 1.6 g Poly, 1.3 g Sat); 92 mg Cholesterol; 31 g Carbohydrate; 5 g Fibre; 35 g Protein; 586 mg Sodium

Spicy Orange Chicken Fingers

Familiar, family-friendly chicken fingers. Fun for the kids but with a complexity of flavours that will woo the adults. We suggest you forgo dip and eat these tasty tidbits as is.

Boneless, skinless chicken breast halves (4 – 6 oz., 113 – 170 g, each)	6	6
Plain yogurt	1/4 cup	60 mL
Grated orange zest	1/2 tsp.	2 mL
Fine dry bread crumbs	3/4 cup	175 mL
Brown sugar, packed	1 tbsp.	15 mL
Chili powder	1 tsp.	5 mL
Ground cumin	1/2 tsp.	2 mL
Seasoned salt	1/4 tsp.	1 mL
Cayenne pepper	1/8 tsp.	0.5 mL

(continued on next page)

Preheat oven to 425°F (220°C). Slice each chicken breast lengthwise into 4 strips. Combine yogurt and orange zest in large shallow bowl. Add chicken. Stir until coated.

Combine remaining 6 ingredients in large resealable freezer bag. Add half of chicken. Toss well. Arrange chicken strips in single layer on large greased baking sheet with sides. Repeat with remaining chicken and crumbs. Discard any remaining crumb mixture. Bake for about 15 minutes until chicken is no longer pink inside. Makes 24 chicken fingers. Serves 6.

1 serving: 197 Calories; 3.0 g Total Fat (0.9 g Mono, 0.6 g Poly, 0.9 g Sat); 67 mg Cholesterol; 13 g Carbohydrate; trace Fibre; 28 g Protein; 235 mg Sodium

Orange-Sauced Chicken

It's time to get saucy! Tender strips of chicken covered in a rich orange sauce with a zippy finish. Almonds add a contrasting crunch. Up the heat factor by adding more fresh chili pepper. Serve on a bed of rice.

Water	1 tbsp.	15 mL
Cornstarch	1 tsp.	5 mL
Canola oil	2 tsp.	10 mL
Boneless, skinless chicken breast halves, thinly sliced	1 lb.	454 g
Paprika	1/2 tsp.	2 mL
Salt, sprinkle		
Pepper, sprinkle		
Orange juice	1/4 cup	60 mL
Frozen concentrated orange juice, thawed	2 tbsp.	30 mL
Grated orange zest (see Tip, page 141)	1 tbsp.	15 mL
Brown sugar, packed	1 tsp.	5 mL
Finely diced fresh hot chili pepper (see Tip, page 59) (or 1/8 tsp., 0.5 mL crushed, dried chiles)	1/2 – 1 tsp.	2 – 5 mL
Sliced natural almonds	1 – 2 tbsp.	15 – 30 mL
Chopped fresh parsley, for garnish		

Stir water into cornstarch in small cup. Set aside.

Heat canola oil in large frying pan on medium. Add chicken. Sprinkle with paprika, salt and pepper. Cook for about 5 minutes, stirring often, until no longer pink inside.

Add next 5 ingredients. Stir. Bring to a boil. Stir cornstarch mixture. Add to chicken mixture. Heat and stir until boiling and thickened.

Sprinkle with almonds and parsley. Serves 4.

1 serving: 186 Calories; 5.0 g Total Fat (2.3 g Mono, 1.3 g Poly, 0.7 g Sat); 66 mg Cholesterol; 8 g Carbohydrate; trace Fibre; 26 g Protein; 64 mg Sodium

Pepper Lime Burgers

This chicken burger flouts convention and dares to be bold! The zippy lime sauce adds a lot of character.

RANCH LIME SAUCE		
Light Ranch dressing	1/2 cup	125 mL
Lime juice	2 tbsp.	30 mL
Grated lime zest	1 tsp.	5 mL
Pepper	1/4 tsp.	1 mL
BURGER		
Large egg, fork-beaten	1	1
Quick-cooking rolled oats	3/4 cup	175 mL
Garlic clove, minced (or 1/4 tsp., 1 mL, powder)	1	1
Salt	1/2 tsp.	2 mL
Lean ground chicken thigh	1 1/2 lbs.	680 g
Whole wheat hamburger buns, split	6	6
Pieces of roasted red pepper, drained and blotted dry	6	6
Green leaf lettuce leaves, halved	3	3

Ranch Lime Sauce: Combine first 4 ingredients in small bowl. Makes about 2/3 cup (150 mL) sauce.

Burger: Preheat gas barbecue to medium (see Note). Combine next 4 ingredients and 1/4 cup (60 mL) of Ranch Lime Sauce in medium bowl. Add chicken. Mix well. Divide into 6 equal portions. Shape into 1/2 inch (12 mm) thick patties. Cook on greased grill for about 5 minutes per side until fully cooked, and internal temperature of chicken reaches 175°F (80°C).

Meanwhile, spread remaining Ranch Lime Sauce on bun halves. Serve patties, topped with red pepper and lettuce, in buns. Makes 6 burgers.

1 burger: 514 Calories; 23.4 g Total Fat (0.9 g Mono, 1.1 g Poly, 1.0 g Sat); 37 mg Cholesterol; 42 g Carbohydrate; 5 g Fibre; 28 g Protein; 1213 mg Sodium

Note: Too cold to barbecue? Patties can be placed on a greased broiling pan and broiled on top rack in oven for about 5 minutes per side until fully cooked, and internal temperature of chicken reaches 175°F (80°C).

Southwestern Turkey Chili

This turkey's gone south of the border! A nice change from your regular chili. Serve Sloppy Joe-style on whole wheat buns or make it a taco salad with shredded lettuce and baked whole wheat tortilla wedges.

Canola oil	2 tsp.	10 mL
Chopped onion	1 cup	250 mL
Garlic clove, minced (or 1/4 tsp., 1 mL, powder)	1	1
Extra-lean ground turkey	1 lb.	454 g
Salt, sprinkle		
Chopped green pepper	1/2 cup	125 mL
Chili powder	2 tsp.	10 mL
Ground cumin	1 tsp.	5 mL
Dried oregano	1/2 tsp.	2 mL
Dried crushed chilies (optional)	1/4 tsp.	1 mL
Can of black beans, rinsed and drained	19 oz.	540 mL
Low-sodium vegetable cocktail juice	2 cups	500 mL
Tomato paste (see Tip, below)	2 tbsp.	30 mL
Ketchup	2 tbsp.	30 mL

Heat canola oil in large frying pan on medium-high. Add next 3 ingredients. Sprinkle with salt. Scramble-fry for about 5 minutes until onion is softened and turkey is starting to brown.

Add next 5 ingredients. Heat and stir for 1 minute.

Add remaining 4 ingredients. Stir well. Bring to a boil. Reduce heat to medium. Boil gently, uncovered, for 5 minutes, stirring occasionally, to blend flavours. Makes about 6 cups (1.5 L).

1 cup (250 mL): 259 Calories; 3.3 g Total Fat (1.0 g Mono, 0.8 g Poly, 0.3 g Sat); 30 mg Cholesterol; 32 g Carbohydrate; 8 g Fibre; 28 g Protein; 379 mg Sodium

If a recipe calls for less than an entire can of tomato paste, freeze the unopened can for 30 minutes. Open both ends and push the contents through one end. Slice off only what you need. Freeze the remaining paste in a resealable freezer bag or plastic wrap for future use.

Mushroom Wine Chicken

The soft and subtle sauce makes this a perfect choice for a more delicate palate. Perfect on a winter's night.

Skinless, boneless chicken breast halves (4 – 6 oz., 113 – 170 g, each)	4	4
Olive oil	**1 tbsp.**	**15 mL**
Salt, sprinkle		
Pepper	**1/4 tsp.**	**1 mL**
Sliced fresh white mushrooms	**2 cups**	**500 mL**
Garlic cloves, minced (or 1/2 tsp., 2 mL, powder)	**2**	**2**
All-purpose flour	**2 tbsp.**	**30 mL**
Low-sodium prepared chicken broth	**1 cup**	**250 mL**
Dry (or alcohol-free) red wine	**1/2 cup**	**125 mL**
Dried thyme	**1/2 tsp.**	**2 mL**

Place chicken breasts between 2 sheets of plastic wrap. Pound with mallet or rolling pin to about 1/2 inch (12 mm) thickness.

Heat olive oil in large frying pan on medium-high. Add chicken. Sprinkle with salt and pepper. Cook for about 3 minutes per side until lightly browned. Transfer to plate. Cover to keep warm.

Add mushrooms and garlic to same frying pan. Cook on medium for about 3 minutes, stirring occasionally, until softened and starting to brown.

Add flour. Heat and stir for 1 minute. Slowly add broth and wine, stirring constantly. Add thyme. Heat and stir until boiling and thickened. Add chicken. Reduce heat to medium-low. Simmer, uncovered, for 5 minutes to blend flavours. Serves 4.

1 serving: 212 Calories; 5.6 g Total Fat (3.0 g Mono, 0.8 g Poly, 1.0 g Sat); 66 mg Cholesterol; 6 g Carbohydrate; 1 g Fibre; 28 g Protein; 75 mg Sodium

Don't keep this good news in the dark—mushrooms are a good source of vitamins B2, B3 and B5. Vitamin B2 is also called riboflavin and aids in the breakdown of carbohydrates, fats and proteins. Vitamin B3 is also known as niacin and aids in the upkeep of healthy skin and nerves. Vitamin B5, also called pantothenic acid, is essential in proper cell metabolism.

Sweet-And-Sour Chicken

With the flavourful combination of mustard, lime and pineapple, this is not your everyday chicken dish! We've made sure there's plenty of sauce for you to serve over egg noodles or rice.

Pineapple juice	1/4 cup	60 mL
Brown sugar, packed	3 tbsp.	50 mL
Balsamic vinegar	2 tbsp.	30 mL
Dijon mustard	2 tbsp.	30 mL
Lime juice	2 tbsp.	30 mL
Cornstarch	2 tsp.	10 mL
Canola oil	2 tsp.	10 mL
Boneless, skinless chicken breast halves, cut into 1 inch (2.5 cm) cubes	1 lb.	454 g
Canola oil	2 tsp.	10 mL
Chopped red pepper	1 cup	250 mL
Chopped onion	1/2 cup	125 mL
Garlic clove, minced (or 1/4 tsp., 1 mL, powder)	1	1

Combine first 6 ingredients in small bowl. Set aside.

Heat wok or large frying pan on medium-high until very hot. Add first amount of canola oil. Add chicken. Stir-fry for about 4 minutes until browned. Transfer to plate.

Add second amount of canola oil to hot wok. Add next 3 ingredients. Stir-fry for about 2 minutes until onion is softened. Add chicken. Stir pineapple juice mixture. Add to chicken mixture. Heat and stir for about 1 minute until sauce is boiling and thickened. Serves 4.

1 serving: 242 Calories; 6.5 g Total Fat (3.1 g Mono, 1.8 g Poly, 0.8 g Sat); 66 mg Cholesterol; 19 g Carbohydrate; 1 g Fibre; 26 g Protein; 169 mg Sodium

Grilled Pepper Chicken

Add flair to your food the easiest way possible—with rustic grill marks! Balsamic vinegar and feta cheese add delicious flavour to colourful sweet peppers and tender chicken.

Boneless, skinless chicken breast halves (4 – 6 oz., 113 g – 170 g, each)	**4**	**4**
Salt, sprinkle		
Pepper, sprinkle		
Small red pepper, quartered lengthwise	1	1
Small orange pepper, quartered lengthwise	1	1
Small yellow pepper, quartered lengthwise	1	1
Olive oil	1 tbsp.	15 mL
Ground oregano	1/2 tsp.	2 mL
Pepper, sprinkle		
Balsamic vinegar	2 tbsp.	30 mL
Crumbled light feta cheese	1/4 cup	60 mL
Finely chopped fresh parsley	2 tsp.	10 mL

Preheat gas barbecue to medium-high (see Note). Sprinkle chicken with salt and pepper. Cook on greased grill for about 3 minutes per side until no longer pink inside.

Meanwhile, put next 3 ingredients into large bowl. Drizzle with olive oil. Sprinkle with oregano and pepper. Toss well. Cook on grill for about 3 minutes per side until tender-crisp.

Transfer chicken and peppers to large bowl. Drizzle with balsamic vinegar. Toss. Transfer to large plate.

Sprinkle with feta and parsley. Serves 4.

1 serving: 196 Calories; 6.5 g Total Fat (3 g Mono, 0.8 g Poly, 1.7 g Sat); 68 mg Cholesterol; 6 g Carbohydrate; 1 g Fibre; 28 g Protein; 201 mg Sodium

Pictured on page 125.

Note: Too cold to barbecue? Chicken can be placed on a greased broiling pan and broiled on top rack in oven for about 5 minutes per side until no longer pink inside.

Mango Salsa Chicken

Refreshing, delicious and pretty to look at! Spicy citrus and mango salsa is the perfect match for tender chicken. The salsa also goes well with salads, wraps, quesadillas and grilled fish.

Boneless, skinless chicken breast halves (4 – 6 oz., 113 g – 170 g, each)	4	4
Olive oil	2 tbsp.	30 mL
Lime juice	1 1/2 tbsp.	25 mL
Grated lime zest	1 1/2 tsp.	7 mL
Cajun seasoning	1 tsp.	5 mL
LIME MANGO SALSA		
Chopped frozen mango, thawed (see Note)	1 cup	250 mL
Finely diced red onion	1/4 cup	60 mL
Garlic clove, minced (or 1/4 tsp., 1 mL, powder)	1	1
Finely diced jalapeño pepper (see Tip, page 59)	2 tbsp.	30 mL
Olive oil	2 tbsp.	30 mL
Lime juice	1 1/2 tbsp.	25 mL
Chopped fresh cilantro or parsley	1 tbsp.	15 mL
Grated lime zest	1 1/2 tsp.	7 mL

Preheat gas barbecue to medium (see Note). Score both sides of each chicken breast several times with sharp knife. Combine next 4 ingredients in small bowl. Brush over chicken breasts. Cook chicken on greased grill for about 6 minutes per side, brushing with lime mixture, until no longer pink inside.

Lime Mango Salsa: Combine all 8 ingredients in small bowl. Makes 1 1/2 cups (375 mL) salsa. Serve with chicken. Serves 4.

1 serving: 281 Calories; 15.5 g Total Fat (10.5 g Mono, 1.6 g Poly, 2.3 g Sat); 65 mg Cholesterol; 10 g Carbohydrate; 1 g Fibre; 26 g Protein; 197 mg Sodium

Pictured on page 89.

Note: If frozen mango is unavailable, fresh or canned mango can be used instead.

Note: Too cold to barbecue? Chicken can be placed on a greased broiling pan and broiled on top rack in oven for about 5 minutes per side until no longer pink inside.

Variation: Use chopped oranges or pineapple instead of mango.

Polynesian Apricot Chicken

Multi-tasking makes quick work of this suppertime favourite—chop the veggies while the chicken is cooking. Sweet and savoury flavours combine with just a touch of heat. Serve over rice for a complete meal.

Dried apricots, quartered	3/4 cup	175 mL
Olive oil	1 tbsp.	15 mL
Boneless, skinless chicken thighs, quartered	1 lb.	454 g
Chopped onion	1 1/2 cups	375 mL
Chopped green pepper	1 cup	250 mL
Garlic clove, minced (or 1/4 tsp., 1 mL, powder)	1	1
Finely grated gingerroot (or 1/4 tsp., 1 mL, ground ginger)	1 tsp.	5 mL
Chili powder	1/2 tsp.	2 mL
Ground cumin	1/2 tsp.	2 mL
Can of diced tomatoes (with juice)	14 oz.	398 mL

Put apricot into small heatproof bowl. Cover with boiling water. Stir. Cover. Set aside.

Heat olive oil in large frying pan on medium. Add chicken. Cook for 8 to 10 minutes, stirring occasionally, until lightly browned. Transfer to plate. Cover to keep warm.

Add next 6 ingredients to same frying pan. Stir. Cook, covered, for about 5 minutes, stirring occasionally, until green pepper is tender-crisp.

Drain apricot. Add to green pepper mixture. Add chicken and tomatoes with juice. Stir. Increase heat to medium-high. Boil gently, uncovered, for about 10 minutes until sauce is slightly thickened. Serves 4.

1 serving: 308 Calories; 12.1 g Total Fat (5.8 g Mono, 2.3 g Poly, 2.9 g Sat); 74 mg Cholesterol; 29 g Carbohydrate; 3 g Fibre; 23 g Protein; 363 mg Sodium

Pictured at right.

1. Polynesian Apricot Chicken, above
2. Mango Salsa Chicken, page 87

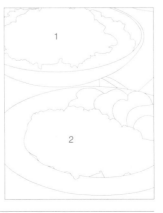

Dressed-Up Turkey Patties

The ordinary becomes extraordinary! Turkey patties are made exotic when paired with a cinnamon-scented tomato sauce. Serve with rice or couscous, add some fresh green beans and you're set.

Large egg, fork-beaten	1	1
Grated zucchini	1/2 cup	125 mL
Parsley flakes	2 tsp.	10 mL
Garlic salt	1/2 tsp.	2 mL
Pepper	1/2 tsp.	2 mL
Extra-lean ground turkey	1 lb.	454 g
Olive oil	2 tsp.	10 mL
Can of stewed tomatoes, drained and broken up	14 oz.	398 mL
Low-sodium prepared chicken broth	1/2 cup	125 mL
Balsamic vinegar	1 tsp.	5 mL
Granulated sugar	1/2 tsp.	2 mL
Ground cinnamon	1/4 tsp.	1 mL
Garlic powder	1/4 tsp.	1 mL

Combine first 5 ingredients in large bowl. Add turkey. Mix well. Divide into 4 equal portions. Shape into 1/2 inch (12 mm) thick patties.

Heat olive oil in large frying pan on medium. Add patties. Cook for about 5 minutes per side until fully cooked, and internal temperature of turkey reaches 175°F (80°C).

Combine remaining 6 ingredients in medium bowl. Add to frying pan. Stir. Bring to a boil. Reduce heat to medium-low. Simmer, covered, for 5 minutes to blend flavours. Transfer patties to serving platter. Carefully process sauce with hand blender or in blender until almost smooth. Pour over patties. Serves 4.

1 serving: 196 Calories; 5.1 g Total Fat (2.2 g Mono, 0.4 g Poly, 0.7 g Sat); 92 mg Cholesterol; 8 g Carbohydrate; 2 g Fibre; 31 g Protein; 197 mg Sodium

1. Orange Chicken Stir-Fry, page 79
2. Aloha Shrimp Stir-Fry, page 104

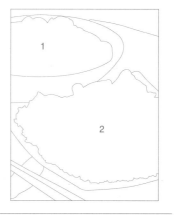

Cranberry-Topped Chicken

Fire up the grill! There's no need to save the vitamin-rich cranberries for the holidays. Ruby red, naturally-thickened cranberry sauce tops lightly seasoned, grilled chicken breasts. If you would like to use fresh parsley and sage in the sauce instead of dried, add 1/2 tsp. (2 mL) of each near the end of cooking.

Olive oil	1 tsp.	5 mL
Finely chopped onion	1/4 cup	60 mL
Garlic clove, minced (or 1/4 tsp., 1 mL, powder)	1	1
CRANBERRY SAUCE		
Fresh (or frozen) cranberries	1 cup	250 mL
Low-sodium prepared chicken broth	1/4 cup	60 mL
Granulated sugar	1/4 cup	60 mL
Parsley flakes	1/8 tsp.	0.5 mL
Dried sage	1/8 tsp.	0.5 mL
Salt, sprinkle		
Cayenne pepper, sprinkle		
Boneless, skinless chicken breast halves (4 – 6 oz., 113 – 170 g, each)	4	4
Seasoned salt, sprinkle		
Pepper, sprinkle		

Preheat gas barbecue to medium (see Note). Heat olive oil in small frying pan on medium. Add onion and garlic. Cook for about 5 minutes, stirring occasionally, until onion is softened.

Cranberry Sauce: Add all 7 ingredients. Stir. Bring to a boil. Boil, uncovered, for about 5 minutes, stirring occasionally, until cranberries split and sauce is slightly thickened. Remove from heat. Cover to keep warm.

Sprinkle chicken with seasoned salt and pepper. Cook on greased grill for about 5 minutes per side until no longer pink inside. Transfer to plate. Spoon sauce over chicken. Serves 4.

1 serving: 202 Calories; 3.1 g Total Fat (1.3 g Mono, 0.5 g Poly, 0.7 g Sat); 66 mg Cholesterol; 17 g Carbohydrate; 1 g Fibre; 26 g Protein; 66 mg Sodium

Pictured on page 54.

Note: Too cold to barbecue? Chicken can be placed on a greased broiling pan and broiled on top rack in oven for about 5 minutes per side until no longer pink inside.

Honey Ginger Salmon

Keep your honey happy and healthy with this delicious and attractive combination! A light, sweet glaze complements salmon garnished with crunchy cucumber salsa—a refreshing choice for supper on a warm summer evening.

Fresh (or frozen, thawed) salmon fillets (about 1 lb., 454 g), skin removed	**4**	**4**
Liquid honey	**1/4 cup**	**60 mL**
Rice vinegar	**2 tbsp.**	**30 mL**
Finely grated gingerroot (or 1/4 tsp., 1 mL, ground ginger)	**1 tsp.**	**5 mL**
CUCUMBER SALSA		
Diced English cucumber	**1 cup**	**250 mL**
Chopped green onion	**1/4 cup**	**60 mL**
Diced yellow pepper	**1/4 cup**	**60 mL**
Liquid honey	**1 tbsp.**	**15 mL**
Rice vinegar	**1 tbsp.**	**15 mL**
Salt	**1/2 tsp.**	**2 mL**
Pepper	**1/4 tsp.**	**1 mL**

Preheat broiler. Place fillets on greased baking sheet with sides. Combine next 3 ingredients in small cup. Brush generously over fillets. Broil on centre rack in oven for 8 to 10 minutes until fish flakes easily when tested with fork.

Cucumber Salsa: Meanwhile, combine all 7 ingredients in small bowl. Makes about 1 1/4 cups (300 mL) salsa. Serve with salmon. Serves 4.

1 serving: 303 Calories; 12.4 g Total Fat (4.4 g Mono, 4.5 g Poly, 2.5 g Sat); 67 mg Cholesterol; 24 g Carbohydrate; 1 g Fibre; 23 g Protein; 363 mg Sodium

Pictured on front cover.

Hook, line and sinker, fish is a great source of lean protein and omega-3 fatty acids, which aid in preventing build-up from forming in your arteries. Truly a heart-friendly food.

Corn And Cod Tacos

A nice light change from heavier ground beef and cheese-filled tacos. Add chopped avocado to the salsa for a nutrient booster. To save time, set out the lettuce, fish, salsa and taco shells so everyone can build their own.

Fresh (or frozen, thawed) cod fillets, any small bones removed	**1 lb.**	**454 g**
Lime juice	**1 tbsp.**	**15 mL**
Ground cumin	**1 tsp.**	**5 mL**
Hard taco shells	**8**	**8**
CORN SALSA		
Frozen kernel corn, thawed (see Tip, page 67)	**1 cup**	**250 mL**
Medium salsa	**1/2 cup**	**125 mL**
Chopped fresh cilantro	**1/4 cup**	**60 mL**
Shredded lettuce, lightly packed	**1 cup**	**250 mL**

Preheat broiler. Arrange fillets in single layer on greased baking sheet with sides. Drizzle with lime juice. Sprinkle with cumin. Broil on centre rack in oven for 8 to 10 minutes until fish flakes easily when tested with fork. Break into small chunks. Set aside.

Arrange taco shells in single layer on separate ungreased baking sheet. Place on bottom rack in hot oven for 1 minute until warm.

Corn Salsa: Meanwhile, combine all 4 ingredients in small bowl. Makes about 1 cup (250 mL) salsa.

Layer lettuce, fish and Corn Salsa, in order given, in taco shells. Makes 8 tacos.

1 taco: 134 Calories; 3.5 g Total Fat (1.3 g Mono, 1.3 g Poly, 0.5 g Sat); 21 mg Cholesterol; 14 g Carbohydrate; 2 g Fibre; 12 g Protein; 155 mg Sodium

Pictured on page 72.

Oven-Poached Salmon Steaks

Simple can be so good! Very mildly flavoured salmon with the perfect complement—a light dill sauce. Wonderful served with a vegetable salad and rice pilaf.

Water	**1 1/2 cups**	**375 mL**
Chopped onion	**1/4 cup**	**60 mL**
Lemon juice	**2 tbsp.**	**30 mL**
Bay leaf, broken in half	**1**	**1**
Fresh (or frozen, thawed) salmon steaks (4 – 5 oz., 113 – 140 g, each), about 1 inch (2.5 cm) thick	**4**	**4**
Pepper, sprinkle		
Plain yogurt	**1/2 cup**	**125 mL**
Chopped fresh dill	**1/4 cup**	**60 mL**
Dijon mustard	**2 tsp.**	**10 mL**
Worcestershire sauce	**1/4 tsp.**	**1 mL**

Preheat oven to 325°F (160°C). Combine first 4 ingredients in 2 cup (500 mL) liquid measure or small microwave-safe bowl. Microwave on high (100%) until boiling. Pour half of water mixture into 2 quart (2 L) shallow baking dish.

Arrange salmon in single layer in baking dish. Sprinkle with pepper. Pour remaining water mixture over salmon. Bake for about 15 minutes until fish flakes easily when tested with fork. Transfer to serving plate. Discard bay leaf and poaching liquid.

Meanwhile, combine remaining 4 ingredients in small cup. Serve with salmon. Serves 4.

1 serving: 233 Calories; 13.3 g Total Fat (4.7 g Mono, 4.5 g Poly, 3.1 g Sat); 71 mg Cholesterol; 3 g Carbohydrate; trace Fibre; 24 g Protein; 117 mg Sodium

Look for yogurts that contain live and active bacterial culture. Studies have shown that these "good" bacteria may help maintain a healthy digestive tract.

Seafood Medley

Ahoy, me hearties! This light stew is perfect for anyone who's angling for a dinner from the high seas! Morsels of seafood in a tomato sauce—reminiscent of cioppino. Serve over rice or pasta.

Canola (or olive) oil	2 tsp.	10 mL
Finely chopped onion	1/2 cup	125 mL
Garlic cloves, minced	2	2
Can of diced tomatoes (with juice)	14 oz.	398 mL
Low-sodium prepared chicken broth	1/2 cup	125 mL
Grated lemon zest	1 tbsp.	15 mL
Ground cumin	1/2 tsp.	2 mL
Pepper	1/8 tsp.	0.5 mL
Chopped capers (optional)	1 tbsp.	15 mL
Fresh (or frozen, thawed) salmon fillet, skin removed, cut into 1 inch (2.5 cm) pieces	6 oz.	170 g
Fresh (or frozen, thawed) halibut fillet, any small bones removed, cut into 1 inch (2.5 cm) pieces	6 oz.	170 g
Fresh (or frozen, thawed) large sea scallops, halved	1/4 lb.	113 g
Chopped fresh parsley	1/4 cup	60 mL

Heat canola oil in large frying pan on medium-high. Add onion and garlic. Cook for about 5 minutes, stirring occasionally, until onion is softened.

Add next 6 ingredients. Stir. Cook, covered, for 3 minutes, stirring occasionally, to blend flavours.

Add remaining 4 ingredients. Stir. Reduce heat to medium-low. Simmer, covered, for about 4 minutes until fish flakes easily when tested with fork and scallops are opaque. Makes about 4 cups (1 L).

1 cup (250 mL): 203 Calories; 8.3 g Total Fat (3.4 g Mono, 2.8 g Poly, 1.3 g Sat); 48 mg Cholesterol; 8 g Carbohydrate; 1 g Fibre; 24 g Protein; 372 mg Sodium

Sesame Ginger Halibut

Light flavours with an Asian twist and an upscale presentation. Snowy white halibut glazed with sesame, ginger and pepper is served alongside tender-crisp, ginger-infused bok choy.

Sesame oil	2 tsp.	10 mL
Water	1 cup	250 mL
Prepared vegetable broth	1/2 cup	125 mL
Chopped green onion	1/2 cup	125 mL
Finely grated gingerroot	1 tbsp.	15 mL
Chopped bok choy	4 cups	1 L
Fresh (or frozen, thawed) halibut fillets (4 – 5 oz., 113 – 140 g each), any small bones removed	4	4
Pepper	1/4 tsp.	1 mL
Tahini (sesame paste)	1 tbsp.	15 mL
Rice vinegar	1 tbsp.	15 mL
Low-sodium soy sauce	2 tsp.	10 mL
Sesame oil	1/2 tsp.	2 mL
Sesame seeds, toasted (see Tip, page 21)	2 tsp.	10 mL

Heat sesame oil in large frying pan on medium-high. Add next 4 ingredients. Bring to a boil. Add bok choy.

Place fillets over bok choy. Sprinkle with pepper. Reduce heat to medium-low. Simmer, covered, for about 3 minutes until bok choy starts to soften.

Combine next 4 ingredients in small cup. Drizzle over fillets. Cook, covered, for about 5 minutes until fish flakes easily when tested with fork. Transfer fillets and bok choy to serving plate, using slotted spoon. Drizzle sauce over top.

Sprinkle with sesame seeds. Serves 4.

1 serving: 184 Calories; 6.9 g Total Fat (2.5 g Mono, 2.7 g Poly, 1.0 g Sat); 36 mg Cholesterol; 4 g Carbohydrate; 1 g Fibre; 25 g Protein; 312 mg Sodium

Halibut Bake

A slightly sweet, creamy spread hides beneath a crispy crumb coating. A dashing dash of dill adds the perfect touch.

Fresh (or frozen, thawed) halibut fillets (4 – 5 oz., 113 – 140 g, each), any small bones removed	4	4
Sweet pickle relish	1/4 cup	60 mL
Light mayonnaise	2 tbsp.	30 mL
Grated Parmesan cheese	2 tbsp.	30 mL
Creamed horseradish	1 tsp.	5 mL
Cornflake crumbs	1/4 cup	60 mL
Fine dry bread crumbs	1/4 cup	60 mL
Dried dillweed	1/2 tsp.	2 mL

Preheat oven to 400°F (205°C). Pat fillets dry with paper towels. Arrange in single layer in greased 3 quart (3 L) shallow baking dish.

Combine next 4 ingredients in small bowl. Spread over fillets.

Combine remaining 3 ingredients in separate small bowl. Sprinkle over fillets. Bake for about 15 minutes until fish flakes easily when tested with fork. Serves 4.

1 serving: 418 Calories; 7.3 g Total Fat (1.6 g Mono, 1.1 g Poly, 1.5 g Sat); 42 mg Cholesterol; 66 g Carbohydrate; 2 g Fibre; 27 g Protein; 1558 mg Sodium

Tarragon-Poached Fish

Silky tarragon with lemon sauce is the perfect match for fish. There will be lots of sauce to serve over rice or noodles. Simply delicious!

Butter (or hard margarine)	2 tbsp.	30 mL
All-purpose flour	2 tbsp.	30 mL
Prepared vegetable broth	1 cup	250 mL
Lemon juice	2 tbsp.	30 mL
Dried tarragon	1 tsp.	5 mL
Fresh (or frozen, thawed) haddock (or cod) fillets (about 1/2 inch, 12 mm, thick), any small bones removed	1 lb.	454 g
Chopped fresh tarragon, for garnish		

Melt butter in large frying pan on medium. Sprinkle with flour. Heat and stir for 1 minute. Slowly add broth, stirring constantly, until boiling and thickened.

(continued on next page)

Add lemon juice and tarragon. Stir.

Pat fillets dry with paper towels. Add to sauce. Reduce heat to medium-low. Simmer, covered, for 5 to 7 minutes until fish flakes easily when tested with fork.

Garnish with tarragon. Serves 4.

1 serving: 168 Calories; 6.6 g Total Fat (1.6 g Mono, 0.5 g Poly, 3.8 g Sat); 80 mg Cholesterol; 4 g Carbohydrate; trace Fibre; 22 g Protein; 235 mg Sodium

Pictured on page 143.

Graham-Crusted Basa

A tantalizing taste surprise! A sweet coating of graham crumbs and crunchy nuts over moist, delicate fish. Just a hint of lemon rounds out this delicious dish.

Graham cracker crumbs	**1/2 cup**	**125 mL**
Finely chopped pecans	**2 tbsp.**	**30 mL**
Grated lemon zest	**1 tsp.**	**5 mL**
Lemon pepper	**1/4 tsp.**	**1 mL**
Milk	**1/4 cup**	**60 mL**
Fresh (or frozen, thawed) basa (or other white fish) fillets (4 – 5 oz., 113 – 140 g, each), any small bones removed	**4**	**4**
Cooking spray		

Preheat oven to 400°F (205°C). Combine first 4 ingredients in shallow bowl.

Measure milk into separate shallow bowl.

Dip fillets into milk. Press both sides of fillets into crumb mixture until coated. Place fillets on greased baking sheet with sides. Discard any remaining milk and crumbs. Spray fillets lightly with cooking spray. Bake for about 10 minutes until fish flakes easily when tested with fork. Serves 4.

1 serving: 229 Calories; 10.5 g Total Fat (4.2 g Mono, 3.6 g Poly, 1.5 g Sat); 69 mg Cholesterol; 9.4 g Carbohydrate; 1 g Fibre; 23 g Protein; 135 mg Sodium

Salmon With Citrus Salsa

Don't you love it when such a minimal effort reaps such a huge reward? This is the type of healthy, yet decadent, meal you would expect to get at a very posh spa. The pairing of citrus and salmon is a delicious and refreshing combination!

QUICK CITRUS SALSA		
Large orange, segmented and chopped (see Note)	1	1
Small ruby red grapefruit, segmented and chopped (see Note)	1	1
Finely chopped red onion	1/4 cup	60 mL
Chopped fresh cilantro or parsley	1 tsp.	5 mL
Small fresh hot chili pepper, finely diced (see Tip, page 59)	1	1
Salt, sprinkle		
Pepper, sprinkle		

SALMON		
Fresh (or frozen, thawed) salmon fillets (about 4 – 5 oz., 113 – 140 g, each), skin removed	4	4
Salt, sprinkle		
Pepper, sprinkle		

Quick Citrus Salsa: Combine all 7 ingredients in small bowl. Makes about 1 1/3 cups (325 mL) salsa. Set aside.

Salmon: Preheat broiler. Sprinkle fillets with salt and pepper. Place on greased baking sheet with sides. Broil on top rack in oven for about 5 minutes until fish flakes easily when tested with fork. Serve with Quick Citrus Salsa. Serves 4.

1 serving: 250 Calories; 12.4 g Total Fat (4.4 g Mono, 4.5 g Poly, 2.5 g Sat); 67 mg Cholesterol; 11 g Carbohydrate; 2 g Fibre; 23 g Protein; 68 mg Sodium

Note: To segment citrus fruits, trim a small slice of peel from both ends so the flesh is exposed. Place the fruit, cut-side down, on a cutting board. Remove the peel with a sharp knife, cutting down and around the flesh, leaving as little pith as possible. Over a small bowl, cut on either side of the membranes to release the segments.

Poached Salmon Kabobs

Delicate salmon skewers on a bed of nutty couscous with a burst of fresh lemon. A very attractive presentation, indeed!

Low-sodium prepared chicken broth	1/2 cup	125 mL
Orange juice	1/2 cup	125 mL
Olive oil	1 tsp.	5 mL
Cayenne pepper, sprinkle (optional)		
Couscous	1 cup	250 mL
Low-sodium prepared chicken broth	2 cups	500 mL
Chopped onion	1/2 cup	125 mL
Garlic cloves, minced (or 3/4 tsp., 4 mL, powder)	3	3
Pepper	1 tsp.	5 mL
Large lemon, cut into 8 wedges	1	1
Fresh (or frozen, thawed) salmon fillets, skin removed, cut into 1 inch (2.5 cm) cubes	1 lb.	454 g
Bamboo skewers (8 inches, 20 cm, each)	4	4
Chopped fresh dill	1 1/2 tsp.	7 mL

Measure first 4 ingredients into medium saucepan. Bring to a boil. Remove from heat. Add couscous. Stir. Cover. Let stand for about 5 minutes until liquid is absorbed.

Meanwhile, combine next 4 ingredients in medium frying pan. Stir. Add 4 lemon wedges. Bring to a boil. Reduce heat to medium-low.

Thread fish onto skewers. Add to broth mixture. Simmer, covered, for about 5 minutes until fish flakes easily when tested with fork. Fluff couscous with fork. Spoon onto serving platter. Place skewers over top.

Sprinkle with dill. Serve with remaining lemon wedges. Serves 4.

1 serving: 439 Calories; 14.4 g Total Fat (5.5 g Mono, 4.8 g Poly, 2.9 g Sat); 67 mg Cholesterol; 48 g Carbohydrate; 5 g Fibre; 31 g Protein; 97 mg Sodium

Despair not, there are some good fats out there. Monounsaturated fats, like those in olive oil, help to reduce the levels of bad cholesterol in your body.

Tomato Shrimp Pasta

A garlic-lover's dream come true! Tangy tomato sauce with lots of shrimp, plenty of pasta and mild chili heat to liven things up. Serve with a sprinkle of grated Parmesan and fresh ground pepper.

Whole wheat spaghetti	8 oz.	225 g
Olive oil	2 tbsp.	30 mL
Garlic cloves, minced (or 3/4 tsp., 4 mL, powder)	3	3
Cans of diced tomatoes (with juice), 14 oz., 398 mL, each	2	2
Dried crushed chilies	1/2 tsp.	2 mL
Frozen uncooked large shrimp (peeled and deveined), thawed	1 lb.	454 g
Grated lemon zest	1 tsp.	5 mL
Chopped fresh parsley	1/4 cup	60 mL

Cook spaghetti in boiling salted water in large uncovered saucepan or Dutch oven for about 8 minutes, stirring occasionally, until tender but firm. Drain. Return to same pot. Cover to keep warm.

Meanwhile, heat olive oil in large frying pan on medium. Add garlic. Cook for 1 minute until fragrant. Add tomatoes with juice and chilies. Stir. Boil gently for about 5 minutes until slightly thickened.

Add shrimp and lemon zest. Return to a boil. Cook and stir about 4 minutes until shrimp turn pink. Add parsley. Stir. Add to spaghetti. Toss. Serves 4.

1 serving: 416 Calories; 9.6 g Total Fat (5.4 g Mono, 1.7 g Poly, 1.4 g Sat); 172 mg Cholesterol; 53 g Carbohydrate; 5 g Fibre; 33 g Protein; 730 mg Sodium

Lemon Sole

You won't be standing on your feet for long—this lemony, breaded sole dish is easy on the soles, not to mention good for the soul! Assembles and bakes quickly.

Fine dry bread crumbs	1 cup	250 mL
Grated zest from 1 small lemon		
Salt, sprinkle		
Pepper, sprinkle		
Large egg	1	1
Fresh (or frozen, thawed) sole fillets (4 – 5 oz., 113 – 140 g, each), any small bones removed	6	6

(continued on next page)

Preheat oven to 400°F (205°C). Combine first 4 ingredients in shallow bowl.

Beat egg in separate shallow bowl.

Dip fillets into egg. Press both sides of fillets into crumb mixture until coated. Place on greased baking sheet with sides. Bake for about 5 minutes until fish flakes easily when tested with fork. Serves 6.

1 serving: 187 Calories; 3.2 g Total Fat (1.1 g Mono, 0.7 g Poly, 0.8 g Sat); 85 mg Cholesterol; 13 g Carbohydrate; 0.5 g Fibre; 25 g Protein; 257 mg Sodium

Fennel Snapper Packets

Good things come in small packets! Get your protein and vegetables all wrapped up in one convenient package. Perfect with a squeeze of lemon.

Thinly sliced fennel bulb (white part only)	1 cup	250 mL
Thinly sliced onion	1/4 cup	60 mL
Chopped fresh parsley (or 3/4 tsp., 4 mL, flakes)	1 tbsp.	15 mL
Olive oil	1 tsp.	5 mL
Salt, sprinkle		
Pepper, sprinkle		
Fresh (or frozen, thawed) snapper fillet, any small bones removed	1/2 lb.	225 g
Dry (or alcohol-free) white wine	2 tbsp.	30 mL
Salt, sprinkle		
Lemon wedges (optional)	2	2

Preheat oven to 400°F (205°C). Combine first 3 ingredients in medium bowl. Drizzle with olive oil. Sprinkle with salt and pepper. Toss well. Divide fennel mixture on 2 sheets of greased heavy-duty (or double layer of regular) foil.

Cut fillet into 2 portions. Place over fennel mixture. Drizzle with wine. Sprinkle with salt. Fold edges of foil together over fish to enclose. Fold ends to seal completely. Place packets, seam-side up, on ungreased baking sheet with sides. Bake for 15 to 20 minutes until fish flakes easily when tested with fork.

Squeeze lemon over top. Serves 2.

1 serving: 211 Calories; 4.2 g Total Fat (2.0 g Mono, 0.7 g Poly, 0.6 g Sat); 42 mg Cholesterol; 16 g Carbohydrate; 6 g Fibre; 26 g Protein; 171 mg Sodium

Aloha Shrimp Stir-Fry

Mahalo nui loa—or thank you very much! Your dinner guests will certainly thank you for bringing this tropical taste to the table! Colourful fresh vegetables and shrimp with a sweet pineapple-ginger glaze. Enjoy with a Mai Tai!

Low-sodium prepared chicken broth	**1/2 cup**	**125 mL**
Reserved pineapple juice	**2 tbsp.**	**30 mL**
Low-sodium soy sauce	**2 tsp.**	**10 mL**
Cornstarch	**2 tsp.**	**10 mL**
Chili paste (sambal oelek)	**1/2 tsp.**	**2 mL**
Canola oil	**2 tsp.**	**10 mL**
Frozen uncooked large shrimp (peeled and deveined), thawed	**1 lb.**	**454 g**
Garlic clove, minced (or 1/4 tsp., 1 mL, powder)	**1**	**1**
Finely grated gingerroot (or 1/8 tsp., 0.5 mL, ground ginger)	**1/2 tsp.**	**2 mL**
Canola oil	**2 tsp.**	**10 mL**
Fresh mixed stir-fry vegetables	**5 cups**	**1.25 L**
Can of pineapple chunks, drained and juice reserved	**19 oz.**	**540 mL**
Sesame seeds, toasted (see Tip, page 21), optional	**1 tbsp.**	**15 mL**

Stir first 5 ingredients in small cup until smooth. Set aside.

Heat wok or large frying pan on medium-high until very hot. Add first amount of canola oil. Add next 3 ingredients. Stir-fry for about 2 minutes until shrimp turn pink. Transfer to small bowl.

Heat second amount of canola oil in same wok. Add vegetables. Stir-fry for about 3 minutes until tender-crisp. Add pineapple and shrimp. Toss. Stir broth mixture. Add to vegetable mixture. Heat and stir for about 1 minute until boiling and slightly thickened.

Sprinkle with sesame seeds. Serves 6.

1 serving: 179 Calories; 4.5 g Total Fat (2.0 g Mono, 1.5 g Poly, 0.5 g Sat); 115 mg Cholesterol; 18 g Carbohydrate; 2 g Fibre; 17 g Protein; 194 mg Sodium

Pictured on page 90.

Eggplant Envelopes

With nary a bill in sight, you'll be delighted to open up these envelopes. Sweet little eggplant packages come bearing tasty gifts—feta cheese, pesto and roasted red pepper. Your nearest and dearest will marvel at the unique presentation.

Medium eggplant (with peel), cut lengthwise into 8 1/4 inch (6 mm) thick slices	**1**	**1**
Basil pesto	**2 tbsp.**	**30 mL**
Crumbled light feta cheese	**3/4 cup**	**175 mL**
Roasted red peppers, drained and blotted dry, chopped	**1/2 cup**	**125 mL**
Olive oil	**1 tbsp.**	**15 mL**
Salt, sprinkle		
Pepper, sprinkle		

Preheat oven to 450°F (230°C). Meanwhile, cook eggplant slices in boiling water in Dutch oven for about 2 minutes until softened. Remove to paper towels to drain.

Lay 1 slice of eggplant vertically on work surface. Place another slice of eggplant crosswise over top to form a cross. Put 1 1/2 tsp. (7 mL) pesto in centre of cross. Sprinkle 3 tbsp. (50 mL) cheese over pesto. Place 2 tbsp. (30 mL) red pepper on top. Fold eggplant ends into centre to enclose filling. Turn over. Place, folded-side down, on greased baking sheet with sides. Repeat with remaining eggplant and fillings.

Brush olive oil over envelopes. Sprinkle with salt and pepper. Bake for about 15 minutes until filling is hot and eggplant starts to turn golden. Serves 4.

1 serving: 117 Calories; 8.5 g Total Fat (5.0 g Mono, 0.7 g Poly, 2.0 g Sat); 5 mg Cholesterol; 8 g Carbohydrate; 4 g Fibre; 4 g Protein; 188 mg Sodium

 Fibre, fibre everywhere—but make sure you have lots to drink! To get the full digestive benefits of fibre, you need to accompany it with plenty of fluids. If you eat a lot of fibre but don't drink enough liquids, it will take much longer to move through your body.

Enchilada Casserole

Lazy day enchiladas! Layers of whole wheat tortillas surround sweet potato and black bean filling. Great taste with minimal effort!

Whole wheat flour tortillas (9 inch, 22 cm, diameter), quartered	**4**	**4**
Can of sweet potatoes, drained	**19 oz.**	**540 mL**
Can of black beans, rinsed and drained	**19 oz.**	**540 mL**
Chunky mild salsa	**1/2 cup**	**125 mL**
Chili powder	**2 tsp.**	**10 mL**
Can of tomato sauce	**14 oz.**	**398 mL**
Chunky mild salsa	**1/2 cup**	**125 mL**
Grated light sharp Cheddar cheese	**1 cup**	**250 mL**
Ripe large avocado, diced	**1**	**1**
Finely chopped green onion	**1/4 cup**	**60 mL**
Light sour cream	**1/2 cup**	**125 mL**

Preheat oven to 450°F (230°C). Arrange half of tortilla pieces in bottom of greased 9 x 13 inch (22 x 33 cm) baking dish.

Mash sweet potatoes in medium bowl. Add next 3 ingredients. Stir. Spread evenly over tortillas in baking dish. Arrange remaining tortilla pieces over top.

Combine tomato sauce and second amount of salsa in small bowl. Pour evenly over tortillas. Bake, uncovered, in oven for 15 minutes. Sprinkle with cheese. Bake for another 5 minutes until heated through and cheese is golden.

Sprinkle avocado and green onion over top.

Serve with sour cream. Serves 6.

1 serving: 465 Calories; 11.4 g Total Fat (3.4 g Mono, 1.3 g Poly, 4.1 g Sat); 17 mg Cholesterol; 81 g Carbohydrate; 14 g Fibre; 21 g Protein; 1294 mg Sodium

Pictured on page 72.

1. Sesame Pork Skewers, page 115
2. Thai Cucumber Salad, page 49
3. Citrus Spice Quinoa Pilaf, page 130

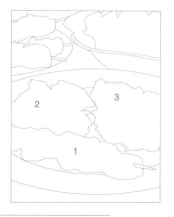

Polenta Vegetable Stacks

Plenty of polenta piled high with grilled vegetables and black beans makes for fast, fresh and healthy comfort food. Try adding some Creamy Chipotle Dressing, page 44, for a zippy southwestern flavour. Store your extra polenta, tightly wrapped, in the fridge for up to one month.

Olive oil	1 tbsp.	15 mL
Tube of plain polenta (2.2 lbs., 1 kg), cut into	1/2	1/2
** 8 rounds, about 1/2 inch (12 mm) thick**		
Slices of jalapeño Monterey Jack cheese	8	8
** (about 6 oz., 170 g), cut in half**		
Olive oil	1 tbsp.	15 mL
Thinly sliced zucchini	1 1/2 cups	375 mL
Garlic cloves, minced (or 1/2 tsp.,	2	2
** 2 mL, powder)**		
Can of diced tomatoes, drained	14 oz.	398 mL
Canned black beans, rinsed and drained	1 cup	250 mL

Lime wedges, for garnish

Preheat broiler. Heat first amount of olive oil in large frying pan on medium-high. Add polenta rounds. Cook for about 2 minutes per side until golden. Transfer to greased 9 × 13 inch (22 × 33 cm) baking dish.

Place half slice of cheese on each polenta round. Cover to keep warm.

Heat second amount of olive oil in same frying pan on medium. Add zucchini and garlic. Cook for about 3 minutes until zucchini is tender-crisp.

Add tomatoes and beans. Cook for about 1 minute until heated through. Spoon over polenta. Place remaining cheese slices on top. Broil on centre rack in oven for about 2 minutes until cheese is melted.

Garnish with lime wedges. Makes 8 stacks. Serves 4.

1 serving: 387 Calories; 20.3 g Total Fat (8.7 g Mono, 1.1 g Poly, 9.1 g Sat); 38 mg Cholesterol; 35.7 g Carbohydrate; 4 g Fibre; 17 g Protein; 562 mg Sodium

Pictured at left.

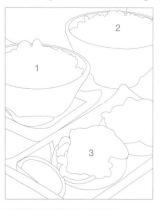

1. Navy Bean Stew, page 110
2. Cumin Lentils, page 111
3. Polenta Vegetable Stacks, above

Navy Bean Stew

You don't have to enlist to enjoy this fresh and hearty stew. Add a slice of lemon for a tiny bit of tang. Serve over soft polenta or with crusty focaccia bread and salad to make this a complete meal.

Canola (or olive) oil	2 tsp.	10 mL
Chopped onion	1 1/2 cups	375 mL
Chopped red pepper	1 1/2 cups	375 mL
Chopped fresh rosemary (or 3/4 tsp., 4 mL, dried, crushed)	1 tbsp.	15 mL
Dried crushed chilies	1/2 tsp.	2 mL
Garlic cloves, minced (or 1/2 tsp., 2 mL, powder)	2	2
Cans of navy beans, rinsed and drained (14 oz., 398 mL, each)	2	2
Can of diced tomatoes (with juice)	14 oz.	398 mL
Water	1 cup	250 mL
Bay leaf	1	1
Coarsely chopped kale leaves, lightly packed (see Tip, below)	6 cups	1.5 L
Chopped fresh parsley	1 tbsp.	15 mL
Grated lemon zest	1 tsp.	5 mL

Heat canola oil in large frying pan on medium. Add onion and red pepper. Cook for about 5 minutes, stirring occasionally, until onion starts to soften.

Add next 3 ingredients. Heat and stir for 1 minute until fragrant.

Add next 4 ingredients. Bring to a boil. Reduce heat to medium-low. Simmer, covered, for 10 minutes to blend flavours.

Add kale. Stir. Simmer, covered, for about 3 minutes until kale is wilted. Discard bay leaf.

Add parsley and lemon zest. Stir. Makes about 7 cups (1.75 L).

1 cup (250 mL): 195 Calories; 2.3 g Total Fat (0.8 g Mono, 0.8 g Poly, 0.3 g Sat); 0 mg Cholesterol; 36 g Carbohydrate; 8 g Fibre; 11 g Protein; 389 mg Sodium

Pictured on page 108.

To remove the centre rib from lettuce or kale, fold the leaf in half along the rib and then cut along the length of the rib.

Cumin Lentils

A mild, but far from tame, introduction to curry flavours and meatless eating. This appetizing and colourful blend of lentils, potatoes, tomatoes and spice is excellent served with warm naan bread or whole wheat pitas.

Diced peeled potato	2 cups	500 mL
Canola oil	4 tsp.	20 mL
Thinly sliced onion	2 cups	500 mL
Thinly sliced celery	1 cup	250 mL
Ground cumin	1 tsp.	5 mL
Turmeric	1/2 tsp.	2 mL
Garlic cloves, minced (or 1/2 tsp., 2 mL, powder)	2	2
Pepper	1/4 tsp.	1 mL
Cans of lentils, rinsed and drained (19 oz., 540 mL, each)	2	2
Chopped tomato	2 cups	500 mL
Prepared vegetable broth	1 cup	250 mL
Chopped fresh parsley (or cilantro), for garnish		

Put potato into microwave-safe dish. Microwave, covered, on high (100%) for about 6 minutes until tender.

Meanwhile, heat canola oil in large frying pan on medium-high. Add onion and celery. Cook for 5 to 10 minutes, stirring often, until onion starts to brown.

Add next 4 ingredients. Heat and stir for 1 minute until fragrant.

Add next 3 ingredients and potato. Stir. Reduce heat to medium. Cook, covered, for about 5 minutes, stirring occasionally, until celery is softened.

Garnish with parsley. Makes about 8 cups (2 L).

1 cup (250 mL): 220 Calories; 3.0 g Total Fat (1.4 g Mono, 1.0 g Poly, 0.3 g Sat); 0 mg Cholesterol; 39 g Carbohydrate; 7 g Fibre; 12 g Protein; 347 mg Sodium

Pictured on page 108.

Cashew Tofu Stir-Fry

Colourful, crunchy and full of vegetable goodness! Serve over rice for a complete meal.

Water	3/4 cup	175 mL
Sweet (or regular) chili sauce	2 tbsp.	30 mL
Cornstarch	1 tbsp.	15 mL
Soy sauce	1 tbsp.	15 mL
Sesame oil (optional)	1 tbsp.	15 mL
Canola oil	1 tbsp.	15 mL
Chopped suey choy (Chinese cabbage)	4 cups	1 L
Sugar snap peas, trimmed	2 cups	500 mL
Sliced onion	1 1/2 cups	375 mL
Sliced red pepper	1 cup	250 mL
Finely grated gingerroot (or 3/4 tsp., 4 mL, ground ginger)	1 tbsp.	15 mL
Package of extra-firm tofu, cut into 3/4 inch (2 cm) pieces	12 1/2 oz.	350 g
Salted cashews	1/2 cup	125 mL

Combine first 5 ingredients in small bowl. Set aside.

Heat large frying pan or wok on medium-high until very hot. Add canola oil. Add next 5 ingredients. Stir-fry for about 2 minutes until vegetables start to soften.

Add tofu and cashews. Stir-fry for 2 to 3 minutes until vegetables are tender-crisp. Stir cornstarch mixture. Add to vegetable mixture. Stir-fry for about 1 minute until boiling and thickened. Serves 4.

1 serving: 297 Calories; 16.6 g Total Fat (8.3 g Mono, 4.8 g Poly, 2.6 g Sat); 0 mg Cholesterol; 27 g Carbohydrate; 5 g Fibre; 13 g Protein; 750 mg Sodium

Tofu, made from soybeans, is rich in protein, high in fibre, low in calories and cholesterol-free. Once you've opened the package of this healthy and satisfying fare, change the water daily and make sure to use it within several days. If you note any trace of a sour odour or taste, your tofu should be given a swift and quick burial—in the garbage can!

Mediterranean Linguine

Let your taste buds take a stroll on the Mediterranean. The distinctive flavours of sun-dried tomatoes, balsamic vinegar and feta cheese are showcased in this easy-to-prepare, yet sophisticated-tasting delight.

Whole wheat linguine	3/4 lb.	340 g
Sun-dried tomatoes in oil, drained and chopped	3/4 cup	175 mL
Garlic cloves, minced (or 3/4 tsp., 4 mL, powder)	3	3
Dried crushed chilies	1/2 tsp.	2 mL
Can of artichoke hearts, drained and quartered	14 oz.	398 mL
Spinach leaves, lightly packed	6 cups	1.5 L
Balsamic vinegar	3 tbsp.	50 mL
Chopped fresh basil	1/4 cup	60 mL
Pine nuts, toasted (see Tip, page 21)	1/2 cup	125 mL
Crumbled light feta cheese	1 cup	250 mL

Cook pasta in boiling salted water in large uncovered saucepan or Dutch oven for about 10 minutes, stirring occasionally, until tender but firm. Drain. Return to same pot. Cover to keep warm.

Meanwhile, heat next 3 ingredients in large frying pan on medium for 1 minute. Add artichokes and spinach. Heat and stir for about 2 minutes until spinach is wilted.

Add next 3 ingredients. Reduce heat to low. Heat and stir for 1 minute until vinegar is evaporated. Add to pasta. Toss.

Sprinkle with feta cheese. Serves 4.

1 serving: 623 Calories; 18.5 g Total Fat (5.8 g Mono, 5.4 g Poly, 4.8 g Sat); 13 mg Cholesterol; 95 g Carbohydrate; 19 g Fibre; 33 g Protein; 680 mg Sodium

Ricotta Rotini

This rich and creamy dish is a pasta-lover's, and cheese-lover's, dream come true. Try with some basil or sun-dried tomato pesto for a more assertive flavour.

Whole wheat rotini	5 cups	1.25 L
Olive oil	2 tsp.	10 mL
Sliced red onion	1 cup	250 mL
Garlic cloves, minced (or 1/2 tsp., 2 mL, powder)	2	2
All-purpose flour	2 tbsp.	30 mL
Can of evaporated milk	13 1/2 oz.	385 mL
Ricotta cheese	1 cup	250 mL
Jar of marinated artichoke hearts, drained and chopped	6 oz.	170 mL
Cherry tomatoes, halved	12	12
Grated Parmesan cheese	1/4 cup	60 mL
Chopped fresh parsley	2 tbsp.	30 mL
Grated Parmesan cheese (optional)	2 – 4 tbsp.	30 – 60 mL

Cook pasta in boiling salted water in large uncovered saucepan or Dutch oven for about 12 minutes, stirring occasionally, until tender but firm. Drain. Return to saucepan. Cover to keep warm.

Meanwhile, heat olive oil in large frying pan on medium. Add onion and garlic. Cook for 5 to 10 minutes, stirring occasionally, until onion is softened.

Sprinkle with flour. Heat and stir for 1 minute.

Slowly add milk, stirring constantly, until mixture is boiling and thickened.

Add next 3 ingredients. Stir. Cook for about 4 minutes, stirring often, until tomato is starting to soften. Add to pasta.

Add first amount of Parmesan cheese and parsley. Stir.

Sprinkle with second amount of Parmesan cheese. Serves 4.

1 serving: 702 Calories; 22.7 g Total Fat (6.9 g Mono, 0.8 g Poly, 22.7 g Sat); 66 mg Cholesterol; 95 g Carbohydrate; 12 g Fibre; 31 g Protein; 333 mg Sodium

Sesame Pork Skewers

The easiest way to make a weekday meal look special? Skewer it! Tender pork skewers with the classic Asian flavours of ginger, garlic and sesame.

Low-sodium prepared chicken broth	1/4 cup	60 mL
Sesame oil	1 tsp.	5 mL
Low-sodium soy sauce	1 tsp.	5 mL
Rice vinegar	1 tsp.	5 mL
Brown sugar, packed	1 tsp.	5 mL
Ground ginger	1/4 tsp.	1 mL
Garlic powder	1/4 tsp.	1 mL
Pork tenderloin, trimmed of fat, cut into 3/4 inch (2 cm) cubes	1 lb.	454 g
Bamboo skewers (8 inches, 20 cm, each), soaked in water for 10 minutes	4	4
Thinly sliced green onion	2 tbsp.	30 mL
Sesame seeds	1 1/2 tsp.	7 mL

Preheat gas barbecue to medium-high. Combine first 7 ingredients in medium bowl.

Add pork. Toss well. Thread pork onto skewers. Cook on greased grill for about 12 minutes, turning occasionally and basting at halftime with any remaining soy sauce mixture, until no longer pink inside. Remove from heat. Let stand, covered, for 5 minutes.

Sprinkle with green onion and sesame seeds. Makes 4 skewers.

1 skewer: 166 Calories; 4.5 g Total Fat (1.9 g Mono, 1 g Poly, 1.2 g Sat); 67 mg Cholesterol; 2 g Carbohydrate; trace Fibre; 28 g Protein; 101 mg Sodium

Pictured on page 107.

Lemon Herb Pork

Pucker up people, this is a must-try for lemon lovers! Zesty lemon and tarragon sauce coats fork-tender pork medallions.

Olive oil	1 tbsp.	15 mL
Pork tenderloin, trimmed of fat, cut into 1/4 inch (6mm) thick slices	1 lb.	454 g
Slices of lemon, halved crosswise	4	4
Chopped fresh parsley (or 1 1/2 tsp., 7 mL, flakes)	2 tbsp.	30 mL
Chopped fresh tarragon (or 3/4 tsp., 4 mL, dried)	1 tbsp.	15 mL
Grated lemon zest	2 tsp.	10 mL
Garlic clove, minced (or 1/4 tsp., 1 mL, powder)	1	1
Dry (or alcohol-free) white wine	1/4 cup	60 mL
Evaporated milk	1/4 cup	60 mL
Salt	1/2 tsp.	2 mL
Pepper	1/4 tsp.	1 mL

Heat olive oil in large frying pan on medium-high. Add pork. Cook for about 1 minute per side until starting to brown. Remove to plate. Cover to keep warm.

Reduce heat to medium. Add next 5 ingredients to same frying pan. Cook and stir for about 1 minute until garlic is golden.

Add wine. Bring to a boil. Cook for about 1 minute until wine is reduced by half.

Add remaining 3 ingredients and pork. Cook and stir until pork is heated through. Serves 4.

1 serving: 213 Calories; 7.5 g Total Fat (4.2 g Mono, 0.6 g Poly, 2.2 g Sat); 72 mg Cholesterol; 3.9 g Carbohydrate; 0.4 g Fibre; 28 g Protein; 314 mg Sodium

Tangy Pineapple Chops

Sweet and sour flavours on pork—the perfect combination! The tangy pineapple topping keeps the pork moist and tasty.

Olive oil	1 tbsp.	15 mL
Finely chopped onion	1 cup	250 mL
Can of crushed pineapple (with juice)	14 oz.	398 mL
Brown sugar, packed	2 tbsp.	30 mL
Apple cider vinegar	2 tbsp.	30 mL
Dijon mustard	1 tbsp.	15 mL
Seasoned salt	1/2 tsp.	2 mL
Boneless pork loin chops, trimmed of fat (about 1 3/4 lbs., 790 g)	6	6
Seasoned salt	1 tsp.	5 mL

Heat olive oil in medium frying pan on medium. Add onion. Cook for 5 to 10 minutes, stirring occasionally, until softened.

Add next 5 ingredients. Bring to a boil. Cook, uncovered, for about 10 minutes, stirring occasionally, until slightly thickened. Cover to keep warm.

Meanwhile, preheat broiler (see Note). Place pork chops on broiling pan. Sprinkle second amount of seasoned salt on both sides of pork chops. Broil on top rack in oven for about 4 to 6 minutes per side until no longer pink inside. Transfer to serving plate. Spoon pineapple sauce over pork chops. Serves 6.

1 serving: 281 Calories; 11.3 g Total Fat (5.8 g Mono, 0.9 g Poly, 3.7 g Sat); 73 mg Cholesterol; 17 g Carbohydrate; 1 g Fibre; 26 g Protein; 427 mg Sodium

Note: Pork chops may be cooked on a gas barbecue on medium for 4 to 6 minutes per side until no longer pink inside.

Pear Chutney Pork Chops

Sugar and spice make these pork chops extra nice! This mild curry is tempered by sweet pear. A perfect dish for those who are new to curry flavours.

All-purpose flour	1 tbsp.	15 mL
Curry powder	1 tsp.	5 mL
Ground cardamom	1/2 tsp.	2 mL
Salt	1/2 tsp.	2 mL
Pepper	1/4 tsp.	1 mL
Boneless pork loin chops, trimmed of fat (about 1 lb., 454 g)	4	4
Canola (or olive) oil	2 tsp.	10 mL
Reserved pear syrup	1/2 cup	125 mL
Brown sugar, packed	3 tbsp.	50 mL
Apple cider vinegar	3 tbsp.	50 mL
Soy sauce	2 tbsp.	30 mL
Can of pear halves in light syrup, drained and syrup reserved, chopped	28 oz.	796 mL

Combine first 5 ingredients in shallow bowl. Remove half of flour mixture to small bowl. Set aside. Press both sides of pork chops into remaining flour mixture until coated.

Heat canola oil in large frying pan on medium. Add pork chops. Cook for 3 to 4 minutes per side until no longer pink inside. Remove chops to serving plate. Cover to keep warm.

Add next 4 ingredients to reserved flour mixture. Stir with whisk until smooth. Add to frying pan. Heat and stir until boiling and slightly thickened.

Add pears. Stir. Bring to a boil. Reduce heat to medium-low. Simmer, uncovered, for about 5 minutes until slightly thickened. Spoon over chops. Serves 4.

1 serving: 353 Calories; 8.9 g Total Fat (4.3 g Mono, 1.4 g Poly, 2.4 g Sat); 72 mg Cholesterol; 44 g Carbohydrate; 3 g Fibre; 25 g Protein; 967 mg Sodium

Pork Chops Cacciatore

A delicious and versatile tomato sauce crowns tender pork. The sauce is perfect served over rice or pasta, and makes a quick and healthy alternative to ready-made pasta sauces.

Canola oil	2 tsp.	10 mL
All-purpose flour	2 tbsp.	30 mL
Pepper, sprinkle		
Boneless fast-fry pork chops (about 1 lb., 454 g)	4	4
Chopped red pepper	1 1/2 cups	375 mL
Chopped onion	1 cup	250 mL
Garlic cloves, minced	2	2
Dry (or alcohol-free) white wine	1/4 cup	60 mL
Can of diced tomatoes (with juice)	14 oz.	398 mL
Low-sodium prepared chicken broth	1/2 cup	125 mL
Brown sugar, packed	1 tbsp.	15 mL
Dried oregano	1 tsp.	5 mL
Dried basil	1/2 tsp.	2 mL

Heat canola oil in large frying pan on medium. Meanwhile, combine flour and pepper in small shallow dish. Press both sides of pork into flour mixture until coated. Add to frying pan. Cook for about 4 minutes per side until browned. Remove to plate.

Add next 3 ingredients to same frying pan. Cook for 5 to 10 minutes, stirring often, until onion is softened.

Add wine, scraping any brown bits from bottom of pan.

Add remaining 5 ingredients. Stir. Add pork chops to frying pan. Simmer, uncovered, for about 5 minutes until pork chops are heated through. Serves 4.

1 serving: 263 Calories; 9.5 g Total Fat (4.4 g Mono, 1.4 g Poly, 2.7 g Sat); 67 mg Cholesterol; 18 g Carbohydrate; 2 g Fibre; 24 g Protein; 317 mg Sodium

Five-Spice Pork Medallions

Five flavours in one spice—you gotta love it! The exotic five-spice crumb coating is wonderful with these tender medallions. Serve with peach-flavoured applesauce for a delicious combination of flavours.

All-purpose flour	1/3 cup	75 mL
Large egg	1	1
Water	1 tbsp.	15 mL
Fine dry bread crumbs	1 cup	250 mL
Chinese five-spice powder	1 tbsp.	15 mL
Pork tenderloin, trimmed of fat, cut diagonally into 1/4 inch (6 mm) slices	1 lb.	454 g

Cooking spray
Salt, sprinkle

Measure flour into shallow bowl. Set aside.

Beat egg and water with fork in small bowl. Set aside.

Preheat oven to 425°F (220°C). Combine bread crumbs and five-spice powder in large resealable freezer bag.

Press each pork slice into flour until lightly coated. Dip into egg mixture. Add, a few at a time, to freezer bag with crumb mixture. Seal bag. Shake until evenly coated. Place on greased baking sheet with sides.

Spray pork with cooking spray. Sprinkle with salt. Bake for 10 to 15 minutes until no longer pink inside. Serves 4.

1 serving: 309 Calories; 5.9 g Total Fat (2.5 g Mono, 0.8 g Poly, 1.7 g Sat); 113 mg Cholesterol; 29 g Carbohydrate; 1 g Fibre; 33 g Protein; 305 mg Sodium

Pork is an excellent source of zinc, which may be one of the most important minerals for food lovers—it helps maintain your senses of smell and taste!

Peach Basil Pork Chops

A taste of summer—with a fresh and appetizing presentation. Use fresh peaches when they are in season, and substitute chicken broth for the peach juice.

Canola oil	1 tbsp.	15 mL
Italian seasoning	1/2 tsp.	2 mL
Paprika	1/2 tsp.	2 mL
Salt, sprinkle		
Boneless pork loin chops, trimmed of fat (about 1 lb., 454 g)	4	4
Chopped onion	1/4 cup	60 mL
Apple cider vinegar	2 tbsp.	30 mL
Can of sliced peaches in juice, drained and juice reserved	14 oz.	398 mL
Reserved peach juice	1/4 cup	60 mL
Chopped fresh basil	2 tbsp.	30 mL

Heat canola oil in large frying pan on medium-high. Combine next 3 ingredients in small cup. Sprinkle on both sides of pork chops. Add pork chops to frying pan. Cook for about 2 minutes until browned. Reduce heat to medium. Turn chops. Cook for about 3 minutes until no longer pink. Remove to plate. Cover to keep warm.

Add onion to same frying pan. Cook and stir for 1 minute. Add vinegar. Stir, scraping any brown bits from bottom of pan. Add peaches and reserved juice. Cook and stir for about 2 minutes until heated through.

Add basil. Stir. Pour over pork chops. Serves 4.

1 serving: 248 Calories; 11.0 g Total Fat (5.4 g Mono, 1.7 g Poly, 2.9 g Sat); 62 mg Cholesterol; 14 g Carbohydrate; 2 g Fibre; 24 g Protein; 49 mg Sodium

Pork And Sweet Potato Toss

Take a trip to the islands with this mild introduction to Caribbean flavours! Jerk-seasoned pork and sweet potatoes are tempered by the sweetness of apple. Try the jerk seasoning on chicken too!

JERK SEASONING

Onion powder	1 tsp.	5 mL
Ground thyme	1/2 tsp.	2 mL
Ground allspice	1/4 tsp.	1 mL
Pepper	1/4 tsp.	1 mL
Cayenne pepper	1/4 tsp.	1 mL
Ground cinnamon	1/8 tsp.	0.5 mL

PORK AND POTATOES

Canola oil	1 tbsp.	15 mL
Pork tenderloin, trimmed of fat, halved lengthwise and cut into 1/4 inch (6 mm) slices	1 lb.	454 g
Chopped peeled sweet potato (or yam)	3 cups	750 mL
Coleslaw mix	2 cups	500 mL
Low-sodium prepared chicken broth	2 tbsp.	30 mL
Medium cooking apples (such as McIntosh), peeled and sliced	2	2
Low-sodium prepared chicken broth	1/4 cup	60 mL
Golden corn syrup	2 tbsp.	30 mL

Jerk Seasoning: Combine all 6 ingredients in small cup. Makes about 2 tsp. (10 mL) seasoning. Set aside.

Pork And Potatoes: Heat canola oil in large frying pan or wok on medium-high. Sprinkle pork with 1/4 tsp. (1 mL) Jerk Seasoning. Add to frying pan. Stir-fry for about 5 minutes until no longer pink.

Add next 3 ingredients. Sprinkle with remaining Jerk Seasoning. Reduce heat to medium. Cook, covered, for about 6 minutes, stirring occasionally, until sweet potato starts to soften.

Add remaining 3 ingredients. Stir. Cook, covered, for 2 to 3 minutes, stirring occasionally, until apple is tender. Serves 4.

1 serving: 315 Calories; 6.6 g Total Fat (3.3 g Mono, 1.5 g Poly, 1.3 g Sat); 67 mg Cholesterol; 35 g Carbohydrate; 4 g Fibre; 30 g Protein; 109 mg Sodium

Apricot Jalapeño Pork

Sweet, tender pork with a lingering heat. For those who like it even spicier, try including the jalapeño seeds and ribs. Excellent served over rice.

Canola oil	2 tsp.	10 mL
Pork tenderloin, trimmed of fat, halved lengthwise and cut into 1/4 inch (6 mm) slices	1 lb.	454 g
Pepper	1/8 tsp.	0.5 mL
Low-sodium prepared chicken broth	1/3 cup	75 mL
Dry (or alcohol-free) white wine	2 tbsp.	30 mL
Apricot jam	3 tbsp.	50 mL
Jalapeño pepper, finely diced (see Tip, page 59)	1	1

Chopped fresh cilantro or parsley, for garnish

Heat canola oil in large frying pan on medium-high. Sprinkle pork with pepper. Add to frying pan. Cook for about 5 minutes, stirring often, until no longer pink inside. Remove to plate. Cover to keep warm.

Add broth and wine to same frying pan. Reduce heat to medium-low. Stir, scraping any brown bits from bottom of pan.

Add jam and jalapeño pepper. Cook and stir for 4 to 5 minutes until sauce is reduced by about half. Spoon over pork.

Garnish with cilantro. Serves 4.

1 serving: 207 Calories; 5.2 g Total Fat (2.7 g Mono, 1 g Poly, 1.2 g Sat); 67 mg Cholesterol; 10 g Carbohydrate; trace Fibre; 27 g Protein; 66 mg Sodium

Pictured on page 18.

Tropical Peppers

This combination of fruit and vegetables makes a colourful side dish that goes well with fish, pork or poultry. Enjoy the simple and mildly sweet flavours of glazed pineapple and bell peppers.

Can of pineapple chunks, drained and juice reserved	**14 oz.**	**398 mL**
Large green pepper, cut into 1 inch (2.5 cm) strips	**1**	**1**
Large red pepper, cut into 1 inch (2.5 cm) strips	**1**	**1**
Large orange pepper, cut into 1 inch (2.5 cm) strips	**1**	**1**
Olive oil	**2 tsp.**	**10 mL**
Salt, sprinkle		
Pepper, sprinkle		
Reserved pineapple juice	**2/3 cup**	**150 mL**
Cornstarch	**1 tsp.**	**5 mL**

Preheat broiler. Put first 4 ingredients into large bowl. Drizzle with olive oil. Sprinkle with salt and pepper. Toss well. Arrange pineapple with peppers, skin side up, in single layer on greased baking sheet with sides. Broil on top rack in oven for about10 minutes until peppers are just starting to blacken and pineapple is hot.

Meanwhile, stir reserved pineapple juice into cornstarch in medium saucepan until smooth. Bring to a boil on medium, stirring constantly, until boiling and thickened. Add peppers and pineapple. Stir until coated. Serves 6.

1 serving: 89 Calories; 1.8 g Total Fat (1.1 g Mono, 0.2 g Poly, 0.3 g Sat); 0 mg Cholesterol; 19 g Carbohydrate; 2 g Fibre; 1 g Protein; 3 mg Sodium

Pictured on front cover.

1. Portobellos And Greens, page 40
2. Basil Pesto Pasta, page 132
3. Grilled Pepper Chicken, page 86

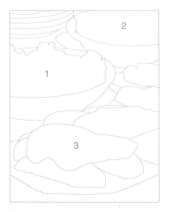

Creamy Curried Zucchini

This is the dish you'll want to invite to all your dinners—it goes well with everything!

Canola oil	1 tbsp.	15 mL
Thinly sliced onion	1 cup	250 mL
Curry powder	1 1/2 tsp.	7 mL
Low-sodium prepared chicken (or vegetable) broth	1/2 cup	125 mL
Medium zucchini, quartered lengthwise and cut into 1/2 inch (12 mm) pieces	2	2
Salt, sprinkle		
Pepper, sprinkle		
Light spreadable cream cheese	2 tbsp.	30 mL

Heat canola oil in large frying pan on medium-high until very hot. Add onion. Stir-fry for about 2 minutes until starting to turn golden.

Add curry powder. Stir-fry for about 1 minute until fragrant.

Add next 4 ingredients. Stir-fry for about 5 minutes until zucchini is tender-crisp. Remove from heat.

Add cream cheese. Stir well. Serves 4.

1 serving: 89 Calories; 5.1 g Total Fat (2.1 g Mono, 1.2 g Poly, 1.2 g Sat); 4 mg Cholesterol; 9 g Carbohydrate; 2 g Fibre; 3 g Protein; 56 mg Sodium

Pictured at left.

Variation: Use 4 cups (1 L) broccoli or cauliflower florets instead of zucchini.

1. Balsamic Beans, page 128
2. Fennel Potatoes, page 129
3. Creamy Curried Zucchini, above

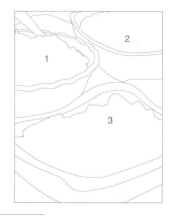

Tangy Asparagus

With its white wine, lemon and garlic flavours, this side dish is guaranteed to impress even the most refined of guests!

Olive oil	2 tbsp.	30 mL
Finely chopped onion	1/2 cup	125 mL
Garlic cloves, minced (or 1/2 tsp., 2 mL, powder)	2	2
Fresh asparagus, trimmed of tough ends and cut into 2 inch (5 cm) pieces	2 lbs.	900 g
Dry (or alcohol-free) white wine	1/4 cup	60 mL
Lemon juice	1/4 cup	60 mL
Salt, sprinkle		
Pepper, sprinkle		

Heat olive oil in large frying pan on medium. Add onion and garlic. Cook for about 2 minutes until onion starts to soften.

Add asparagus. Cook and stir for about 3 minutes until almost tender-crisp.

Add remaining 4 ingredients. Heat and stir for 1 minute to blend flavours. Serves 4.

1 serving: 139 Calories; 7.2 g Total Fat (5.0 g Mono, 0.8 g Poly, 1.0 g Sat); 0 mg Cholesterol; 15 g Carbohydrate; 4 g Fibre; 6 g Protein; 6 mg Sodium

Balsamic Beans

Complementary colours of red and green make this dish appealing to the eye. Complementary flavours of beans and balsamic vinegar make this dish appealing to the palate.

Frozen cut green beans	5 cups	1.25 L
Olive oil	1 tbsp.	15 mL
Thinly sliced red onion	1/4 cup	60 mL
Garlic clove, minced (or 1/4 tsp., 1 mL, powder)	1	1
Can of diced tomatoes, drained	14 oz.	398 mL
Balsamic vinegar	3 tbsp.	50 mL
Parsley flakes	1 tsp.	5 mL
Dried basil	1/2 tsp.	2 mL

Cook beans in boiling salted water in large partially covered saucepan for about 6 minutes, stirring occasionally, until tender but firm. Drain. Return to same pot. Cover to keep warm.

(continued on next page)

Meanwhile, heat olive oil in medium frying pan on medium. Add onion and garlic. Cook for about 5 minutes until onion is softened.

Add remaining 4 ingredients. Heat and stir for 2 minutes to blend flavours. Add to beans. Toss. Serves 4.

1 serving: 108 Calories; 3.5 g Total Fat (2.5 g Mono, 0.3 g Poly, 0.5 g Sat); 0 mg Cholesterol; 16 g Carbohydrate; 5 g Fibre; 3 g Protein; 430 mg Sodium

Pictured on page 126.

Fennel Potatoes

Tender vegetables and potatoes tossed together with a hint of lemon pepper and the delicate licorice taste of fennel.

Olive oil	2 tbsp.	30 mL
Thinly sliced fennel bulb (white part only)	2 cups	500 mL
Red baby potatoes, cut into 8 wedges each	1 lb.	454 g
Lemon pepper	1/2 tsp.	2 mL
Roasted red pepper, drained and blotted dry, cut into strips	1 cup	250 mL
Prepared chicken broth	3 tbsp.	50 mL

Heat olive oil in large frying pan on medium-high. Add next 3 ingredients. Cook for about 5 minutes, stirring often, until potato and fennel start to brown.

Add red pepper and broth. Stir. Reduce heat to medium. Cook, covered, for about 10 minutes, stirring occasionally, until potato is tender. Serves 4.

1 serving: 213 Calories; 7.4 g Total Fat (5.0 g Mono, 0.7 g Poly, 0.9 g Sat); 0 mg Cholesterol; 35 g Carbohydrate; 8 g Fibre; 5 g Protein; 261 mg Sodium

Pictured on page 126.

Honey-Roasted Carrots

These honey-kissed carrots are a guaranteed hit for those with a sweet tooth.

Baby carrots	**2 lbs.**	**900 g**
Liquid honey	**2 tbsp.**	**30 mL**
Olive oil	**2 tsp.**	**10 mL**
Salt, sprinkle		
Pepper, sprinkle		

Preheat oven to 450°F (230°C). Combine all 5 ingredients in large bowl. Toss well. Arrange in single layer on greased baking sheet with sides. Bake in oven for about 15 minutes until tender-crisp. Serves 4.

1 serving: 140 Calories; 3.5 g Total Fat (1.7 g Mono, 0.8 g Poly, 0.5 g Sat); 0 mg Cholesterol; 27 g Carbohydrate; 4 g Fibre; 2 g Protein; 79 mg Sodium

Citrus Spice Quinoa Pilaf

You'll be keen on this fluffy quinoa (pronounced KEEN–wah) pilaf scented with lemon and thyme. Quinoa is available in the bulk or health food sections of grocery stores.

Low-sodium prepared chicken broth	**2 cups**	**500 mL**
Quinoa, rinsed and drained	**1 cup**	**250 mL**
Bay leaf	**1**	**1**
Olive oil	**1 tbsp.**	**15 mL**
Diced butternut squash	**2 cups**	**500 mL**
Chopped onion	**1 cup**	**250 mL**
Chopped fresh thyme (or 1/2 tsp., 2 mL, dried)	**2 tsp.**	**10 mL**
Dried crushed chilies	**1/4 tsp.**	**1 mL**
Salt, sprinkle		
Lemon juice	**2 tbsp.**	**30 mL**
Grated lemon zest	**2 tsp.**	**10 mL**

Combine first 3 ingredients in medium saucepan. Bring to a boil. Reduce heat to medium-low. Simmer, covered, for about 15 minutes until broth is absorbed. Discard bay leaf.

Meanwhile, heat olive oil in large frying pan on medium. Add next 5 ingredients. Cook, covered, for 5 to 10 minutes, stirring occasionally, until squash and onion are softened and lightly browned. Remove from heat.

Add lemon juice, lemon zest and quinoa. Stir. Serves 4.

1 serving: 272 Calories; 6.4 g Total Fat (3.3 g Mono, 1.4 g Poly, 0.9 g Sat); 0 mg Cholesterol; 49 g Carbohydrate; 6 g Fibre; 8 g Protein; 33 mg Sodium

Pictured on page 107.

Lemon Leek Linguine

A very intriguing dinner companion (for salmon or chicken, at least) and a very tasty pasta dish for you! Serve immediately.

Whole wheat linguine	3/4 lb.	340 g
Olive oil	2 tsp.	10 mL
Sliced leek (white part only)	2 cups	500 mL
Garlic cloves, minced	2	2
Low-sodium prepared chicken broth	1/2 cup	125 mL
Dry (or alcohol-free) white wine	1/3 cup	75 mL
Grated lemon zest	2 tsp.	10 mL
Pepper	1/2 tsp.	2 mL
Evaporated milk	1/2 cup	125 mL
Grated Parmesan cheese	1/4 cup	60 mL
Chopped fresh dill	2 tbsp.	30 mL

Cook pasta in boiling salted water in uncovered Dutch oven or large pot for 10 to 12 minutes, stirring occasionally, until tender but firm. Drain, reserving 1/4 cup (60 mL) cooking water. Return to same pot. Cover to keep warm.

Meanwhile, heat olive oil in large frying pan on medium. Add leek and garlic. Cook, covered, for about 5 minutes, stirring occasionally, until leek is softened.

Add next 4 ingredients. Bring to a boil. Heat and stir for 2 minutes.

Add evaporated milk. Stir. Heat until hot, but not boiling. Add to pasta. Add reserved cooking water. Stir well. Transfer to serving bowl.

Sprinkle with Parmesan cheese and dill. Serves 4.

1 serving: 423 Calories; 5.7 g Total Fat (2.4 g Mono, 0.8 g Poly, 1.8 g Sat); 5 mg Cholesterol; 78 g Carbohydrate; 9 g Fibre; 17 g Protein; 146 mg Sodium

Basil Pesto Pasta

Make this in the summer when you harvest your herb garden. Less oil than traditional pesto makes this a healthier version. Excellent with grilled chicken.

Whole wheat linguine	8 oz.	225 g
Fresh basil, lightly packed	1 cup	250 mL
Salted, roasted shelled pumpkin seeds	1/4 cup	60 mL
Water	1/4 cup	60 mL
Olive oil	2 tbsp.	30 mL
Lemon juice	2 tbsp.	30 mL
Garlic cloves, minced (or 1/2 tsp., 2 mL, powder)	2	2
Chopped fresh spinach leaves, lightly packed	2 cups	500 mL
Grated Parmesan cheese	1/4 cup	60 mL

Cook pasta in boiling salted water in large uncovered saucepan or Dutch oven for about 12 minutes, stirring occasionally, until tender but firm. Drain, reserving 1/2 cup (125 mL) cooking water. Return to same pot. Cover to keep warm.

Meanwhile, process next 6 ingredients in blender or food processor until smooth.

Add spinach, Parmesan cheese and basil mixture to pasta. Toss, adding reserved cooking water a little at a time, if needed, to moisten. Serve immediately. Serves 4.

1 serving: 372 Calories; 15.6 g Total Fat (7.5 g Mono, 3.8 g Poly, 3.4 g Sat); 5 mg Cholesterol; 47 g Carbohydrate; 6 g Fibre; 17 g Protein; 218 mg Sodium

Pictured on page 125.

Rice And Peas Parmesan

Talk about well-rounded! This side dish covers all your food groups— and has the taste of fresh peas. Use converted whole grain rice for an added nutty flavour but allow a little longer for cooking.

Olive (or canola) oil	1 tsp.	5 mL
Finely chopped onion	1 cup	250 mL
Low-sodium prepared chicken broth	2 1/4 cups	550 mL
Converted white rice	1 cup	250 mL
Chopped deli smoked turkey (or ham) slices	1/2 cup	125 mL
Pepper	1/4 tsp.	1 mL
Frozen peas, thawed (see Tip, page 67)	1 cup	250 mL
Grated Parmesan cheese	1/3 cup	75 mL
Chopped fresh parsley	1/3 cup	75 mL

Heat olive oil in medium saucepan on medium-high. Add onion. Cook for about 3 minutes until starting to brown.

(continued on next page)

Add next 4 ingredients. Bring to a boil. Reduce heat to medium-low. Simmer, covered, for about 20 minutes, without stirring, until rice is tender.

Stir remaining 3 ingredients into rice mixture. Serves 4.

1 serving: 290 Calories; 4.8 g Total Fat (1.8 g Mono, 0.4 g Poly, 1.9 g Sat); 13 mg Cholesterol; 48 g Carbohydrate; 3 g Fibre; 13 g Protein; 382 mg Sodium

Asparagus Spaghetti

Get a double dose of nutrients with a helping of whole wheat spaghetti and healthful asparagus. This side dish should please all tastes—it's a little bit sweet and a little bit spicy.

Whole wheat spaghetti	8 oz.	225 g
Fresh asparagus, trimmed of tough ends and cut into 2 inch (5 cm) pieces	1 lb.	454 g
Orange juice	1 tbsp.	15 mL
Cornstarch	1 tsp.	5 mL
Olive oil	2 tsp.	10 mL
Garlic cloves, minced (or 1/2 tsp., 2 mL powder)	2	2
Orange juice	1 cup	250 mL
Rice vinegar	2 tsp.	10 mL
Grated lemon zest	1 tsp.	5 mL
Dried crushed chilies	1/8 – 1/4 tsp.	0.5 – 1 mL
Chopped fresh chives, for garnish		

Cook spaghetti in boiling salted water in large uncovered saucepan or Dutch oven for about 8 minutes, stirring occasionally, until partially cooked. Add asparagus. Stir. Cook for about 3 minutes until spaghetti is tender but firm. Drain. Return to same pot. Cover to keep warm.

Meanwhile, stir first amount of orange juice into cornstarch in small cup. Set aside.

Heat olive oil in small frying pan on medium. Add garlic. Cook for about 2 minutes, stirring occasionally, until fragrant.

Add next 4 ingredients. Stir. Simmer for 5 minutes to blend flavours. Stir cornstarch mixture. Add to garlic mixture. Heat and stir for 1 to 2 minutes until boiling and thickened. Pour over spaghetti and asparagus. Toss well.

Garnish with chives. Serves 6.

1 serving: 101 Calories; 2.0 g Total Fat (1.2 g Mono, 0.3 g Poly, 0.3 g Sat); 0 mg Cholesterol; 19 g Carbohydrate; 2 g Fibre; 4 g Protein; 3 mg Sodium

Fragrant Rice

Subtle Asian-influenced aromas give this dish its scent-ual name. You can use converted whole grain rice in place of converted white rice for added health benefits. Adjust the cooking time accordingly.

Water	2 cups	500 mL
Converted white rice	1 cup	250 mL
Salt	1/4 tsp.	1 mL
Finely chopped celery	1/4 cup	60 mL
Sliced green onion	1/4 cup	60 mL
Low-sodium soy sauce	2 tbsp.	30 mL
Lime juice	2 tsp.	10 mL
Liquid honey	2 tsp.	10 mL
Garlic clove, minced (or 1/4 tsp., 1 mL, powder)	1	1
Finely grated gingerroot (or 1/4 tsp., 1 mL, ground ginger)	1 tsp.	5 mL
Sesame oil (optional)	1 tsp.	5 mL

Chopped green onion, for garnish

Measure first 3 ingredients into small saucepan. Bring to a boil. Reduce heat to medium-low. Simmer, covered, for about 20 minutes, without stirring, until water is absorbed and rice is tender.

Meanwhile, combine next 8 ingredients in small bowl. Add to rice. Stir well. Cover. Let stand for 5 minutes to blend flavours. Fluff with fork.

Garnish with green onion. Serves 4.

1 serving: 200 Calories; 1.5 g Total Fat (0.5 g Mono, 0.6 g Poly, 0.3 g Sat); 0 mg Cholesterol; 42 g Carbohydrate; 1 g Fibre; 4 g Protein; 371 mg Sodium

Pictured on front cover.

Roasted Brussels Sprouts

Just toss together and bake! Roasting brings out the sweetness of vegetables for an easy and delicious side dish.

Frozen baby Brussels sprouts (do not thaw)	4 cups	1 L
Sliced red onion, cut 1/4 inch (6 mm) thick	1/2 cup	125 mL
Diced cooked ham	1/2 cup	125 mL
Olive oil	1 tbsp.	15 mL
Salt, sprinkle		
Pepper, sprinkle		

(continued on next page)

Preheat oven to 400°F (205°C). Combine all 6 ingredients in large bowl. Toss well. Arrange in single layer on large greased baking sheet with sides. Bake in oven for about 20 minutes, stirring once at halftime, until Brussels sprouts are tender. Serves 6.

1 serving: 85 Calories; 4.5 g Total Fat (2.6 g Mono, 0.6 g Poly, 1.1 g Sat); 7 mg Cholesterol; 7 g Carbohydrate; 3 g Fibre; 6 g Protein; 146 mg Sodium

Butternut Squash Toss

This toss will never leave you at a loss for what to make for dinner! Its pretty colours and contrasting textures are sure to please the palate.

Butternut squash, cut into 1/2 inch (12 mm) pieces (about 3 cups, 750 mL)	1 1/2 lbs.	680 g
Balsamic vinegar	1 tbsp.	15 mL
Brown sugar, packed	1 tbsp.	15 mL
Olive oil	2 tsp.	10 mL
Pepper	1/4 tsp.	1 mL
Fresh spinach leaves, lightly packed, chopped	3 cups	750 mL
Olive oil	1 tbsp.	15 mL
Lemon juice	1 tbsp.	15 mL
Salt, sprinkle		
Raw pumpkin seeds, toasted (see Tip, page 21)	2 tbsp.	30 mL
Crumbled blue cheese	1 oz.	28 g

Toss first 5 ingredients in large microwave-safe bowl. Microwave, covered, on high (100%) for 10 minutes. Stir. Microwave, covered, for another 3 to 5 minutes until squash is tender-crisp.

Add next 4 ingredients. Stir. Microwave, covered, on high (100%) for 30 seconds until spinach is wilted. Transfer to serving dish.

Sprinkle pumpkin seeds and blue cheese over centre of squash mixture. Serves 4.

1 serving: 214 Calories; 10.9 g Total Fat (5.6 g Mono, 2.0 g Poly, 2.7 g Sat); 5 mg Cholesterol; 27 g Carbohydrate; 5 g Fibre; 6 g Protein; 127 mg Sodium

Pepper-Sauced Rotini

A sure-fire attraction, this easy and elegant rotini will delight one and all.

Whole wheat rotini	2 cups	500 mL
Large red pepper, quartered	1	1
Garlic clove, peeled	1	1
Lime juice	2 tbsp.	30 mL
Olive oil	1 tbsp.	15 mL
Tomato paste (see Tip, page 83)	2 tsp.	10 mL
Pepper	1/8 tsp.	0.5 mL
Grated Parmesan cheese	1/4 cup	60 mL

Cook pasta in boiling salted water in large uncovered saucepan for about 10 minutes, stirring occasionally, until tender but firm. Drain, reserving 2 tbsp. (30 mL) cooking water. Return to same pot. Cover to keep warm.

Meanwhile, put red pepper and garlic into small microwave-safe bowl. Microwave, covered, on high (100%) for about 5 minutes until softened. Let stand for 5 minutes. Remove and discard skin from red pepper. Transfer to blender or food processor.

Add next 4 ingredients. Process until smooth.

Add Parmesan cheese, red pepper mixture and reserved cooking water to pasta. Stir well. Serves 4.

1 serving: 223 Calories; 6.5 g Total Fat (3.1 g Mono, 0.4 g Poly, 1.7 g Sat); 5 mg Cholesterol; 34 g Carbohydrate; 5 g Fibre; 8 g Protein; 129 mg Sodium

Ginger-Lime Carrots

A brightly-coloured gingery treat with the goodness of carrots! With the added bonus of natural sweetening from apple juice, this recipe needs no added sugar!

Apple juice	1 tbsp.	15 mL
Cornstarch	2 tsp.	10 mL
Sliced carrot (about 1/4 inch, 6 mm, thick)	3 cups	750 mL
Apple juice	1 cup	250 mL
Minced crystallized ginger	1 tbsp.	15 mL
Salt, sprinkle		
Lime juice	1 tbsp.	15 mL

(continued on next page)

137

Stir first amount of apple juice into cornstarch in small cup. Set aside.

Combine next 4 ingredients in medium saucepan. Bring to a boil. Reduce heat to medium. Boil gently, partially covered, for about 10 minutes until carrot is tender-crisp. Stir cornstarch mixture. Add to carrot mixture. Heat and stir until boiling and thickened. Remove from heat.

Add lime juice. Stir. Serves 4.

1 serving: 181 Calories; 0.5 g Total Fat (trace Mono, 0.2 g Poly, 0.1 g Sat); 0 mg Cholesterol; 44 g Carbohydrate; 3 g Fibre; 1 g Protein; 84 mg Sodium

Black Bean And Corn Skillet

A great side dish for your next barbecue! This light and colourful dish is very versatile—it can be served at room temperature or chilled. If you like the tangy taste of balsamic or want to really feel the heat in your cayenne, opt for the larger measurement options.

Olive oil	1 tbsp.	15 mL
Frozen kernel corn	2 cups	500 mL
Diced zucchini	3/4 cup	175 mL
Diced red pepper	1/2 cup	125 mL
Garlic clove, minced (or 1/4 tsp., 1 mL, powder)	1	1
Cayenne pepper	1/8 – 1/4 tsp.	0.5 – 1 mL
Can of black beans, rinsed and drained	19 oz.	540 mL
Finely chopped green onion	1/4 cup	60 mL
Balsamic vinegar	1 – 2 tbsp.	15 – 30 mL
Grated lemon zest	2 tsp.	10 mL
Chopped fresh thyme (or 1/4 tsp., 1 mL, dried)	1 tsp.	5 mL

Heat olive oil in large frying pan on medium. Add next 5 ingredients. Cook for 8 to 10 minutes, stirring occasionally, until vegetables are tender-crisp.

Add remaining 5 ingredients. Heat and stir for 2 minutes to blend flavours. Serves 4.

1 serving: 299 Calories; 4.8 g Total Fat (2.7 g Mono, 0.9 g Poly, 0.8 g Sat); 0 mg Cholesterol; 53 g Carbohydrate; 12 g Fibre; 15 g Protein; 330 mg Sodium

Pictured on page 18.

• SIDES •

Quick Fruit Compote

Very versatile! Serve hot or cold, as a dessert or as a condiment. Makes a great topping for pancakes or yogurt. Doubles easily and keeps well in the refrigerator, so make a big batch to keep on hand for a quick snack.

White grape juice (see Note)	3/4 cup	175 mL
Coarsely chopped dried apricot	1/2 cup	125 mL
Large pear, peeled and cut into 1/2 inch (12 mm) pieces	1	1
Medium cooking apple (such as McIntosh), peeled and diced	1	1
Medium orange, peeled and cut into 1/2 inch (12 mm) pieces	1	1
Fresh (or frozen) cranberries	1 cup	250 mL
Orange liqueur (or orange juice)	1 tbsp.	15 mL

Combine first 4 ingredients in medium saucepan. Bring to a boil. Reduce heat to medium-low. Simmer, uncovered, for about 5 minutes until softened.

Add orange and cranberries. Stir gently. Cook for about 5 minutes until cranberries begin to split.

Stir in liqueur. Makes about 3 cups (750 mL).

1 cup (250 mL): 204 Calories; 0.3 g Total Fat (trace Mono, 0.1 g Poly, 0.1 g Sat); 0 mg Cholesterol; 50 g Carbohydrate; 7 g Fibre; 2 g Protein; 21 mg Sodium

Note: If necessary, add up to another 1/4 cup (60 mL) white grape juice to get the desired consistency.

HOLIDAY FRUIT COMPOTE: Add 2 tbsp. (30 mL) finely chopped crystallized ginger, a 4 inch (10 cm) stick of cinnamon and 4 whole cloves with first 4 ingredients. Discard cinnamon stick and cloves before serving.

Cranberry may just be your bladder's best friend. It makes your bladder slippery so anything nasty that wants to stick around, attach to your bladder walls and cause problems has a heck of a time hanging on.

Bread Puddings

With sweet apples and a kiss of cinnamon, this one's a real beauty. Best served with a scoop of vanilla frozen yogurt.

Chopped dried apple	1/2 cup	125 mL
Apple juice	1/4 cup	60 mL
Large eggs	2	2
Can of skim evaporated milk	13 1/2 oz.	385 mL
Brown sugar, packed	3 tbsp.	50 mL
Vanilla extract	1 tsp.	5 mL
Ground cinnamon	1/2 tsp.	2 mL
Ground nutmeg, sprinkle		
Salt, just a pinch		
Whole grain bread slices, cubed	4	4
(about 3 cups, 750 mL)		
Brown sugar, packed	4 tsp.	20 mL

Preheat oven to 375°F (190°C). Combine apples and apple juice in small microwave-safe bowl. Microwave, uncovered, on medium (50%) for 45 seconds.

Meanwhile, beat eggs in medium bowl. Stir in next 6 ingredients. Add bread cubes and apple mixture. Stir. Spoon into 4 greased 1 cup (250 mL) ramekins or ovenproof bowls.

Sprinkle with second amount of brown sugar. Place ramekins on baking sheet with sides. Bake in oven for about 20 minutes until top is golden and a knife inserted in centre comes out clean. Let stand for 3 to 4 minutes until set. Serves 4.

1 serving: 327 Calories; 3.5 g Total Fat (1.5 g Mono, 0.6 g Poly, 1.0 g Sat); 93 mg Cholesterol; 61 g Carbohydrate; 3 g Fibre; 13 g Protein; 433 mg Sodium

Pecan-Stuffed Dates

These sweet dates with a creamy pecan and cinnamon filling are the ideal energy snack for those on the go. Can be stored in the refrigerator for up to 1 week in a sealed container for a quick treat. Use large, moist fresh dates for best results.

Large whole dates	**12**	**12**
Chopped pecans, toasted (see Tip, page 21)	**1/4 cup**	**60 mL**
Light spreadable cream cheese	**2 tbsp.**	**30 mL**
Ground cinnamon	**1/4 tsp.**	**1 mL**

Cut dates in half lengthwise almost, but not quite through to other side. Press open. Remove pits.

Combine remaining 3 ingredients in small bowl. Spoon 1 tsp. (5 mL) into each date. Press closed. Makes 12 dates.

1 date: 82 Calories; 2.3 g Total Fat (1.0 g Mono, 0.6 g Poly, 0.5 g Sat); 1 mg Cholesterol; 17 g Carbohydrate; 2 g Fibre; 1 g Protein; 13 mg Sodium

Melon Banana Splits

No one's going to split when this fun and fruity treat is served. Think of it as an artistic way of getting your fruit. Refreshing, delicious and very healthy!

Large bananas, halved crosswise	**2**	**2**
Chopped watermelon	**1 1/3 cups**	**325 mL**
Chopped honeydew	**1 1/3 cups**	**325 mL**
Chopped cantaloupe	**1 1/3 cups**	**325 mL**
Vanilla yogurt	**1 cup**	**250 mL**
Fresh blueberries	**1/4 cup**	**60 mL**
Chopped fresh pineapple (or canned tidbits, drained)	**1/4 cup**	**60 mL**
Fresh raspberries	**1/4 cup**	**60 mL**
Caramel ice cream topping (optional)	**2 tbsp.**	**30 mL**

Cut banana halves lengthwise to make 8 pieces. Place 2 banana pieces on opposite sides of 4 banana split dishes or shallow bowls.

Drop spoonfuls of next 3 ingredients in separate mounds between banana pieces.

Drizzle yogurt over melon.

Sprinkle next 3 ingredients over yogurt.

Drizzle with ice cream topping. Serves 4.

1 serving: 175 Calories; 1.4 g Total Fat (0.1 g Mono, 0.2 g Poly, 0.6 g Sat); 3 mg Cholesterol; 40 g Carbohydrate; 3 g Fibre; 4 g Protein; 54 mg Sodium

Orange Soufflé Clouds

These individual soufflés will have you floating high. Ensure your beaters and bowl are grease-free.

Granulated sugar	2 tbsp.	30 mL
Skim milk	1 cup	250 mL
Granulated sugar	3 tbsp.	50 mL
Cornstarch	2 tbsp.	30 mL
Egg yolk (large), fork-beaten	1	1
Orange juice	1/3 cup	75 mL
Grated orange zest (see Tip, below)	1 tbsp.	15 mL
Egg whites (large), room temperature	5	5
Cream of tartar	1/2 tsp.	2 mL
Granulated sugar	3 tbsp.	50 mL

Preheat oven to 400°F (205°C). Sprinkle first amount of sugar into greased 6 oz. (170 mL) ramekin. Tilt ramekin to coat bottom and sides with sugar. Gently tap excess sugar into another greased ramekin. Repeat 5 more times to prepare a total of 6 sugar-coated ramekins. Discard excess sugar from last ramekin once coated. Place ramekins on baking sheet with sides. Set aside.

Combine next 3 ingredients in small saucepan on medium. Heat and stir for about 5 minutes until boiling and thickened.

Combine next 3 ingredients in small cup. Add to milk mixture, stirring constantly with whisk for about 1 minute until thick. Transfer to medium bowl.

Beat egg whites and cream of tartar in large bowl until soft peaks form. Add third amount of sugar 1 tbsp. (15 mL) at a time, beating constantly until stiff peaks form and sugar is dissolved. Fold about 1/3 of egg white mixture into hot milk mixture until almost combined. Fold milk mixture into remaining egg whites until no white streaks remain. Spoon into ramekins. Smooth tops. Bake in oven for about 12 minutes, without opening oven door, until very puffed and tops are golden. Serves 6.

1 serving: 117 Calories; 0.9 g Total Fat (0.4 g Mono, 0.1 g Poly, 0.3 g Sat); 32 mg Cholesterol; 22 g Carbohydrate; trace Fibre; 5 g Protein; 68 mg Sodium

Pictured on page 143.

TART LEMON SOUFFLÉ CLOUDS: Use same amounts of lemon juice and lemon zest instead of orange juice and orange zest.

When a recipe calls for both the zest and juice of a citrus fruit, be sure to grate the zest before juicing.

Dessert Quesadillas

Guiltless but oh, so good! You can't go wrong with this banana and chocolate-filled whole wheat quesadilla. Use dark chocolate chips for a healthier choice. Serve with vanilla frozen yogurt. Peanut butter lovers must try the Banana Nut variation!

Granulated sugar	2 tsp.	10 mL
Ground cinnamon	1/8 tsp.	0.5 mL
Small bananas, thinly sliced	2	2
Lemon juice	2 tsp.	10 mL
Whole wheat flour tortillas (9 inch, 22 cm, diameter)	4	4
Dark (or semi-sweet) chocolate chips	1/4 cup	60 mL
Cooking spray		

Preheat oven to 350°F (175°C). Combine sugar and cinnamon in small cup. Set aside.

Put banana slices and lemon juice into small bowl. Toss gently.

Arrange banana slices on half of each tortilla. Sprinkle chocolate chips over banana. Fold tortillas in half to cover filling. Transfer to ungreased baking sheet with sides.

Spray tortillas with cooking spray. Sprinkle cinnamon mixture over top. Bake in oven for about 5 minutes until chocolate chips are melted. Cut tortillas into wedges. Serves 4.

1 serving: 262 Calories; 6.0 g Total Fat (0.1 g Mono, 0.4 g Poly, 3.2 g Sat); 0 mg Cholesterol; 58 g Carbohydrate; 5 g Fibre; 7 g Protein; 299 mg Sodium

BANANA NUT QUESADILLAS: Spread 1 tbsp. (15 mL) peanut butter on half of each tortilla before arranging banana slices.

1. Sweet Pea Soup, page 58
2. Orange Soufflé Clouds, page 141
3. Summer Salad, page 42
4. Tarragon-Poached Fish, page 98

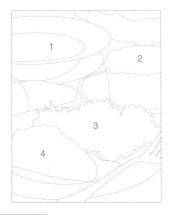

Oatmeal Cranberry Cookies

Quell the inner cookie monster when a craving hits. Full of oats, wheat germ, pecans and cranberries, this cookie is a guilt-free treat. A small ice cream scoop helps portion the dough quickly and evenly.

Butter (or hard margarine), softened	1/2 cup	125 mL
Brown sugar, packed	1/2 cup	125 mL
Large egg	1	1
Vanilla extract	1/2 tsp.	2 mL
Quick-cooking rolled oats	1 cup	250 mL
All-purpose flour	2/3 cup	150 mL
Wheat germ	1/2 cup	125 mL
Baking powder	1 tsp.	5 mL
Salt	1/2 tsp.	2 mL
Dried cranberries	3/4 cup	175 mL
Chopped pecans	1/4 cup	60 mL

Preheat oven to 375°F (190°C). Cream butter and brown sugar in medium bowl. Add egg and vanilla. Beat until smooth.

Add next 5 ingredients. Beat on low until well combined.

Add cranberries and pecans. Stir. Drop, using 1 tbsp. (15 mL) for each, about 1 inch (2.5 cm) apart onto 2 greased cookie sheets. Flatten slightly with a fork. Bake on separate racks in oven for about 10 minutes, switching position of cookie sheets at halftime, until golden. Remove cookies from cookie sheets and place on wire racks to cool. Makes about 36 cookies.

1 cookie: 76 Calories; 3.8 g Total Fat (1.1 g Mono, 0.3 g Poly, 1.8 g Sat); 12 mg Cholesterol; 9 g Carbohydrate; 1 g Fibre; 1 g Protein; 56 mg Sodium

Pictured at left.

1. Pineapple Coconut Meringues, page 146
2. Strawberry Angel Cups, page 147
3. Oatmeal Cranberry Cookies, above
4. Date Crispies, page 146

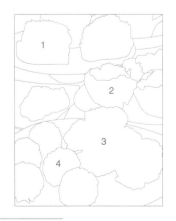

Pineapple Coconut Meringues

Tropical flavours abound! Sweet meringue with almonds and coconut tops a warm pineapple slice.

Can of pineapple slices, drained	14 oz.	398 mL
Sliced natural almonds	1/4 cup	60 mL
Egg whites (large), room temperature	2	2
Vanilla extract	1/2 tsp.	2 mL
Granulated sugar	2 tbsp.	30 mL
Medium unsweetened coconut	1/3 cup	75 mL
Sliced natural almonds	1/4 cup	60 mL
Medium unsweetened coconut	3 tbsp.	50 mL

Preheat oven to 400°F (205°C). Arrange 4 stacks of 2 pineapple slices in greased 9 inch (22 cm) pie plate. Sprinkle almonds over top. Set aside.

Beat egg whites in medium bowl until soft peaks form. Add vanilla. Add sugar 1 tbsp. (15 mL) at a time, beating constantly until stiff peaks form and sugar is dissolved.

Fold first amount of coconut and second amount of almonds into egg white mixture. Spoon onto pineapple.

Sprinkle with second amount of coconut. Bake in oven for about 10 minutes until meringue is golden. Serves 4.

1 serving: 226 Calories; 12.2 g Total Fat (4.1 g Mono, 1.6 g Poly, 5.8 g Sat); 0 mg Cholesterol; 26 g Carbohydrate; 4 g Fibre; 5 g Protein; 32 mg Sodium

Pictured on page 144.

Date Crispies

Another "I can't believe this is good for me" treat. Chewy and crispy, they're sure to satisfy all manner of cravings. Store them in the fridge—if they're still around after a few hours!

Butter (or hard margarine)	1 tbsp.	15 mL
Chopped pitted dates	1/2 cup	125 mL
Granulated sugar	1/4 cup	60 mL
Large egg, fork-beaten	1	1
Crisp rice cereal	1 1/2 cups	375 mL
Salted, roasted sunflower seeds	1/4 cup	60 mL

Melt butter in small saucepan on medium. Add next 3 ingredients. Cook for about 3 minutes, stirring constantly, until thickened. Remove from heat.

(continued on next page)

Add cereal and sunflower seeds. Stir. Let stand for about 10 minutes until cool enough to handle. Shape into 1 inch (2.5 cm) balls (see Note). Makes 18 crispies.

1 crispy: 53 Calories; 1.8 g Total Fat (0.5 g Mono, 0.7 g Poly, 0.6 g Sat); 12 mg Cholesterol; 9 g Carbohydrate; 1 g Fibre; 1 g Protein; 53 mg Sodium

Pictured on page 144.

Note: Coat hands lightly with cooking spray to prevent date mixture from sticking to them while forming into balls.

Strawberry Angel Cups

Individual pieces of heaven. The toasted cups put a unique spin on classic strawberry shortcake. For those who love the taste of orange liqueur, add just a little bit more!

Slices of angel food cake, about 1/2 inch (12 mm) thick	**12**	**12**
Finely chopped fresh strawberries	**1 cup**	**250 mL**
Icing (confectioner's) sugar	**2 tbsp.**	**30 mL**
Orange liqueur	**1 tbsp.**	**15 mL**
Frozen light whipped topping, thawed	**3/4 cup**	**175 mL**

Preheat oven to 350°F (175°C). Press cake slices into bottom and sides of 12 greased muffin cups. Bake on bottom rack in oven for about 15 minutes until bottoms are golden. Remove to wire rack to cool. Cups become crisp as they cool.

Combine next 3 ingredients in small bowl. Stir.

Spoon whipped topping into cups. Spoon strawberry mixture over topping. Makes 12 angel cups.

1 angel cup: 99 Calories; 0.8 g Total Fat (trace Mono, 0.1 g Poly, 0.5 g Sat); 0 mg Cholesterol; 21 g Carbohydrate; 1 g Fibre; 2 g Protein; 213 mg Sodium

Pictured on page 144.

When choosing strawberries, indulge your urge to select only the reddest and most juicy-looking specimens—these brilliant berries don't continue to ripen after they're picked.

Chocolate Almond Puffs

With just enough chocolate to make the worries of the day go away, these flourless puffs are crisp on the outside and soft on the inside.

Ground almonds	2 cups	500 mL
Granulated sugar	3/4 cup	175 mL
Ground ginger	1/4 tsp.	1 mL
Salt	1/8 tsp.	0.5 mL
Egg whites (large), room temperature	3	3
Almond extract	1/4 tsp.	1 mL
Bittersweet chocolate baking squares (1 oz., 28 g, each), finely chopped	4	4

Preheat oven to 350°F (175°C). Process first 4 ingredients in food processor (see Note) until well combined.

Add egg whites and extract. Process until mixture just starts to come together. Do not overmix. Transfer to medium bowl.

Add chocolate. Stir. Drop, using 1 tbsp. (15 mL) for each, about 1 inch (2.5 cm) apart onto 2 parchment paper-lined cookie sheets. Bake on separate racks in oven for about 12 minutes, switching position of cookie sheets at halftime, until tops puff up and bottoms are golden. Let stand on cookie sheets for about 5 minutes. Remove puffs and place on wire racks to cool. Makes about 30 puffs.

1 puff: 75 Calories; 4.8 g Total Fat (2.0 g Mono, 0.8 g Poly, 1.1 g Sat); 0 mg Cholesterol; 8 g Carbohydrate; 1 g Fibre; 2 g Protein; 13 mg Sodium

Note: If you don't have a food processor, an electric mixer can be used instead.

Egg whites are high in protein, and contain none of the cholesterol found in egg yolks. Try using egg whites instead of whole eggs in baking, or in omelettes and other egg dishes. But if cholesterol is not a going concern for you, don't throw out your yolks just yet—although they do contain cholesterol, they also have many beneficial nutrients as well.

Raspberry Parfait Fool

Don't let the name fool you. With yogurt and non-fat pudding replacing the traditional whipped cream, this version of the classic English treat is a smart dessert choice!

Box of instant non-fat vanilla pudding powder (4 serving size)	1	1
Milk	1 cup	250 mL
Vanilla yogurt	1 cup	250 mL
Lemon juice	1 tbsp.	15 mL
Grated lemon zest	1 tsp.	5 mL
Frozen (or fresh) whole raspberries	1 1/2 cups	375 mL
Flaked hazelnuts, toasted (see Tip, page 21)	2 tbsp.	30 mL

Combine pudding powder and milk in medium bowl. Beat on low for about 2 minutes until smooth and thickened.

Add next 3 ingredients. Beat for 1 minute.

Fold in raspberries. Spoon into 4 serving dishes.

Sprinkle with hazelnuts. Serves 4.

1 serving: 151 Calories; 4.0 g Total Fat (1.9 g Mono, 0.3 g Poly, 1.0 g Sat); 7 mg Cholesterol; 24 g Carbohydrate; 3 g Fibre; 6 g Protein; 366 mg Sodium

Measurement Tables

Throughout this book measurements are given in Conventional and Metric measure. To compensate for differences between the two measurements due to rounding, a full metric measure is not always used. The cup used is the standard 8 fluid ounce. Temperature is given in degrees Fahrenheit and Celsius. Baking pan measurements are in inches and centimetres as well as quarts and litres. An exact metric conversion is given below as well as the working equivalent (Standard Measure).

OVEN TEMPERATURES

Fahrenheit (°F)	Celsius (°C)
175°	80°
200°	95°
225°	110°
250°	120°
275°	140°
300°	150°
325°	160°
350°	175°
375°	190°
400°	205°
425°	220°
450°	230°
475°	240°
500°	260°

SPOONS

Conventional Measure	Metric Exact Conversion Millilitre (mL)	Metric Standard Measure Millilitre (mL)
1/8 teaspoon (tsp.)	0.6 mL	0.5 mL
1/4 teaspoon (tsp.)	1.2 mL	1 mL
1/2 teaspoon (tsp.)	2.4 mL	2 mL
1 teaspoon (tsp.)	4.7 mL	5 mL
2 teaspoons (tsp.)	9.4 mL	10 mL
1 tablespoon (tbsp.)	14.2 mL	15 mL

CUPS

	Metric Exact Conversion Millilitre (mL)	Metric Standard Measure Millilitre (mL)
1/4 cup (4 tbsp.)	56.8 mL	60 mL
1/3 cup (5 1/3 tbsp.)	75.6 mL	75 mL
1/2 cup (8 tbsp.)	113.7 mL	125 mL
2/3 cup (10 2/3 tbsp.)	151.2 mL	150 mL
3/4 cup (12 tbsp.)	170.5 mL	175 mL
1 cup (16 tbsp.)	227.3 mL	250 mL
4 1/2 cups	1022.9 mL	1000 mL (1 L)

PANS

Conventional Inches	Metric Centimetres
8x8 inch	20x20 cm
9x9 inch	22x22 cm
9x13 inch	22x33 cm
10x15 inch	25x38 cm
11x17 inch	28x43 cm
8x2 inch round	20x5 cm
9x2 inch round	22x5 cm
10x4 1/2 inch tube	25x11 cm
8x4x3 inch loaf	20x10x7.5 cm
9x5x3 inch loaf	22x12.5x7.5 cm

DRY MEASUREMENTS

Conventional Measure Ounces (oz.)	Metric Exact Conversion Grams (g)	Metric Standard Measure Grams (g)
1 oz.	28.3 g	28 g
2 oz.	56.7 g	57 g
3 oz.	85.0 g	85 g
4 oz.	113.4 g	125 g
5 oz.	141.7 g	140 g
6 oz.	170.1 g	170 g
7 oz.	198.4 g	200 g
8 oz.	226.8 g	250 g
16 oz.	453.6 g	500 g
32 oz.	907.2 g	1000 g (1 kg)

CASSEROLES (Canada & Britain)

Standard Size Casserole	Exact Metric Measure
1 qt. (5 cups)	1.13 L
1 1/2 qts. (7 1/2 cups)	1.69 L
2 qts. (10 cups)	2.25 L
2 1/2 qts. (12 1/2 cups)	2.81 L
3 qts. (15 cups)	3.38 L
4 qts. (20 cups)	4.5 L
5 qts. (25 cups)	5.63 L

CASSEROLES (United States)

Standard Size Casserole	Exact Metric Measure
1 qt. (4 cups)	900 mL
1 1/2 qts. (6 cups)	1.35 L
2 qts. (8 cups)	1.8 L
2 1/2 qts. (10 cups)	2.25 L
3 qts. (12 cups)	2.7 L
4 qts. (16 cups)	3.6 L
5 qts. (20 cups)	4.5 L

Recipe Index

Recipe Notes

Recipe Notes

Recipe Notes

Company's Coming®

Easy Healthy Recipes

Fruit or vegetables in every recipe • Lower in sodium & fat

Jean Paré
LIFESTYLE SERIES

Easy Healthy Recipes

Easy Healthy Recipes

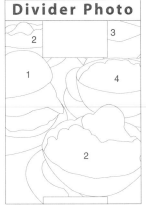

Divider Photo

1. Grilled Veggie Burgers, page 60
2. Pear Cranberry Crumble, page 134
3. Chicken And Bacon Pea Soup, page 39
4. Antipasto, page 149

We gratefully acknowledge the following suppliers for their generous support of our Test and Photography Kitchens:

Broil King Barbecues
Corelle®
Hamilton Beach® Canada
Lagostina®
Proctor Silex® Canada
Tupperware®

Our special thanks to the following businesses for providing various props for photography:

Browne & Co.
Canhome Global
Casa Bugatti
Cherison Enterprises Inc.
Danesco Inc.
Emile Henry
Klass Works
Mikasa Home Store
Out Of The Fire Studio
Pfaltzgraff Canada
Pier 1 Imports
Pyrex® Storage
Totally Bamboo
Tupperware®
Winners Stores

Cooking tonight?

A selection of
feature recipes
is only a
click away—
absolutely **FREE!**

Visit us at

www.companyscoming.com

Table of contents

 Denotes recipes with 2 or more servings of fruit and/or vegetables per portion. The specific number of servings per portion is given inside the icon.

foreword

A healthy lifestyle doesn't mean we need to climb mountains, run marathons, or follow the latest fad diet. It means eating well and staying active if we want to feel better and have more energy.

It makes sense that a balanced diet is a good place to start. But what are the right foods to choose? Canada's Food Guide to Healthy Eating (page 9 has more information) outlines the average nutritional needs of a healthy diet. One particular recommendation caught our attention and became the focus of *Easy Healthy Recipes*.

Eating lots of fruit and vegetables is a key element to reducing health risks such as heart disease and cancer. When cooking for the family though, it can be a struggle to stay on track, particularly when it comes to meeting the recommended 5 to 10 servings of fruit and vegetables a day.

Easy Healthy Recipes offers a wide selection of dishes, each emphasizing fibre-rich fruit and vegetables. In fact, each recipe includes at least one full fruit or vegetable serving per portion.

We've used this icon to identify those recipes with multiple fruit or vegetable servings.

The recipes themselves are lower in salt, fat and sugar, plus they're simple to prepare and adventurous in variety and taste. Some use more common vegetables like green beans, zucchini and squash, while others explore the intriguing tastes of less familiar vegetables like bok choy, eggplant and fennel. Or choose from an assortment of recipes using fruit— its sweet flavour offering just the right touch to beverages, soups, salads, main dishes, desserts and snacks.

Long-standing advice that we eat all our vegetables, or that an apple a day keeps the doctor away, may not be far wrong. Healthy eating is the first step to living stronger and better. *Easy Healthy Recipes*—the title says it all. Every dish is a step in the right direction.

Jean Paré

Nutrition Information Guidelines

Each recipe is analyzed using the most current version of the Canadian Nutrient File from Health Canada, which is based on the United States Department of Agriculture (USDA) Nutrient Database.

- If more than one ingredient is listed (such as "hard margarine or butter"), or if a range is given (1 – 2 tsp., 5 – 10 mL), only the first ingredient or first amount is analyzed.

- For meat, poultry and fish, the serving size per person is based on the recommended 4 oz. (113 g) uncooked weight (without bone), which is 2 – 3 oz. (57 – 85 g) cooked weight (without bone)—approximately the size of a deck of playing cards.

- Milk used is 1% M.F. (milk fat), unless otherwise stated.

- Cooking oil used is canola oil, unless otherwise stated.

- Ingredients indicating "sprinkle," "optional," or "for garnish" are not included in the nutrition information.

Margaret Ng, B.Sc. (Hon.), M.A.
Registered Dietitian

Common Sense Eating

Healthy eating is all about making wise food choices, watching portion sizes and getting lots of variety.

Daily choices

Balance your meals and eating throughout the day. That means starting with breakfast—even something simple like a bowl of enriched cereal with fruit. Try to limit your caffeine intake each day—change your coffee break to a juice break. And don't forget, water is still your best thirst quencher. A mid-morning snack is a good idea, but reach for something healthy like a fruit or vegetable. Skipping lunch can often leave you with less energy in the afternoon. Plan to eat something nutritious at lunchtime to give you a boost midway through your day. And remember to eat a balanced meal at dinner.

Portion sizes

Look closely at the portions on your plate—often those portions are at least double the recommended serving sizes. Here are a few tips:

1. Use smaller plates. Our instinct is to fill a plate with food, which can be considerably more than we really need.

2. Occasionally measure your portions to find out how large a serving size is. A recipe itself is a good place to start. If there are 4 of you at the table and the dish serves 6, you should have leftovers.

3. In restaurants, order half-portions when possible, or share a full portion with a friend.

4. Don't feel a need to finish your meal. Eat slowly, enjoy every bite and stop when you are full, not when the plate is empty.

Variety

Eating a variety of foods enables you to enjoy different flavours and also provides you with a full range of vitamins and minerals. Choose wisely from the different food groups and look for healthy, appealing substitutes to your favourite, but not-so-healthy, treats. For example, a low-fat muffin can fulfill that urge for a doughnut, or a glass of low-fat chocolate milk will satisfy a craving for chocolate.

These small adjustments are simple, common sense habits that will make a big difference to your health and energy. Before you know it, you'll be reaching for healthier food without a second thought—and your body will thank you for it.

Fruit and vegetable serving sizes

It's not hard to fit 5 to 10 servings of fruit and vegetables into your day. These examples represent one serving as outlined in *Canada's Food Guide to Healthy Eating*:

1 medium-sized fruit or vegetable (about the size of a tennis ball)
1 cup (250 mL) salad greens
1/2 cup (125 mL) fresh, frozen or canned fruits or vegetables
1/2 cup (125 mL) 100% fruit or vegetable juice
1/4 cup (60 mL) dried fruit

Canada's Food Guide to Healthy Eating

Canada's Food Guide to Healthy Eating outlines the healthy nutritional food choices available to us. The Food Guide stresses the need to eat a variety of foods from each food group in order to receive a full range of vitamins and minerals. Consider your age, lifestyle and calorie requirements when making your selections. For example, an active teenage boy will need a higher number of daily servings than a moderately active 40-year-old woman.

Use the Food Guide (available online at Health Canada) to help you make healthy food choices, and look for healthy, low-fat, low-salt choices within each food group. For instance, an apple pie may fall into the category of a fruit serving, but unsweetened applesauce is a much better, low-fat alternative. Here are some other ideas for each food group:

Grain products (5 to 12 servings a day)
A single slice of bread or 3/4 cup (175 mL) of hot cereal constitutes 1 serving size. Try to choose whole grains because they contain more fibre and zinc than refined grain products. Look for cereals and pasta enriched with iron and B vitamins. Although cookies, cakes and croissants fall into this category, they aren't considered a smart choice, so save these treats as an occasional indulgence.

Vegetables and fruit (5 to 10 servings a day)
A half-cup (125 mL) of juice or medium-size carrot is all it takes to make up 1 serving in this important category. Colour is key here: Dark green, leafy vegetables and orange vegetables and fruit are all rich in vitamin A and folacin. Vividly coloured fruits and vegetables are higher in antioxidants and phytochemicals, and fruits like apples, strawberries and citrus offer soluble fibre—all valuable for reducing the risk of heart disease and some cancers. Canned produce contains the same amount of nutrients, but rinse the vegetables to reduce the salt and choose fruit that has been canned in its own juices.

Milk products (Daily: children—2 to 3 servings; youth—3 to 4 servings; adults—2 to 4 servings; pregnant and breast-feeding women—3 to 4 servings)

One cup (250 mL) of milk or 3/4 cup (175 mL) of yogurt constitutes 1 serving. Look for lower fat or fat-free alternatives in this category. The fat content in milk will not change the amount of vitamins A and D, but keep in mind that milk products like yogurt and cheese don't have added vitamin D.

Meat and alternatives (2 to 3 servings a day)
Pay attention to serving size and fat content: one serving of cooked meat or fish weighs only 2 to 3 ounces (57 to 85 g)—about the size of a deck of cards. Red meat is a better source of iron than poultry, but choose lean cuts, if possible. As an alternative, legumes (peas, beans and lentils) provide significant amounts of starch and fibre. The Food Guide recommends you try to include legumes in your menu plan at least once or twice a week.

Other foods
The Food Guide also recognizes foods that fall outside the four main food groups. Things like condiments, cooking oils, candy, snack foods, soft drinks and alcohol can be high in fat, salt or sugar. These should only be an occasional choice.

Making Healthier Choices

Many health organizations agree that eating the right foods can help reduce the risk of heart attacks, stroke, hypertension and some forms of cancer. It begins with finding the right balance of food choices that works for you and your family. Include a wide variety of foods and remember:

Follow Canada's Food Guide to Healthy Eating

Choose more frequently from the first two food groups: whole grain products and enriched cereals, and colourful selections of fruit and vegetables. Fruit and vegetables, in particular, play a key role in fighting heart disease, hypertension and some cancers because they are naturally rich in antioxidants, phytochemicals and fibre, and low in fat and sodium.

Reduce the fat

Whenever possible, choose low-fat dairy products, leaner cuts of meat and foods prepared with little or no cooking oil. Remove skin from poultry and limit your use of gravies and other high-fat sauces. Think about adding legumes once or twice to the weekly menu as an alternative to a meat serving, and try to minimize consumption of high-fat snack foods whenever possible.

Watch the salt

Avoid processed foods such as pre-packaged dinners, mixes and soups when you can. Add salt to your food at the table and not while cooking or, better yet, flavour with herbs and spices instead. And make cured meat, such as bacon, ham and salami, an occasional choice.

You'll notice none of the recommendations include eliminating any one kind of food. The primary goal of healthy eating is to create good eating habits you can live with. Beyond these key points, *Canada's Food Guide to Healthy Eating* also suggests including regular physical activity as part of your daily schedule. Start making healthier choices today and the benefits will last a lifetime.

Apricot Breakfast Drink

Golden and creamy, with a frothy layer on top. A satisfying start to your day!

Can of apricot halves in light syrup (do not drain)	**14 oz.**	**398 mL**
Ice cubes	**16**	**16**
Milk	**1 cup**	**250 mL**
Low-fat plain yogurt	**1/2 cup**	**125 mL**
Liquid honey	**2 tbsp.**	**30 mL**
Ground nutmeg	**1/8 tsp.**	**0.5 mL**

Process all 6 ingredients in blender until smooth. Makes about 5 cups (1.25 L). Pour into 3 large glasses. Serves 3.

1 serving: 173 Calories; 1.1 g Total Fat (0.3 g Mono, 0.1 g Poly, 0.6 g Sat); 4 mg Cholesterol; 38 g Carbohydrate; 1 g Fibre; 6 g Protein; 79 mg Sodium

Pictured on page 71.

Cherry Almond Delight

A thick, sweet, lavender-coloured drink that might remind you of Cherries Jubilee. Add more milk to thin, if desired.

Can of pitted Bing cherries in heavy syrup (do not drain), chilled	**14 oz.**	**398 mL**
Light vanilla ice cream	**1 cup**	**250 mL**
Milk	**3/4 cup**	**175 mL**
Ground cinnamon (optional)	**1/4 tsp.**	**1 mL**
Almond flavouring	**1/8 tsp.**	**0.5 mL**

Process all 5 ingredients in blender until smooth. Makes about 3 3/4 cups (925 mL). Pour into 2 chilled large glasses. Serves 2.

1 serving: 360 Calories; 9 g Total Fat (2.6 g Mono, 0.4 g Poly, 5.5 g Sat); 35 mg Cholesterol; 67 g Carbohydrate; 2 g Fibre; 7 g Protein; 111 mg Sodium

Pictured on page 17.

Instead of buying yogurt and fruit combinations that often contain added sugar, cut up and stir fresh fruit into low-fat or plain yogurt for a lower calorie option.

Banana Smoothie

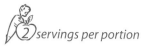

2 servings per portion

This creamy, sunny yellow drink is a great way to say "Good morning."

Can of sliced peaches in pear juice (do not drain)	**14 oz.**	**398 mL**
Vanilla frozen yogurt	**1 cup**	**250 mL**
Ripe medium banana, cut up (see Tip, below)	**1**	**1**
Wheat germ	**1 tbsp.**	**15 mL**
Ice cubes	**4**	**4**

Process all 5 ingredients in blender until smooth. Makes about 3 1/2 cups (875 mL). Pour into 2 chilled large glasses. Serves 2.

1 serving: 319 Calories; 6.4 g Total Fat (1.7 g Mono, 0.5 g Poly, 3.8 g Sat); 10 mg Cholesterol; 64 g Carbohydrate; 4 g Fibre; 7 g Protein; 71 mg Sodium

BANANA SLUSHY: Peel and cut banana into 2 inch (5 cm) pieces. Freeze until firm. Process with other ingredients as directed.

Creamy Raspberry Cooler

Pink, thick and creamy. Delightfully refreshing any time of day.

Container of frozen raspberries in syrup, partially thawed (see Note)	**15 oz.**	**425 g**
Low-fat raspberry yogurt	**3/4 cup**	**175 mL**
Milk	**1/2 cup**	**125 mL**

Process all 3 ingredients in blender until smooth. Makes about 3 1/4 cups (800 mL). Pour into 2 large glasses. Serves 2.

1 serving: 306 Calories; 1.2 g Total Fat (0.3 g Mono, 0.2 g Poly, 0.6 g Sat); 5 mg Cholesterol; 69 g Carbohydrate; 9 g Fibre; 8 g Protein; 103 mg Sodium

Pictured on page 125 and on back cover.

Note: If you prefer a seedless cooler, thaw raspberries completely and press through sieve into medium bowl to remove seeds. Cooler will not be as thick.

Overripe bananas provide rich flavour to beverages. To use, peel and cut bananas into 2 inch (5 cm) pieces. Arrange in single layer in ungreased 9 x 13 inch (22 x 33 cm) pan. Freeze until firm. Store in resealable freezer bag. Use 4 pieces for 1 medium banana.

Strawberry Lemonade

2 servings per portion

This frothy pink drink tends to separate quickly, but it's so good it won't last long enough to tell!

Pink lemonade	**2 cups**	**500 mL**
Fresh strawberries	**2 cups**	**500 mL**
Ice		

Process lemonade and strawberries in blender until smooth. Makes about 3 3/4 cups (925 mL).

Pour over ice in 2 large glasses. Garnish each with a fresh strawberry. Serves 2.

1 serving: 150 Calories; 0.6 g Total Fat (0.1 g Mono, 0.3 g Poly, 0.1 g Sat); 0 mg Cholesterol; 38 g Carbohydrate; 3 g Fibre; 1 g Protein; 9 mg Sodium

Pictured on page 17.

Peach Cooler

Cool and fizzy—just peachy any time!

Canned sliced peaches in pear juice, drained	**1/2 cup**	**125 mL**
Ice cubes	**16**	**16**
Club soda (or lemon lime soft drink)	**1 cup**	**250 mL**
White grape juice	**1 cup**	**250 mL**

Process peaches in blender until smooth. Spoon into 2 large glasses. Put 8 ice cubes in each glass.

Slowly add 1/2 cup (125 mL) each club soda and grape juice to each glass. Stir gently. Makes about 2 1/3 cups (575 mL). Serves 2.

1 serving: 97 Calories; 0.2 g Total Fat (0 g Mono, 0.1 g Poly, 0 g Sat); 0 mg Cholesterol; 24 g Carbohydrate; 1 g Fibre; 1 g Protein; 33 mg Sodium

Chocolate Peach Smoothie

An irresistible combination that will jump-start your day.

Can of sliced peaches in pear juice (do not drain)	**14 oz.**	**398 mL**
Milk	**1 cup**	**250 mL**
Low-fat vanilla yogurt	**1/3 cup**	**75 mL**
Chocolate syrup	**2 tbsp.**	**30 mL**

Process all 4 ingredients in blender until smooth. Makes about 3 1/2 cups (875 mL). Pour into 2 large glasses. Serves 2.

1 serving: 227 Calories; 2.4 g Total Fat (0.7 g Mono, 0.1 g Poly, 1.5 g Sat); 7 mg Cholesterol; 48 g Carbohydrate; 2 g Fibre; 8 g Protein; 116 mg Sodium

Dairy-Free Berry Smoothie

Just a little different, but very berry good!

Rice milk (such as Rice Dream)	**1 1/2 cups**	**375 mL**
Frozen mixed berries	**1 cup**	**250 mL**
Blueberry syrup (or liquid honey)	**2 tbsp.**	**30 mL**

Process all 3 ingredients in blender until smooth. Makes about 2 1/4 cups (550 mL). Pour into 2 medium glasses. Serves 2.

1 serving: 191 Calories; 1.9 g Total Fat (1.2 g Mono, 0.3 g Poly, 0.2 g Sat); 0 mg Cholesterol; 45 g Carbohydrate; 3 g Fibre; 1 g Protein; 87 mg Sodium

Banana Melon Shake

Frothy and refreshing. Nutmeg adds the perfect touch.

Milk	**2 cups**	**500 mL**
Chopped cantaloupe	**1 cup**	**250 mL**
Frozen ripe medium banana (see Tip, page 12)	**1**	**1**
Light vanilla ice cream	**1/2 cup**	**125 mL**
Ground nutmeg	**1/8 tsp.**	**0.5 mL**

(continued on next page)

Process all 5 ingredients in blender until smooth. Makes about 4 cups (1 L). Pour into 4 chilled medium glasses. Serves 4.

1 serving: 131 Calories; 3.6 g Total Fat (1 g Mono, 0.2 g Poly, 2.1 g Sat); 13 mg Cholesterol; 21 g Carbohydrate; 1 g Fibre; 6 g Protein; 83 mg Sodium

Yogurt Mango Shake

Lime and mango offer a taste of the tropics. Great for sunny days or when you need an armchair vacation.

Can of sliced mango with syrup (do not drain)	**14 oz.**	**398 mL**
Vanilla frozen yogurt	**1 cup**	**250 mL**
Milk	**3/4 cup**	**175 mL**
Grated lime zest	**1/2 tsp.**	**2 mL**
Ice cubes	**4**	**4**

Process all 5 ingredients in blender until smooth. Makes about 3 1/2 cups (875 mL). Pour into 2 large glasses. Serves 2.

1 serving: 367 Calories; 7 g Total Fat (2 g Mono, 0.3 g Poly, 4.3 g Sat); 14 mg Cholesterol; 73 g Carbohydrate; 2 g Fibre; 8 g Protein; 153 mg Sodium

Pictured on page 17.

Tropical Soy Shake

Shake up your day with this pineapple smoothie.

Can of pineapple chunks (do not drain)	**14 oz.**	**398 mL**
Soy milk	**1 cup**	**250 mL**
Frozen ripe medium banana (see Tip, page 12)	**1**	**1**
Ice cubes	**4**	**4**
Ground nutmeg, sprinkle (optional)		

Process all 5 ingredients in blender until smooth. Makes about 4 cups (1 L). Pour into 4 medium glasses. Serves 4.

1 serving: 110 Calories; 1.4 g Total Fat (0.2 g Mono, 0.6 g Poly, 0.2 g Sat); 0 mg Cholesterol; 24 g Carbohydrate; 2 g Fibre; 2 g Protein; 9 mg Sodium

Apricot Lassi

Start or end your day with this sweet, tangy lassi. An easy-to-make refreshment—morning, noon or night.

Can of apricot halves in light syrup (do not drain)	**14 oz.**	**398 mL**
Low-fat plain yogurt	**1 cup**	**250 mL**
Milk	**1/2 cup**	**125 mL**
Liquid honey	**3 tbsp.**	**50 mL**
Ground almonds	**3 tbsp.**	**50 mL**
Ground cinnamon	**1/8 tsp.**	**0.5 mL**
Ice cubes	**4**	**4**

Process all 7 ingredients in blender until smooth. Makes about 3 3/4 cups (925 mL). Pour into 2 large glasses. Serves 2.

1 serving: 333 Calories; 4.1 g Total Fat (2.4 g Mono, 0.7 g Poly, 0.8 g Sat); 5 mg Cholesterol; 68 g Carbohydrate; 2 g Fibre; 11 g Protein; 133 mg Sodium

1. Yogurt Mango Shake, page 15
2. Cherry Almond Delight, page 11
3. Strawberry Lemonade, page 13

Orange Poppy Seed Coleslaw

Crisp and crunchy with a tasty orange dressing. It's worth a try!

Shredded red cabbage, lightly packed	3 cups	750 mL
Thinly sliced celery	1/2 cup	125 mL
Medium orange, segmented and cut into bite-size pieces	1	1
Green onions, chopped	4	4
ORANGE POPPY SEED DRESSING		
Orange juice	2 tbsp.	30 mL
Liquid honey	1 tbsp.	15 mL
Dijon mustard	1 tbsp.	15 mL
Olive (or cooking) oil	1 tbsp.	15 mL
Poppy seeds	2 tsp.	5 mL
Pepper	1/4 tsp.	1 mL

Put first 4 ingredients into large bowl. Toss gently.

Orange Poppy Seed Dressing: Combine all 6 ingredients in jar with tight-fitting lid. Shake well. Makes about 1/3 cup (75 mL) dressing. Drizzle over salad. Toss gently. Serves 6.

1 serving: 59 Calories; 3 g Total Fat (1.8 g Mono, 0.7 g Poly, 0.4 g Sat); 0 mg Cholesterol; 8 g Carbohydrate; 1 g Fibre; 1 g Protein; 49 mg Sodium

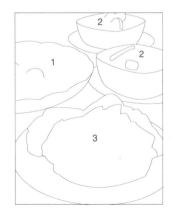

1. Asparagus And Radish Salad, page 24
2. Veggie Rice Salad, page 28
3. Apple Celery Salad, page 28

Bean, Ham And Potato Salad

2 servings per portion

A well-rounded salad with a zesty dressing that's a change from the ordinary. Fabulously full of flavour!

Red baby potatoes, quartered (about 6)	**1 lb.**	**454 g**
Boiling water		
Fresh (or frozen) whole green beans	**2 cups**	**500 mL**
Boiling water		
Ice water		
Cherry (or grape) tomatoes, halved	**20**	**20**
Low-fat deli ham, cut into thin strips	**6 oz.**	**170 g**
Chopped red onion	**1/2 cup**	**125 mL**
MUSTARD DRESSING		
Orange juice	**3 tbsp.**	**50 mL**
Finely chopped gherkin (or dill pickle)	**2 tbsp.**	**30 mL**
Light sour cream	**2 tbsp.**	**30 mL**
Dijon mustard (with whole seeds)	**1 tbsp.**	**15 mL**
Ground cumin	**1/2 tsp.**	**2 mL**
Garlic clove, minced (or 1/4 tsp., 1 mL, powder)	**1**	**1**

Cook potato in boiling water in medium saucepan until just tender. Drain. Cool.

Partially cook green beans in boiling water in medium saucepan for about 5 minutes until bright green. Drain. Immediately plunge into ice water in medium bowl. Let stand for about 10 minutes until cold. Drain well. Cut green beans into 2 inch (5 cm) pieces.

Combine tomato, ham and onion in large bowl. Add potato and green beans. Toss gently.

Mustard Dressing: Combine all 6 ingredients in jar with tight-fitting lid. Shake well. Makes about 1/2 cup (125 mL) dressing. Drizzle over salad. Toss gently. Serves 6.

1 serving: 163 Calories; 4.3 g Total Fat (2 g Mono, 0.6 g Poly, 1.5 g Sat); 17 mg Cholesterol; 24 g Carbohydrate; 3 g Fibre; 9 g Protein; 431 mg Sodium

Pictured on page 53.

Shell Shrimp Salad

Mild creamy dressing coats peas and pasta—a perfect pair with succulent shrimp.

Tiny shell pasta	1 1/2 cups	375 mL
Boiling water	8 cups	2 L
Salt	1 tsp.	5 mL
Frozen peas	3 cups	750 mL
Cooked salad shrimp	6 oz.	170 g
Diced celery	1/2 cup	125 mL
Finely chopped red onion	2 tbsp.	30 mL
Large hard-cooked eggs, chopped	3	3
HORSERADISH DRESSING		
Light mayonnaise	2/3 cup	150 mL
Ketchup	2 tbsp.	30 mL
Milk	1 tbsp.	15 mL
Granulated sugar	1 tsp.	5 mL
Creamed horseradish	1 tsp.	5 mL
Onion powder	1/4 tsp.	1 mL
Chopped or torn romaine lettuce, lightly packed	6 cups	1.5 L

Cook pasta in boiling water and salt in large uncovered pot or Dutch oven for 6 to 8 minutes, stirring occasionally, until tender but firm. Add peas during last 3 minutes of cooking time. Drain. Rinse with cold water. Drain well. Transfer to large bowl.

Add next 4 ingredients. Toss gently.

Horseradish Dressing: Combine first 6 ingredients in small bowl. Makes about 1 cup (250 mL) dressing. Drizzle over pasta mixture. Toss gently.

Spread lettuce evenly on large serving platter. Spoon pasta mixture onto lettuce. Serves 6.

1 serving: 319 Calories; 12.3 g Total Fat (6.2 g Mono, 3.4 g Poly, 1.6 g Sat); 163 mg Cholesterol; 35 g Carbohydrate; 2 g Fibre; 17 g Protein; 362 mg Sodium

To toast nuts, seeds or coconut, spread evenly in ungreased shallow pan. Bake in 350ºF (175ºC) oven for 5 to 10 minutes, stirring or shaking often, until desired doneness.

Ambrosia Fruit Salad

A classic combination that's always a favourite. Use coloured marshmallows for a rainbow effect the kids will enjoy.

Low-fat peach yogurt	1 cup	250 mL
Light sour cream	1/2 cup	125 mL
Can of fruit cocktail, drained	14 oz.	398 mL
Can of mandarin orange segments, drained	10 oz.	284 mL
Can of pineapple tidbits, drained	8 oz.	227 mL
Miniature marshmallows	1 cup	250 mL
Medium sweetened coconut, toasted (see Tip, page 21)	1/4 cup	60 mL

Combine yogurt and sour cream in large bowl.

Add next 4 ingredients. Stir gently.

Sprinkle with coconut. Serves 4.

1 serving: 199 Calories; 4 g Total Fat (1.4 g Mono, 0.2 g Poly, 4.2 g Sat); 8 mg Cholesterol; 39 g Carbohydrate; 2 g Fibre; 5 g Protein; 82 mg Sodium

Beet Coleslaw

A little different from the ordinary, but sure to be a hit! Refreshing dill and tangy lemon make a memorable dressing.

ZESTY DILL DRESSING		
Light mayonnaise	1/2 cup	125 mL
Lemon juice	1 tbsp.	15 mL
Chopped fresh dill (or 1/4 tsp., 1 mL, dill weed)	1 tsp.	5 mL
Dry mustard	1/2 tsp.	2 mL
Shredded green cabbage, lightly packed	2 cups	500 mL
Can of sliced beets, drained and chopped	14 oz.	398 mL
1% cottage cheese	1 cup	250 mL
Shredded red cabbage, lightly packed	1 cup	250 mL

(continued on next page)

Zesty Dill Dressing: Combine first 4 ingredients in small bowl. Makes about 1/2 cup (125 mL) dressing.

Put remaining 4 ingredients into large bowl. Drizzle with dressing. Toss well. Serves 8.

1 serving: 87 Calories; 5.3 g Total Fat (3 g Mono, 1.5 g Poly, 0.5 g Sat); 1 mg Cholesterol; 6 g Carbohydrate; 1 g Fibre; 5 g Protein; 307 mg Sodium

Pictured on page 126.

Poppy Seed Fruit Bowl

2 servings per portion

Avocado adds a nice touch to an array of juicy fruit coated in creamy dressing. Use any seasonal fruit.

POPPY SEED DRESSING

Low-fat vanilla (or plain) yogurt	1 cup	250 mL
Liquid honey	1 tbsp.	15 mL
Lemon juice	2 tsp.	10 mL
Poppy seeds	2 tsp.	10 mL
Ground ginger	1/4 tsp.	1 mL
Mandarin oranges, segmented	8	8
Red medium grapefruits, segmented and cut into bite-size pieces	4	4
Ripe medium avocados, cut into 1/2 inch (12 mm) pieces	2	2
Seedless red grapes	1 cup	250 mL
Seedless green grapes	1 cup	250 mL

Poppy Seed Dressing: Combine first 5 ingredients in small bowl. Makes about 1 cup (250 mL) dressing.

Put remaining 5 ingredients into large bowl. Drizzle with dressing. Toss gently. Serves 10.

1 serving: 171 Calories; 7.2 g Total Fat (4.1 g Mono, 1 g Poly, 1.4 g Sat); 1 mg Cholesterol; 28 g Carbohydrate; 4 g Fibre; 3 g Protein; 20 mg Sodium

Pictured on page 125 and on back cover.

Asparagus And Radish Salad

Zesty lemon and mustard dressing adds the perfect punch to crisp asparagus. Looks pretty with a sprinkling of sesame seeds.

Fresh asparagus, trimmed of tough ends and cut into 2 inch (5 cm) pieces	**1 lb.**	**454 g**
Boiling water		
Ice water		
Thinly sliced radish	**1 cup**	**250 mL**
Sesame seeds, toasted (see Tip, page 21)	**2 tbsp.**	**30 mL**
LEMON DRESSING		
Olive (or cooking) oil	**2 tbsp.**	**30 mL**
Finely chopped shallots (or green onion)	**2 tbsp.**	**30 mL**
White wine vinegar	**1 tbsp.**	**15 mL**
Lemon juice	**1 tbsp.**	**15 mL**
Liquid honey	**2 tsp.**	**10 mL**
Dijon mustard	**1 tsp.**	**5 mL**
Garlic clove, minced (or 1/4 tsp., 1 mL, powder)	**1**	**1**
Grated lemon zest	**1/4 tsp.**	**1 mL**
Pepper, sprinkle		

Partially cook asparagus in boiling water in large saucepan for about 5 minutes until bright green. Drain. Immediately plunge into ice water in large bowl. Let stand for about 10 minutes until cold. Drain well. Transfer to medium bowl.

Add radish and sesame seeds. Toss.

Lemon Dressing: Combine all 9 ingredients in jar with tight-fitting lid. Shake well. Makes about 1/3 cup (75 mL) dressing. Drizzle over salad. Toss well. Serves 4.

1 serving: 139 Calories; 9.7 g Total Fat (6.1 g Mono, 1.7 g Poly, 1.3 g Sat); 0 mg Cholesterol; 12 g Carbohydrate; 3 g Fibre; 4 g Protein; 12 mg Sodium

Pictured on page 18.

Mushroom Cranberry Salad

A delicious blend of both sweet and tart. Using a variety of mushrooms, such as oyster, brown and white, adds interest. Try a mixture of green and red leaf lettuce for a colourful contrast.

Olive (or cooking) oil	**1 tbsp.**	**15 mL**
Sliced fresh mushrooms (your favourite)	**4 cups**	**1 L**
Red wine vinegar	**1 tbsp.**	**15 mL**
Liquid honey	**1 tbsp.**	**15 mL**
Chopped or torn green leaf lettuce, lightly packed	**5 cups**	**1.25 L**
Crumbled light feta cheese (about 4 oz., 113 g)	**3/4 cup**	**175 mL**
CRANBERRY DRESSING		
Olive (or cooking) oil	**3 tbsp.**	**50 mL**
Jellied cranberry sauce, warmed	**3 tbsp.**	**50 mL**
Red wine vinegar	**2 tbsp.**	**30 mL**

Heat olive oil in large frying pan on medium. Add mushrooms. Cook for 5 to 10 minutes, stirring often, until mushrooms are softened.

Add vinegar and honey. Heat and stir for about 1 minute until mushrooms are coated and liquid is evaporated. Transfer to large bowl. Cool slightly.

Add lettuce and cheese. Toss gently.

Cranberry Dressing: Combine all 3 ingredients in jar with tight-fitting lid. Shake well. Makes about 1/2 cup (125 mL) dressing. Drizzle over salad. Toss gently. Serves 8.

1 serving: 133 Calories; 10.2 g Total Fat (5.7 g Mono, 0.8 g Poly, 3.1 g Sat); 13 mg Cholesterol; 9 g Carbohydrate; 1 g Fibre; 3 g Protein; 169 mg Sodium

Reduce fat in your diet by using less dressing or a low-fat dressing on your salad. Measure your salad dressing rather than pouring it straight from the bottle.

Warm Mushroom Salad

servings per portion

Lots of great flavours in this salad. Perfect for mushroom fans!

Red wine vinegar	1 tbsp.	15 mL
Liquid honey, warmed	1 tbsp.	15 mL
Garlic cloves, minced (or 1/2 tsp., 2 mL, powder)	2	2
Small brown mushrooms	2 cups	500 mL
Small white mushrooms	2 cups	500 mL
Mixed salad greens, lightly packed	4 cups	1 L
Jar of roasted red peppers, drained, blotted dry, cut into thin strips	12 oz.	340 mL
Fresh bean sprouts	1 cup	250 mL
Basil pesto	1 tbsp.	15 mL
Red wine vinegar	1 tbsp.	15 mL

Combine first 3 ingredients in large bowl. Add both mushrooms. Toss until coated. Spread in single layer in greased baking sheet with sides. Bake in 450ºF (230ºC) oven for about 10 minutes, stirring once, until mushrooms start to soften. Return to same large bowl.

Add salad greens, red pepper and bean sprouts. Toss.

Combine pesto and second amount of vinegar in small bowl. Drizzle over salad. Toss well. Serves 8.

1 serving: 48 Calories; 1 g Total Fat (0.4 g Mono, 0.2 g Poly, 0.1 g Sat); 0 mg Cholesterol; 9 g Carbohydrate; 2 g Fibre; 3 g Protein; 66 mg Sodium

Pictured on page 54.

Spinach And Raspberry Salad

An imaginative combination of fruit and vegetables. Scrumptious with grilled steak.

Fresh spinach, stems removed, lightly packed	5 cups	1.25 L
Fresh raspberries	1 cup	250 mL
Thinly sliced fresh white mushrooms	1 cup	250 mL
Sliced natural almonds, toasted (see Tip, page 21)	1/3 cup	75 mL

(continued on next page)

RASPBERRY VINAIGRETTE

Fresh raspberries	1/4 cup	60 mL
Raspberry (or red wine) vinegar	2 tbsp.	30 mL
Olive (or cooking) oil	1 tbsp.	15 mL
Granulated sugar	1 tsp.	5 mL
Dijon mustard	1 tsp.	5 mL
Pepper	1/4 tsp.	1 mL

Put first 4 ingredients into large bowl. Toss gently.

Raspberry Vinaigrette: Process all 6 ingredients in blender or food processor until smooth. Makes about 1/2 cup (125 mL) dressing. Drizzle over salad. Toss gently. Serves 6.

1 serving: 84 Calories; 5.9 g Total Fat (3.8 g Mono, 1.1 g Poly, 0.7 g Sat); 0 mg Cholesterol; 7 g Carbohydrate; 3 g Fibre; 3 g Protein; 37 mg Sodium

Minted Pea Salad

A salad that's sure to "pea-lease!" Great with your favourite barbecue meal.

Sugar snap peas, trimmed	2 cups	500 mL
Snow peas, trimmed	2 cups	500 mL
Boiling water		
Ice water		
Pea sprouts	1 cup	250 mL
MINT DRESSING		
Cooking oil	3 tbsp.	50 mL
Lemon juice	2 tbsp.	30 mL
Mint jelly	1 tbsp.	15 mL
Dijon mustard (with whole seeds)	1 tbsp.	15 mL
Granulated sugar	1 tsp.	5 mL

Partially cook both peas in boiling water in medium saucepan for about 5 minutes until bright green. Drain. Immediately plunge into ice water in medium bowl. Let stand for about 10 minutes until cold. Drain well. Blot dry with paper towels. Transfer to large bowl.

Add pea sprouts. Toss.

Mint Dressing: Combine all 5 ingredients in jar with tight-fitting lid. Shake well. Makes about 1/2 cup (125 mL) dressing. Drizzle over salad. Toss well. Serves 6.

1 serving: 120 Calories; 7.3 g Total Fat (4.1 g Mono, 2.3 g Poly, 0.6 g Sat); 0 mg Cholesterol; 11 g Carbohydrate; 2 g Fibre; 3 g Protein; 46 mg Sodium

Veggie Rice Salad

A fresh-tasting salad with an Asian flair. Fresh herbs add lots of colour.

Cooked long grain brown rice (about 2/3 cup, 150 mL, uncooked)	2 cups	500 mL
Thinly sliced English cucumber (with peel)	1 cup	250 mL
Chopped red pepper	1 cup	250 mL
Chopped celery	1 cup	250 mL
Can of sliced water chestnuts, drained	8 oz.	227 mL
Chopped green onion	1/3 cup	75 mL
LIME HERB DRESSING		
Lime juice	3 tbsp.	50 mL
Chopped fresh cilantro or parsley	2 tbsp.	30 mL
Chopped fresh mint leaves	2 tbsp.	30 mL
Sweet chili sauce	1 tbsp.	15 mL
Cooking oil	1 tbsp.	15 mL
Fish sauce	1/2 tsp.	2 mL
Garlic clove, minced (or 1/4 tsp., 1 mL, powder)	1	1

Put first 6 ingredients into large bowl. Toss.

Lime Herb Dressing: Combine all 7 ingredients in jar with tight-fitting lid. Shake well. Makes about 1/3 cup (75 mL) dressing. Drizzle over salad. Toss well. Serves 6.

1 serving: 135 Calories; 3.1 g Total Fat (1.6 g Mono, 1 g Poly, 0.3 g Sat); 0 mg Cholesterol; 25 g Carbohydrate; 3 g Fibre; 3 g Protein; 95 mg Sodium

Pictured on page 18.

Apple Celery Salad

3 servings per portion

A Waldorf-style salad full of sweet apple, crisp celery and crunchy walnuts—all coated with a creamy cinnamon dressing.

YOGURT CINNAMON DRESSING		
Low-fat plain yogurt	1 cup	250 mL
Lemon juice	1 tbsp.	15 mL
Liquid honey	1 tbsp.	15 mL
Ground cinnamon	1/4 tsp.	1 mL

(continued on next page)

Medium cooking apples (such as McIntosh), with peel, cores removed, quartered, sliced	3	3
Thinly sliced celery	1 cup	250 mL
Chopped walnuts, toasted (see Tip, page 21)	1/4 cup	60 mL
Romaine (or iceberg) lettuce leaves	4	4

Yogurt Cinnamon Dressing: Combine first 4 ingredients in large bowl. Makes about 1 cup (250 mL) dressing.

Add next 3 ingredients. Stir until coated.

Place 1 lettuce leaf on each of 4 plates. Spoon apple mixture onto each leaf. Serves 4.

1 serving: 177 Calories; 6.2 g Total Fat (1.4 g Mono, 3.3 g Poly, 1 g Sat); 4 mg Cholesterol; 28 g Carbohydrate; 3 g Fibre; 6 g Protein; 74 mg Sodium

Pictured on page 18.

Cottage Cheese Crunch

A tasty way to dress up cottage cheese for lunch.

Tart medium cooking apples (such as Granny Smith), with peel, cores removed, diced	2	2
1% cottage cheese	1 cup	250 mL
Shredded cabbage, lightly packed	1 cup	250 mL
Salted roasted sunflower seeds	3 tbsp.	50 mL
Chopped pecans, toasted (see Tip, page 21)	3 tbsp.	50 mL
Light mayonnaise	2 tbsp.	30 mL
Pepper	1/4 tsp.	1 mL

Put all 7 ingredients into large bowl. Toss gently. Serves 4.

1 serving: 167 Calories; 9.9 g Total Fat (4.5 g Mono, 3.7 g Poly, 1.2 g Sat); 3 mg Cholesterol; 11 g Carbohydrate; 2 g Fibre; 10 g Protein; 351 mg Sodium

Tofu Spinach Salad

An Asian-inspired salad topped with crunchy fried noodles.

Package of rice stick noodles (8 oz., 225 g, size)	1/4	1/4
Cooking oil, for deep-frying		
Fresh spinach, stems removed, lightly packed	5 cups	1.25 L
Thinly sliced snow peas	1 1/3 cups	325 mL
Grated carrot	2/3 cup	150 mL
Coarsely chopped salted peanuts	1/2 cup	125 mL
Peanut (or cooking) oil	2 tsp.	10 mL
Package of firm tofu, drained and cut into 1/2 inch (12 mm) cubes	12 1/4 oz.	350 g
Low-sodium soy sauce	1 tbsp.	15 mL
Liquid honey	1 tbsp.	15 mL
GINGER DRESSING		
Peanut (or cooking) oil	1/4 cup	60 mL
Rice vinegar	2 tbsp.	30 mL
Liquid honey	2 tbsp.	30 mL
Sweet chili sauce	1 tbsp.	15 mL
Finely grated, peeled gingerroot (or 1/4 tsp., 1 mL, ground ginger)	1 tsp.	5 mL
Dried crushed chilies	1/2 tsp.	2 mL
Pepper	1/8 tsp.	0.5 mL

Separate noodles slightly. Deep-fry in hot (375ºF, 190ºC) cooking oil for about 1 minute until puffed. Remove with slotted spoon to paper towels to drain.

Put next 4 ingredients into large bowl. Toss. Set aside.

Heat peanut oil in large frying pan on medium. Add tofu. Cook for about 5 minutes, stirring often, until golden.

Add soy sauce and honey. Stir until coated. Add to spinach mixture. Toss gently.

Ginger Dressing: Combine all 7 ingredients in jar with tight-fitting lid. Shake well. Makes about 2/3 cup (150 mL) dressing. Drizzle over salad. Toss gently. Break up noodles. Sprinkle over top. Serves 8.

1 serving: 248 Calories; 17.2 g Total Fat (7.1 g Mono, 6.4 g Poly, 2.7 g Sat); 0 mg Cholesterol; 17 g Carbohydrate; 2 g Fibre; 10 g Protein; 180 mg Sodium

Warm Chicken Salad

A rich, colourful meal salad full of earthy flavour. A sure hit!

GARLIC AND HERB MARINADE

Balsamic vinegar	3 tbsp.	50 mL
Olive (or cooking) oil	2 tbsp.	30 mL
Chopped fresh oregano leaves (or 3/4 tsp., 4 mL, dried)	1 tbsp.	15 mL
Garlic cloves, minced (or 1/2 tsp., 2 mL, powder)	2	2
Garlic and herb no-salt seasoning (such as Mrs. Dash)	1/2 tsp.	2 mL
Pepper	1/4 tsp.	1 mL
Boneless, skinless chicken breast halves, chopped	1 lb.	454 g
Cooked whole wheat rotini (or other spiral) pasta (about 2 1/4 cups, 550 mL, uncooked)	3 cups	750 mL
Sliced brown (or white) mushrooms	2 cups	500 mL
Fresh spinach, stems removed, lightly packed	2 cups	500 mL
Crumbled light feta cheese (about 5 oz., 140 g)	1 cup	250 mL
Roasted red peppers, drained, blotted dry, cut into thin strips	1/2 cup	125 mL

Garlic And Herb Marinade: Combine first 6 ingredients in medium bowl. Makes about 1/3 cup (75 mL) marinade. Add chicken. Stir until coated. Cover. Marinate in refrigerator for 20 minutes, stirring occasionally. Heat large frying pan on medium-high until hot. Add chicken with marinade. Cook for about 5 minutes, stirring occasionally, until chicken is no longer pink inside. Transfer to large bowl.

Add remaining 5 ingredients. Toss well. Serves 4.

1 serving: 457 Calories; 18.1 g Total Fat (7.5 g Mono, 1.6 g Poly, 7.4 g Sat); 84 mg Cholesterol; 35 g Carbohydrate; 5 g Fibre; 41 g Protein; 217 mg Sodium

Spiced Beef Soup

This rich broth seasoned with cumin and coriander provides a spicy taste of the East. Serve with pappadums (PAH-pah-duhms), thin bread made with lentil flour.

Cooking oil	1 tbsp.	15 mL
Beef stew meat, cut into 1/2 inch (12 mm) pieces	3/4 lb.	340 g
Cooking oil	2 tsp.	10 mL
Chopped onion	1 1/2 cups	375 mL
Ground cumin	2 tsp.	10 mL
Ground coriander	2 tsp.	10 mL
Ground ginger	1 tsp.	5 mL
Dried crushed chilies	1 tsp.	5 mL
Can of diced tomatoes (with juice)	28 oz.	796 mL
Low-sodium prepared beef broth	4 cups	1 L
Can of chickpeas (garbanzo beans), rinsed and drained	19 oz.	540 mL
Medium zucchini (with peel), chopped	1	1
Chopped fresh mint leaves (or 1 1/2 tsp., 7 mL, dried)	2 tbsp.	30 mL
Liquid honey	2 tsp.	10 mL
Grated lemon zest	1 tsp.	5 mL

Heat first amount of cooking oil in large pot or Dutch oven on medium-high. Add beef. Cook for 5 to 10 minutes, stirring occasionally, until browned. Transfer to large bowl. Cover to keep warm.

Heat second amount of cooking oil in same large pot on medium. Add onion. Cook for 5 to 10 minutes, stirring often, until softened.

Add next 4 ingredients. Heat and stir for about 1 minute until fragrant.

Add beef, tomatoes and broth. Stir. Bring to a boil on medium-high. Reduce heat to medium-low. Cover. Simmer for 20 minutes, stirring occasionally.

Add chickpeas. Stir. Cover. Simmer for about 20 minutes until beef is very tender.

Add remaining 4 ingredients. Stir. Cook, uncovered, on medium for about 5 minutes until zucchini is tender. Serves 8.

1 serving: 200 Calories; 7.9 g Total Fat (3.5 g Mono, 1.5 g Poly, 1.8 g Sat); 24 mg Cholesterol; 19 g Carbohydrate; 3 g Fibre; 15 g Protein; 605 mg Sodium

Pictured on page 35.

Thai-Style Pork Soup

Spicy curry heats up this hearty soup. A great starter for an Asian meal.

Cooking oil	1 tbsp.	15 mL
Pork tenderloin, trimmed of fat and cut into thin strips (see Tip, page 101)	1/2 lb.	225 g
Red curry paste	1 tbsp.	15 mL
Low-sodium prepared chicken broth	4 cups	1 L
Can of cut baby corn, drained	14 oz.	398 mL
Thinly sliced red pepper	1 cup	250 mL
Fish sauce	1 tsp.	5 mL
Brown sugar, packed	1 tsp.	5 mL
Fresh spinach, stems removed, lightly packed	2 cups	500 mL
Finely shredded basil (or 1 1/2 tsp., 7 mL, dried)	2 tbsp.	30 mL
Lime juice	1 tbsp.	15 mL

Heat cooking oil in large pot or Dutch oven on medium-high. Add pork. Cook for about 5 minutes, stirring occasionally, until browned. Transfer to small bowl. Cover to keep warm.

Heat and stir curry paste in same large pot on medium for about 1 minute until fragrant.

Add next 5 ingredients. Stir. Bring to a boil on medium-high. Reduce heat to medium-low. Cover. Simmer for about 5 minutes until red pepper is softened.

Add pork and spinach. Stir. Simmer for about 2 minutes, stirring occasionally, until pork is heated through and spinach is wilted.

Add basil and lime juice. Stir. Serves 4.

1 serving: 199 Calories; 7.7 g Total Fat (3.9 g Mono, 1.8 g Poly, 1.2 g Sat); 35 mg Cholesterol; 17 g Carbohydrate; 3 g Fibre; 18 g Protein; 907 mg Sodium

Pictured on page 35.

Curried Squash Soup

2 servings per portion

Squash your worries about what to feed the family with this velvety-textured golden soup.

Cooking oil	2 tsp.	10 mL
Chopped onion	2 cups	500 mL
Curry powder	1 1/2 tbsp.	25 mL
Finely grated, peeled gingerroot (or 1/2 tsp., 2 mL, ground ginger)	2 tsp.	10 mL
Chopped butternut squash	7 cups	1.75 L
Low-sodium prepared chicken broth	6 cups	1.5 L
Light sour cream	1/4 cup	60 mL
Pepper	1/4 tsp.	1 mL

Heat cooking oil in large pot or Dutch oven on medium. Add onion. Cook for 5 to 10 minutes, stirring often, until softened.

Add curry powder and ginger. Heat and stir for about 1 minute until fragrant.

Add squash and broth. Bring to a boil. Reduce heat to medium-low. Cover. Simmer for about 30 minutes, stirring occasionally, until squash is softened. Remove from heat. Cool slightly. Carefully process with hand blender, or in blender in 2 batches, until smooth. Return to same large pot.

Add sour cream and pepper. Heat and stir on medium until heated through. Serves 8.

1 serving: 108 Calories; 2.1 g Total Fat (1 g Mono, 0.5 g Poly, 0.8 g Sat); 2 mg Cholesterol; 21 g Carbohydrate; 3 g Fibre; 4 g Protein; 489 mg Sodium

1. Spiced Beef Soup, page 32
2. Cabbage Lover's Soup, page 37
3. Thai-Style Pork Soup, page 33

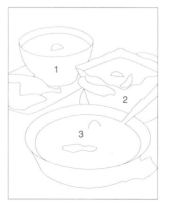

Cabbage Lover's Soup

servings per portion

Get your fill of cabbage with this Italian-style soup. Serve with crusty rolls.

Cooking oil	2 tsp.	10 mL
Chopped cabbage	4 cups	1 L
Thinly sliced leek (white part only)	1 cup	250 mL
Thinly sliced celery	1 cup	250 mL
Diced carrot	1 cup	250 mL
Prepared vegetable broth	8 cups	2 L
Can of diced tomatoes (with juice)	14 oz.	398 mL
Italian seasoning	1 tsp.	5 mL
Fusilli (or other spiral) pasta (about 4 oz., 113 g)	1 cup	250 mL

Heat cooking oil in large pot or Dutch oven on medium-high. Add next 4 ingredients. Cook for 5 to 10 minutes, stirring occasionally, until vegetables start to soften.

Add broth, tomatoes and seasoning. Stir. Bring to a boil. Reduce heat to medium-low. Cover. Simmer for 20 to 30 minutes until vegetables are tender-crisp.

Add pasta. Cook, uncovered, on medium-high for about 10 minutes, stirring occasionally, until pasta is tender but firm. Serves 8.

1 serving: 121 Calories; 2.3 g Total Fat (1 g Mono, 0.6 g Poly, 0.4 g Sat); 0 mg Cholesterol; 20 g Carbohydrate; 3 g Fibre; 6 g Protein; 995 mg Sodium

Pictured on page 35.

1. Mediterranean Sub, page 59
2. Tomato And Zucchini Soup, page 44
3. Apple Carrot Cake, page 141

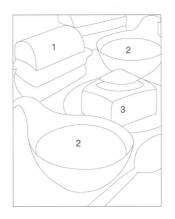

Cool And Zesty Soup

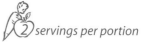

2 servings per portion

Garnish individual servings of this gazpacho-style soup with croutons or diced hard-cooked egg. Delightfully refreshing.

Medium tomatoes, peeled (see Tip, below) and coarsely chopped	**5**	**5**
English cucumber (with peel), coarsely chopped	**1**	**1**
Coarsely chopped red onion	**2/3 cup**	**150 mL**
Roasted red peppers, drained, blotted dry, chopped	**1/3 cup**	**75 mL**
Lemon juice	**1 tbsp.**	**15 mL**
Chopped fresh dill	**1 tbsp.**	**15 mL**
Balsamic vinegar	**1/2 tbsp.**	**7 mL**
Granulated sugar	**3/4 tsp.**	**4 mL**
Garlic cloves, minced	**2**	**2**
Hot pepper sauce	**1/2 tsp.**	**2 mL**
Pepper	**1/8 tsp.**	**0.5 mL**
Can of tomato juice	**19 oz.**	**540 mL**

Put first 11 ingredients into food processor. Pulse with on/off motion until vegetables are finely chopped. Transfer 2 cups (500 mL) tomato mixture to large bowl. Process remaining mixture until almost smooth. Transfer to same large bowl.

Add tomato juice. Stir well. Cover. Chill for at least 3 hours until cold. Serves 8.

1 serving: 43 Calories; 0.4 g Total Fat (0.1 g Mono, 0.2 g Poly, 0.1 g Sat); 0 mg Cholesterol; 10 g Carbohydrate; 2 g Fibre; 2 g Protein; 289 mg Sodium

To peel tomatoes, cut an X on the bottom, just through the skin. Plunge into boiling water for 30 seconds, then immediately into a bowl of ice water. Peel.

Chicken And Bacon Pea Soup

Back bacon adds rich, smoky flavour to this hearty soup. Serve with salad or crusty bread.

Cooking oil	2 tsp.	10 mL
Chopped red pepper	1 cup	250 mL
Chopped green onion	1 cup	250 mL
Boneless, skinless chicken thighs, cut into 1/2 inch (12 mm) pieces	6 oz.	170 g
Chopped lean back bacon	1/3 cup	75 mL
Paprika	1/2 tsp.	2 mL
Pepper	1/2 tsp.	2 mL
All-purpose flour	2 tbsp.	30 mL
Milk	2 cups	500 mL
Low-sodium prepared chicken broth	2 cups	500 mL
Frozen peas	1 cup	250 mL
Light sour cream	2 tbsp.	30 mL

Heat cooking oil in large saucepan on medium. Add next 6 ingredients. Cook for 5 to 10 minutes, stirring occasionally, until chicken is no longer pink inside.

Add flour. Heat and stir for 1 minute.

Slowly add milk and broth, stirring constantly. Heat and stir until boiling and thickened. Reduce heat to medium-low. Simmer, uncovered, for 10 minutes, stirring occasionally.

Add peas and sour cream. Stir. Cover. Simmer for about 5 minutes, stirring occasionally, until peas are heated through. Serves 6.

1 serving: 149 Calories; 5 g Total Fat (2.1 g Mono, 1 g Poly, 1.7 g Sat); 33 mg Cholesterol; 13 g Carbohydrate; 2 g Fibre; 13 g Protein; 361 mg Sodium

Pictured on front cover.

Creamy Mushroom Soup

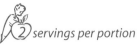 *servings per portion*

A long-time favourite you'll make again and again. Process longer if you prefer a smoother soup.

Sliced fresh mushrooms (your favourite)	**6 cups**	**1.5 L**
Cooking oil	**2 tsp.**	**10 mL**
Pepper, sprinkle		
Cooking oil	**2 tsp.**	**10 mL**
Chopped green onion	**1/2 cup**	**125 mL**
Garlic cloves, minced	**2**	**2**
All-purpose flour	**3 tbsp.**	**50 mL**
Low-sodium prepared chicken broth	**2 cups**	**500 mL**
Milk	**2 cups**	**500 mL**
Dry white (or alcohol-free) wine	**1/4 cup**	**60 mL**
Reduced-sodium chicken bouillon powder	**2 tsp.**	**10 mL**
Ground thyme (optional)	**1/8 tsp.**	**0.5 mL**
Pepper	**1/4 tsp.**	**1 mL**

Put mushrooms into medium bowl. Add first amount of cooking oil. Stir until coated. Spread in single layer in greased baking sheet with sides. Sprinkle with first amount of pepper. Bake in 400°F (205°C) oven for about 10 minutes until mushrooms are softened. Do not drain.

Heat second amount of cooking oil in large pot or Dutch oven on medium. Add green onion and garlic. Cook for about 5 minutes, stirring often, until green onion is softened.

Add flour. Heat and stir for 1 minute. Slowly add next 3 ingredients, stirring constantly until boiling and thickened.

Add mushrooms with liquid and remaining 3 ingredients. Heat and stir for 3 to 4 minutes. Reduce heat to medium-low. Cover. Simmer for 5 minutes. Remove from heat. Cool slightly. Carefully process in blender or food processor until mushrooms are finely chopped. Return to same large pot. Heat and stir on medium for about 5 minutes until heated through. Serves 6.

1 serving: 116 Calories; 4.5 g Total Fat (2.2 g Mono, 1.1 g Poly, 0.9 g Sat); 4 mg Cholesterol; 12 g Carbohydrate; 1 g Fibre; 6 g Protein; 392 mg Sodium

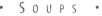

Chicken And Corn Chowder

A light, creamy broth loaded with tender chicken and colourful vegetables. A little Cheddar makes it even better—sprinkle some over top, too!

Cooking oil	1 tbsp.	15 mL
Boneless, skinless chicken thighs, chopped	3/4 lb.	340 g
Chopped red pepper	1 cup	250 mL
Chopped celery	1/2 cup	125 mL
All-purpose flour	3 tbsp.	50 mL
Low-sodium prepared chicken broth	2 cups	500 mL
Milk	2 cups	500 mL
Reduced-sodium chicken bouillon powder	4 tsp.	20 mL
Pepper	1/4 tsp.	1 mL
Frozen kernel corn	1 cup	250 mL
Chopped green onion	1/4 cup	60 mL
Grated light sharp Cheddar cheese	1/2 cup	125 mL

Heat cooking oil in large pot or Dutch oven on medium. Add chicken. Cook for 5 to 10 minutes, stirring occasionally, until browned.

Add red pepper and celery. Stir. Cover. Cook for about 5 minutes until vegetables start to soften.

Add flour. Heat and stir for 1 minute.

Slowly add broth, stirring constantly and scraping any brown bits from bottom of pot. Add milk, bouillon powder and pepper. Heat and stir for about 7 minutes, until boiling and thickened.

Add corn and green onion. Heat and stir for about 2 minutes until heated through.

Add cheese. Heat and stir until cheese is melted. Serves 4.

1 serving: 333 Calories; 13.4 g Total Fat (5 g Mono, 2.7 g Poly, 4.4 g Sat); 85 mg Cholesterol; 25 g Carbohydrate; 2 g Fibre; 29 g Protein; 889 mg Sodium

Spicy Bean Soup

A marvelous Mexican-style soup that's perfect with tortilla chips.

Cooking oil	1 tsp.	5 mL
Chorizo sausages, casings removed, chopped	2	2
Cooking oil	1 tbsp.	15 mL
Finely chopped red onion	1 1/2 cups	375 mL
Finely chopped red pepper	1 1/2 cups	375 mL
Garlic cloves, minced (or 1/2 tsp., 2 mL, powder)	2	2
Chili powder	1 tbsp.	15 mL
Ground cumin	2 tsp.	10 mL
Low-sodium prepared chicken broth	6 cups	1.5 L
Can of diced tomatoes (with juice)	28 oz.	796 mL
Can of red kidney beans, rinsed and drained	19 oz.	540 mL
Frozen kernel corn	1 cup	250 mL
Pepper	1/4 tsp.	1 mL
Light sour cream	3 tbsp.	50 mL
Chopped fresh cilantro or parsley (optional)	3 tbsp.	50 mL

Heat first amount of cooking oil in large pot or Dutch oven on medium. Add sausage. Scramble-fry for about 5 minutes until browned. Transfer with slotted spoon to paper towels to drain. Discard drippings.

Heat second amount of cooking oil in same large pot. Add onion, red pepper and garlic. Cook for 5 to 10 minutes, stirring often, until onion is softened.

Add chili powder and cumin. Heat and stir for about 1 minute until fragrant.

Add sausage and next 5 ingredients. Stir. Bring to a boil on medium-high. Reduce heat to medium-low. Cover. Simmer for about 15 minutes, stirring occasionally.

Add sour cream and cilantro. Stir. Serves 8.

1 serving: 221 Calories; 10.2 g Total Fat (4.8 g Mono, 1.6 g Poly, 3.2 g Sat); 16 mg Cholesterol; 23 g Carbohydrate; 5 g Fibre; 12 g Protein; 944 mg Sodium

Curried Lentil Vegetable Soup

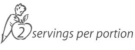 *servings per portion*

Cool mint and yogurt topping adds a nice tangy freshness to this thick, mildly spiced soup.

MINTY YOGURT TOPPING		
Low-fat plain yogurt	1/2 cup	125 mL
Chopped fresh mint leaves (or 1 1/2 tsp., 7 mL, dried)	2 tbsp.	30 mL
Cooking oil	1 tbsp.	15 mL
Finely chopped onion	1 1/2 cups	375 mL
Mild curry paste	2 tbsp.	30 mL
Low-sodium prepared chicken (or prepared vegetable) broth	8 cups	2 L
Dried red split lentils	1 1/2 cups	375 mL
Cauliflower florets	4 cups	1 L
Frozen kernel corn	1 cup	250 mL
Frozen peas	1 cup	250 mL
Fresh spinach, stems removed, lightly packed	2 cups	500 mL

Minty Yogurt Topping: Combine yogurt and mint in small bowl. Chill. Makes about 1/2 cup (125 mL) topping.

Heat cooking oil in large pot or Dutch oven on medium. Add onion. Cook for 5 to 10 minutes, stirring often, until softened.

Add curry paste. Heat and stir for about 1 minute until fragrant.

Add broth and lentils. Stir. Bring to a boil on medium-high. Reduce heat to medium-low. Cover. Simmer for 15 minutes.

Add cauliflower. Stir. Cover. Simmer for about 10 minutes until cauliflower and lentils are tender.

Add corn and peas. Stir. Cover. Simmer for about 5 minutes until heated through.

Add spinach. Stir. Simmer, uncovered, for about 2 minutes until spinach is wilted. Garnish individual servings with topping. Serves 8.

1 serving: 248 Calories; 4.3 g Total Fat (1.9 g Mono, 1.2 g Poly, 0.5 g Sat); 1 mg Cholesterol; 38 g Carbohydrate; 7 g Fibre; 18 g Protein; 704 mg Sodium

Tomato And Zucchini Soup

2 servings per portion

Caramelized onion adds a simple sweetness to this satisfying tomato soup. Great for lunch.

Olive (or cooking) oil	1 tbsp.	15 mL
Thinly sliced onion	2 cups	500 mL
Red wine vinegar	2 tsp.	10 mL
Granulated sugar	2 tsp.	10 mL
Pepper	1/4 tsp.	1 mL
Can of diced tomatoes (with juice)	28 oz.	796 mL
Low-sodium prepared chicken	2 cups	500 mL
(or prepared vegetable) broth		
Medium zucchini (with peel), chopped	2	2
Frozen kernel corn	1 cup	250 mL
Chopped fresh basil	1/4 cup	60 mL

Heat olive oil in large saucepan on medium. Add onion. Cook for about 20 minutes, stirring often, until caramelized.

Add vinegar, sugar and pepper. Heat and stir for about 1 minute until sugar is dissolved.

Add next 4 ingredients. Stir. Bring to a boil on medium-high. Reduce heat to medium-low. Cover. Simmer for 5 to 10 minutes, stirring occasionally, until zucchini is tender.

Add basil. Stir. Serves 6.

1 serving: 112 Calories; 3 g Total Fat (1.8 g Mono, 0.5 g Poly, 0.4 g Sat); 0 mg Cholesterol; 20 g Carbohydrate; 3 g Fibre; 4 g Protein; 436 mg Sodium

Pictured on page 36.

Carrot And Orange Soup

2 servings per portion

A golden harvest soup, perfectly seasoned with thyme.

Cooking oil	1 tbsp.	15 mL
Finely chopped carrot	4 cups	1 L
Finely chopped onion	1 1/2 cups	375 mL
Prepared vegetable broth	5 cups	1.25 L
Dried thyme	1/2 tsp.	2 mL
Pepper	1/4 tsp.	1 mL

(continued on next page)

Orange juice	1/2 cup	125 mL
Light sour cream	1/4 cup	60 mL
Grated orange zest	1/2 tsp.	2 mL

Heat cooking oil in large pot or Dutch oven on medium-high. Add carrot and onion. Cook for 5 to 10 minutes, stirring often, until onion is softened.

Add broth, thyme and pepper. Stir. Cover. Bring to a boil. Boil gently for about 10 minutes, stirring occasionally, until carrot is tender.

Add remaining 3 ingredients. Stir. Remove from heat. Cool slightly. Carefully process with hand blender, or in blender in 2 batches, until smooth. Return to same large pot. Heat and stir on medium-high for 1 to 2 minutes until heated through. Serves 6.

1 serving: 104 Calories; 3.8 g Total Fat (2 g Mono, 0.9 g Poly, 1.3 g Sat); 2 mg Cholesterol; 14 g Carbohydrate; 3 g Fibre; 4 g Protein; 722 mg Sodium

Curried Yam Soup

 *servings per portion*

Spicy curry and sweet yam make a nice blend. Serve with warm whole wheat rolls.

Cooking oil	1 tbsp.	15 mL
Chopped onion	1 1/2 cups	375 mL
Curry powder	1 tbsp.	15 mL
Chopped peeled yam (or sweet potato)	4 cups	1 L
Low-sodium prepared chicken broth	4 cups	1 L
Salt	1/4 tsp.	1 mL
Pepper	1/4 tsp.	1 mL
Low-fat plain yogurt	3 tbsp.	50 mL

Heat cooking oil in large pot or Dutch oven on medium. Add onion. Cook for about 20 minutes, stirring often, until caramelized.

Add curry powder. Heat and stir for about 1 minute until fragrant.

Add next 4 ingredients. Stir. Cover. Bring to a boil. Reduce heat to medium-low. Simmer for about 20 minutes, stirring occasionally, until yam is tender. Remove from heat. Cool slightly. Carefully process with hand blender, or in blender in 2 batches, until smooth. Return to same large pot.

Add yogurt. Heat and stir on medium for about 2 minutes until heated through. Serves 4.

1 serving: 269 Calories; 4.2 g Total Fat (2.1 g Mono, 1.2 g Poly, 0.3 g Sat); 0 mg Cholesterol; 52 g Carbohydrate; 8 g Fibre; 7 g Protein; 812 mg Sodium

Minted Beef And Noodles

servings per portion

Curried beef skewers nestle on a bed of rice noodles and colourful veggies. Exotic flavours make this perfect for a summer meal on the patio.

SWEET AND SPICY MARINADE

Sweet chili sauce	1 tbsp.	15 mL
Fish sauce	1 tbsp.	15 mL
Curry paste	2 tsp.	10 mL
Finely grated, peeled gingerroot	1 tsp.	5 mL
Garlic cloves, minced (or 1/2 tsp., 2 mL, powder)	2	2
Beef top sirloin steak, cut lengthwise into 1/4 inch (6 mm) slices	1 lb.	454 g
Bamboo skewers (8 inches, 20 cm, each), soaked in water for 10 minutes	8	8
Rice vermicelli	4 oz.	113 g
Boiling water		
English cucumber (with peel), halved lengthwise, seeds removed, thinly sliced	1	1
Julienned carrot (see Note)	1 cup	250 mL
Fresh bean sprouts	1 cup	250 mL
Chopped fresh mint leaves (or 3/4 tsp., 4 mL, dried)	1 tbsp.	15 mL

SPICY LIME DRESSING

Lime juice	1/4 cup	60 mL
Sweet chili sauce	2 tbsp.	30 mL
Curry paste	4 tsp.	20 mL
Peanut (or cooking) oil	2 tsp.	10 mL
Coarsely chopped unsalted peanuts, toasted (see Tip, page 21)	2 tbsp.	30 mL

Sweet And Spicy Marinade: Combine first 5 ingredients in small cup. Makes about 2 tbsp. (30 mL) marinade.

Put beef into large resealable freezer bag. Pour marinade over top. Seal bag. Turn until coated. Marinate in refrigerator for at least 6 hours or overnight, turning occasionally.

Preheat electric grill for 5 minutes or gas barbecue to medium (see Note). Thread beef slices, accordion-style, onto skewers. Cook on greased grill for 3 to 4 minutes per side until desired doneness. Transfer to large plate. Cover to keep warm.

(continued on next page)

Put vermicelli into large bowl. Pour boiling water over top until covered. Let stand for about 5 minutes until vermicelli is tender. Drain. Rinse with cold water. Drain well. Return to same large bowl.

Add next 4 ingredients. Toss.

Spicy Lime Dressing: Combine first 4 ingredients in jar with tight-fitting lid. Shake well. Makes about 1/4 cup (60 mL) dressing. Drizzle over vermicelli mixture. Toss well. Remove to large serving dish. Arrange beef skewers on top.

Sprinkle with peanuts. Serves 4.

1 serving: 531 Calories; 17.4 g Total Fat (7.5 g Mono, 2.4 g Poly, 4.9 g Sat); 56 mg Cholesterol; 65 g Carbohydrate; 4 g Fibre; 29 g Protein; 517 mg Sodium

Pictured on page 89.

Note: To julienne vegetables, cut into 1/8 inch (3 mm) strips that resemble matchsticks.

Note: Skewers may be broiled in oven. Place on greased broiler pan. Broil about 4 inches (10 cm) from heat in oven for 3 to 4 minutes per side until desired doneness.

MINTED CHICKEN AND NOODLES: Omit beef. Use same amount of boneless, skinless chicken breast halves, cut into 1/4 inch (6 mm) slices.

Beef Pot Roast

Oh, so tender roast in a rich, wine-flavoured "jus." A warming meal.

Boneless blade (or chuck) roast	2 lbs.	900 g
Garlic cloves, quartered lengthwise	4	4
Italian seasoning	1 tsp.	5 mL
Pepper, sprinkle		
Cooking oil	1 tbsp.	15 mL
Chopped carrot	2 cups	500 mL
Chopped parsnip	2 cups	500 mL
Chopped onion	2 cups	500 mL
Low-sodium prepared beef broth	1 1/4 cups	300 mL
Chopped yellow turnip	1 cup	250 mL
Dry red (or alcohol-free) wine	1/2 cup	125 mL

Cut 16 shallow slits in roast at random. Insert 1 piece of garlic into each slit. Sprinkle roast with seasoning and pepper.

Heat cooking oil in large pot or Dutch oven on medium-high. Add roast. Cook for about 5 minutes, turning occasionally, until browned on all sides. Transfer to large plate.

Combine remaining 6 ingredients in same large pot. Return roast to pot. Bring to a boil on medium. Reduce heat to medium-low. Cover. Simmer for 1 3/4 to 2 hours, turning roast at halftime, until tender. Remove roast to large plate. Cover to keep warm. Remove vegetables with slotted spoon to large serving bowl. Cover to keep warm. Bring liquid in pot to a boil on medium-high. Boil, uncovered, for 10 to 15 minutes until reduced by about half. Remove to small serving bowl. Cut roast into thin slices. Serve with vegetables and "jus." Serves 8 (2 to 3 oz., 57 to 85 g, each of roast beef).

1 serving: 334 Calories; 18.7 g Total Fat (8.4 g Mono, 1.2 g Poly, 6.9 g Sat); 66 mg Cholesterol; 17 g Carbohydrate; 3 g Fibre; 22 g Protein; 275 mg Sodium

 Keep a daily food diary to track what you eat and when. This journal will help identify things to improve upon once you compare it to Canada's Food Guide.

Ginger Pear Pork

Tender chunks of pear in a well-seasoned sauce dress up pork for dinner. Serve with brown rice.

Pork tenderloin, trimmed of fat	**1 lb.**	**454 g**
Pepper	**1/4 tsp.**	**1 mL**
Olive (or cooking) oil	**1 tbsp.**	**15 mL**
Chopped onion	**2 tbsp.**	**30 mL**
Finely grated, peeled gingerroot	**1 tbsp.**	**15 mL**
Fresh medium pears, peeled, cores removed, diced	**2**	**2**
Apple cider	**1 cup**	**250 mL**
Lime juice	**1 tbsp.**	**15 mL**
Liquid honey	**1 tsp.**	**5 mL**
Chopped fresh thyme leaves (or 1/4 tsp., 1 mL, dried)	**1 tsp.**	**5 mL**

Sprinkle tenderloin with pepper. Heat olive oil in medium frying pan on medium-high. Add tenderloin. Cook for about 5 minutes, turning occasionally, until browned on all sides. Reduce heat to medium. Cover. Cook for 10 to 12 minutes until meat thermometer inserted into thickest part of tenderloin reads 155°F (68°C). Remove to large plate. Cover with foil. Let stand for 10 minutes. Internal temperature should rise to at least 160°F (70°C).

Heat and stir onion and ginger in same medium frying pan for about 1 minute until onion is softened.

Add pear. Cook for 1 to 2 minutes, stirring occasionally, until pear starts to soften.

Add remaining 4 ingredients. Bring to a boil. Boil gently, uncovered, for about 8 minutes, until pear is softened and liquid is almost evaporated. Remove to small serving bowl. Cut tenderloin crosswise into 1/2 inch (12 mm) slices. Serve with sauce. Makes 4 servings (2 to 3 oz., 57 to 85 g, each of pork).

1 serving: 254 Calories; 8.4 g Total Fat (4.7 g Mono, 0.8 g Poly, 2.1 g Sat); 72 mg Cholesterol; 20 g Carbohydrate; 3 g Fibre; 24 g Protein; 63 mg Sodium

Wine And Rosemary Chicken

Tender chicken in a subtle white wine and rosemary sauce. Garnish with a sprig of rosemary for a pretty presentation.

Cooking oil	2 tsp.	10 mL
Boneless, skinless chicken thighs, halved	1 lb.	454 g
Baby carrots	1 1/2 cups	375 mL
Chopped onion	1 cup	250 mL
Dry white (or alcohol-free) wine	1 cup	250 mL
Low-sodium prepared chicken broth	1/2 cup	125 mL
Fresh rosemary sprigs	2	2
Garlic cloves, minced (or 1/2 tsp., 2 mL, powder)	2	2
Lemon pepper	1/2 tsp.	2 mL
Water	1 tbsp.	15 mL
Cornstarch	2 tsp.	10 mL
Light sour cream	2 tbsp.	30 mL

Heat cooking oil in large pot or Dutch oven on medium-high. Add chicken. Cook for about 10 minutes, stirring occasionally, until browned.

Add next 7 ingredients. Stir. Bring to a boil. Reduce heat to medium-low. Cover. Simmer for about 40 minutes, stirring occasionally, until chicken and carrots are tender.

Stir water into cornstarch in small cup until smooth. Add to chicken mixture. Heat and stir on medium for about 1 minute until sauce is boiling and thickened. Discard rosemary sprigs.

Add sour cream. Stir well. Serves 4.

1 serving: 285 Calories; 9.7 g Total Fat (3.7 g Mono, 2.5 g Poly, 2.6 g Sat); 104 mg Cholesterol; 13 g Carbohydrate; 2 g Fibre; 26 g Protein; 206 mg Sodium

Low-fat and non-fat dairy products have less fat and calories but still provide the protein and calcium essential to healthy eating. Be sure to read the labels and choose products with a lower percent M.F. (milk fat) or B.F. (butter fat).

Braised Lamb Chops

A splash of wine and a little thyme are all it takes to make a full-bodied "jus" for moist, tender lamb and tender-crisp vegetables. Serve with oven-roasted potatoes for a complete meal.

All-purpose flour	3 tbsp.	50 mL
Cajun seasoning	1 1/2 tbsp.	25 mL
Lamb loin chops (about 2 lbs., 900 g)	8	8
Cooking oil	1 tbsp.	15 mL
Baby carrots	2 cups	500 mL
Low-sodium prepared chicken broth	1 cup	250 mL
Dry white (or alcohol-free) wine	1/2 cup	125 mL
Medium onions, cut into thin wedges	2	2
Chopped fresh thyme leaves (or 3/4 tsp., 4 mL, dried)	1 tbsp.	15 mL
Greek seasoning	1/2 tsp.	2 mL
Bay leaves	2	2
Pepper	1/4 tsp.	1 mL
Frozen cut green beans	1 cup	250 mL

Combine flour and Cajun seasoning in large shallow dish. Press both sides of each lamb chop into flour mixture until coated.

Heat cooking oil in large pot or Dutch oven on medium-high. Add chops. Cook for 2 to 3 minutes per side until browned.

Add next 8 ingredients. Stir. Bring to a boil. Reduce heat to medium-low. Cover. Simmer for about 1 1/4 hours, stirring occasionally, until chops are tender. Remove cover. Bring to a boil on medium. Boil gently for about 15 minutes until sauce is thickened. Discard bay leaves.

Add green beans. Stir. Cover. Cook for 3 to 5 minutes until green beans are tender-crisp. Serves 8.

1 serving: 372 Calories; 27.4 g Total Fat (11.4 g Mono, 2.6 g Poly, 11.3 g Sat); 70 mg Cholesterol; 11 g Carbohydrate; 2 g Fibre; 17 g Protein; 393 mg Sodium

Artichoke Tomato Chicken

Chicken never tasted so good. Enjoy this light, summery dish with a salad on the side.

Boneless, skinless chicken breast halves (4 – 6 oz., 113 – 170 g, each)	**4**	**4**
Garlic and herb no-salt seasoning (such as Mrs. Dash), sprinkle		
Pepper, sprinkle		
Cooking oil	**1 tbsp.**	**15 mL**
Can of artichoke hearts, drained and quartered	**14 oz.**	**398 mL**
Roma (plum) tomatoes, thickly sliced lengthwise	**4**	**4**
Chopped fresh oregano leaves	**1 tbsp.**	**15 mL**
Balsamic vinegar	**1 tsp.**	**5 mL**
Granulated sugar	**1 tsp.**	**5 mL**
Garlic and herb no-salt seasoning (such as Mrs. Dash), sprinkle		

Sprinkle both sides of each chicken breast half with first amount of seasoning and pepper.

Heat cooking oil in large frying pan on medium-high. Add chicken. Cook for 3 to 4 minutes per side until browned. Arrange in single layer in greased 1 1/2 quart (1.5 L) shallow baking dish.

Layer artichoke evenly on top of chicken. Layer tomato slices evenly on top of artichoke.

Sprinkle remaining 4 ingredients over top. Bake, uncovered, in 350ºF (175ºC) oven for about 30 minutes until chicken is no longer pink inside. Serves 4.

1 serving: 269 Calories; 6.7 g Total Fat (2.7 g Mono, 1.9 g Poly, 1 g Sat); 81 mg Cholesterol; 19 g Carbohydrate; 5 g Fibre; 35 g Protein; 198 mg Sodium

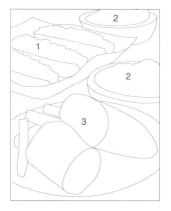

1. Crab-Stuffed Zucchini, page 64
2. Bean, Ham And Potato Salad, page 20
3. Turkey Wraps, page 61

Pumpkin Enchiladas

A subtle bite of chili in a pumpkin-packed tortilla. A tasty autumn dinner.

Cooked long grain white rice (about 1/2 cup, 125 mL, uncooked)	1 1/2 cups	375 mL
Thinly sliced green onion	1 cup	250 mL
Frozen peas	1 cup	250 mL
Grated Monterey Jack cheese	1/2 cup	125 mL
Flour tortillas (9 inch, 22 cm, diameter)	6	6
PUMPKIN SAUCE		
Can of pure pumpkin (no spices)	14 oz.	398 mL
Water	1 1/2 cups	375 mL
Chili powder	2 tsp.	10 mL
Grated Monterey Jack cheese	1 cup	250 mL

Combine first 4 ingredients in large bowl. Spoon across centre of each tortilla. Fold sides over filling. Roll up from bottom to enclose. Arrange in single layer in greased 3 quart (3 L) shallow baking dish.

Pumpkin Sauce: Combine pumpkin, water and chili powder in medium bowl. Makes about 3 cups (750 mL) sauce. Spread evenly over enchiladas.

Sprinkle with cheese. Bake in 450°F (230°C) oven for about 15 minutes until heated through. Broil 6 inches (15 cm) from heat in oven for about 5 minutes until cheese is melted and golden. Serves 6.

1 serving: 370 Calories; 12.6 g Total Fat (3.9 g Mono, 1.6 g Poly, 6.3 g Sat); 27 mg Cholesterol; 50 g Carbohydrate; 5 g Fibre; 15 g Protein; 405 mg Sodium

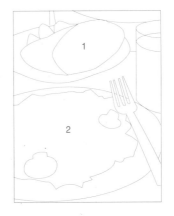

1. Crunchy Chicken Pitas, page 58
2. Warm Mushroom Salad, page 26

Ruby Chard Pork

2 servings per portion

Earthy ruby chard and pleasantly sweet fruit complement tender pork medallions in this colourful dish.

Olive (or cooking) oil	1 tbsp.	15 mL
Pork tenderloin, trimmed of fat and cut into 1/2 inch (12 mm) medallions	1 lb.	454 g
Lemon juice	2 tbsp.	30 mL
Garlic cloves, minced (or 1/2 tsp., 2 mL, powder)	2	2
Ruby chard, coarsely chopped and lightly packed	2 lbs.	900 g
Currants	1/2 cup	125 mL
Chopped dried apricot	1/3 cup	75 mL
Pepper	1/8 tsp.	0.5 mL
Orange juice	2 tbsp.	30 mL
Cornstarch	2 tsp.	10 mL
Pine nuts, toasted (see Tip, page 21)	1/4 cup	60 mL

Heat olive oil in large pot or Dutch oven on medium-high. Add pork medallions. Cook for about 2 minutes per side until browned. Transfer to large plate. Cover to keep warm.

Heat and stir lemon juice and garlic in same large pot on medium for about 1 minute until fragrant.

Add next 4 ingredients. Cover. Cook for about 5 minutes until chard starts to wilt. Stir carefully. Cover. Cook for another 5 minutes until stalks are tender-crisp.

Stir orange juice into cornstarch in small cup until smooth. Add to chard mixture. Add pork medallions. Heat and stir until sauce is boiling and thickened. Remove to large serving dish.

Sprinkle with pine nuts. Serves 4.

1 serving: 321 Calories; 13.9 g Total Fat (6.7 g Mono, 3 g Poly, 2.9 g Sat); 72 mg Cholesterol; 23 g Carbohydrate; 6 g Fibre; 31 g Protein; 540 mg Sodium

Spiced Salmon And Salsa

Cool as a cucumber, the salsa tames the heat of deliciously spicy salmon.

Cajun seasoning	1 tbsp.	15 mL
Lemon pepper	2 tsp.	10 mL
Salmon fillets, skin removed	4	4
MELON CUCUMBER SALSA		
Diced cantaloupe	3/4 cup	175 mL
Diced honeydew	3/4 cup	175 mL
English cucumber (with peel), quartered lengthwise, seeds removed, diced	1/4	1/4
Finely chopped red onion	1/3 cup	75 mL
Lime juice	3 tbsp.	50 mL
Chopped fresh cilantro or parsley (or 1 1/2 tsp., 7 mL, dried)	2 tbsp.	30 mL
Hot pepper sauce	1/2 tsp.	2 mL
Pepper, sprinkle		

Combine seasoning and lemon pepper in small bowl. Rub on both sides of each fillet. Let stand for 15 minutes. Preheat electric grill for 5 minutes or gas barbecue to medium-high (see Note). Cook fillets on greased grill for 3 to 4 minutes per side until fish flakes easily when tested with fork.

Melon Cucumber Salsa: Combine all 8 ingredients in medium bowl. Makes about 2 cups (500 mL) salsa. Serve with salmon. Serves 4.

1 serving: 587 Calories; 24.8 g Total Fat (8.1 g Mono, 9.8 g Poly, 3.8 g Sat); 211 mg Cholesterol; 10 g Carbohydrate; 1 g Fibre; 77 g Protein; 800 mg Sodium

Note: Salmon may be broiled in oven. Place on greased broiler pan. Broil about 4 inches (10 cm) from heat in oven for 3 to 4 minutes per side until fish flakes easily when tested with fork.

Bake, broil, roast, grill or microwave food instead of frying. Or use a non-stick frying pan with little or no oil, and drain off excess fat after frying.

Crunchy Chicken Pitas

Creamy, crunchy filling stuffed into a whole wheat pita. A delicious light lunch.

CRUNCHY CHICKEN FILLING

Grated carrot	3/4 cup	175 mL
Finely chopped cooked chicken	3/4 cup	175 mL
Finely chopped celery	1/2 cup	125 mL
Chopped dill pickle	6 tbsp.	100 mL
Grated light sharp Cheddar cheese	1/3 cup	75 mL
Light mayonnaise	1/4 cup	60 mL
Sliced almonds, toasted (see Tip, page 21)	2 tbsp.	30 mL
Pepper, sprinkle		
Whole wheat pita bread (7 inch, 18 cm, diameter), halved	1	1
Lettuce leaves (your choice)	2	2

Crunchy Chicken Filling: Combine first 8 ingredients in medium bowl. Makes about 1 3/4 cups (425 mL) filling.

Line each pita bread half with 1 lettuce leaf. Spoon filling into each half. Makes 2 chicken pitas.

1 chicken pita: 388 Calories; 18.9 g Total Fat (9.4 g Mono, 4.3 g Poly, 4 g Sat); 60 mg Cholesterol; 29 g Carbohydrate; 5 g Fibre; 27 g Protein; 883 mg Sodium

Pictured on page 54.

Onion Zucchini Frittata

A hearty dish of flavourful onion and zucchini baked with Parmesan cheese and basil.

Olive (or cooking) oil	1 tbsp.	15 mL
Thinly sliced onion	2 1/2 cups	625 mL
Red wine vinegar	2 tsp.	5 mL
Liquid honey	2 tsp.	5 mL
Large eggs	6	6
Grated Parmesan cheese	1/2 cup	125 mL
Pepper	1/4 tsp.	1 mL

(continued on next page)

| Thinly sliced zucchini (with peel) | 1 1/2 cups | 375 mL |
| Finely shredded fresh basil (or 1 1/4 tsp., 6 mL, dried) | 1 1/2 tbsp. | 25 mL |

Heat olive oil in large frying pan on medium. Add onion. Cook for 10 to 15 minutes, stirring often, until onion is softened and browned.

Add vinegar and honey. Stir well. Remove from heat. Let stand until cool.

Beat eggs, Parmesan cheese and pepper with whisk in large bowl.

Add zucchini, basil and onion mixture. Stir. Pour into greased 8 x 8 inch (20 x 20 cm) pan. Bake in 350°F (175°C) oven for 30 to 40 minutes until knife inserted in centre comes out clean. Let stand in pan for 5 minutes. Cuts into 8 pieces.

1 piece: 132 Calories; 7.6 g Total Fat (3.3 g Mono, 0.8 g Poly, 2.7 g Sat); 167 mg Cholesterol; 8 g Carbohydrate; 1 g Fibre; 8 g Protein; 173 mg Sodium

Mediterranean Sub

A sea of rich Mediterranean flavour awaits in this satisfying sandwich.

Hummus	3 tbsp.	50 mL
Section of baguette (8 inch, 20 cm, length), split	1	1
Fresh spinach (or arugula), stems removed, lightly packed	3/4 cup	175 mL
Roasted red peppers, drained, blotted dry, cut into thin strips	1/3 cup	75 mL
Thinly sliced red onion, separated into rings	1/4 cup	60 mL
Ripe medium olives, thinly sliced	4	4
Low-fat deli ham slices	2	2
Pepper, sprinkle		

Spread hummus on both baguette halves.

Layer next 5 ingredients, in order given, on bottom half.

Sprinkle with pepper. Cover with top half. Makes 1 submarine sandwich. Serves 2.

1 serving: 470 Calories; 10.6 g Total Fat (5.4 g Mono, 2.1 g Poly, 2.1 g Sat); 18 mg Cholesterol; 72 g Carbohydrate; 5 g Fibre; 22 g Protein; 1413 mg Sodium

Pictured on page 36.

Grilled Veggie Burgers

 *servings per portion*

Mildly spiced mayonnaise adds zip to layers of grilled veggies nestled in whole grain buns.

Red medium pepper, quartered, seeds and ribs removed	1	1
Medium yam (or sweet potato), peeled and cut into 1/8 inch (3 mm) slices	1	1
Medium zucchini (with peel), cut lengthwise into 1/4 inch (6 mm) slices	1	1
Cooking oil	1 tsp.	5 mL
Thinly sliced onion	1 cup	250 mL
Sweet chili sauce	2 tsp.	10 mL
Lime juice	2 tsp.	10 mL
CHILI LIME MAYONNAISE		
Light mayonnaise	1/4 cup	60 mL
Sweet chili sauce	2 tbsp.	30 mL
Lime juice	1 tbsp.	15 mL
Whole grain buns, split and toasted	4	4
Fresh spinach, stems removed, lightly packed	1 cup	250 mL

Preheat electric grill for 5 minutes or gas barbecue to medium-high. Cook red pepper, skin-side up, on greased grill for about 10 minutes until tender-crisp. Transfer to small bowl. Cover to keep warm.

Spray both sides of each yam slice with cooking spray. Cook on greased grill for about 3 minutes per side until tender. Transfer to large plate. Cover to keep warm.

Spray both sides of each zucchini slice with cooking spray. Cook on greased grill for about 2 minutes per side until tender and grill marks appear. Transfer to separate large plate. Cut zucchini slices in half crosswise. Cover to keep warm.

Heat cooking oil in large frying pan on medium. Add onion. Cook for 5 to 10 minutes, stirring often, until softened.

Add first amounts of chili sauce and lime juice. Stir. Remove from heat. Cover to keep warm.

Chili Lime Mayonnaise: Combine mayonnaise, chili sauce and lime juice in small bowl. Makes about 1/3 cup (75 mL) mayonnaise. Spread on both halves of each bun.

(continued on next page)

Divide and layer onion mixture, yam slices, red pepper, zucchini and spinach on bottom half of each bun. Cover with top halves. Makes 4 veggie burgers.

1 veggie burger: 216 Calories; 7.4 g Total Fat (3.8 g Mono, 2.5 g Poly, 0.7 g Sat); 0 mg Cholesterol; 35 g Carbohydrate; 4 g Fibre; 5 g Protein; 408 mg Sodium

Pictured on front cover.

GRILLED VEGGIE BURRITOS: Omit buns. Spread Chili Lime Mayonnaise on each of 4 whole wheat flour tortillas, almost to edge. Divide and layer prepared onion mixture, yam slices, red pepper, zucchini and spinach across centre of each tortilla. Fold sides over filling. Roll up from bottom to enclose. Makes 4 veggie burritos.

Turkey Wraps

Turkey salad with a cranberry twist—all wrapped up for lunch.

Whole cranberry sauce	**1/4 cup**	**60 mL**
Light sour cream	**1/4 cup**	**60 mL**
Light mayonnaise	**1/4 cup**	**60 mL**
Whole wheat flour tortillas (or your favourite), 9 inch (22 cm) diameter	**4**	**4**
Finely shredded iceberg lettuce, lightly packed	**1 cup**	**250 mL**
Chopped roasted turkey	**1 1/4 cups**	**300 mL**
Finely chopped celery	**1/2 cup**	**125 mL**
Finely chopped green onion	**1/2 cup**	**125 mL**
Raisins	**1/2 cup**	**125 mL**
Sliced almonds, toasted (see Tip, page 21)	**1/4 cup**	**60 mL**

Combine cranberry sauce, sour cream and mayonnaise in large bowl. Spread 1 1/2 tbsp. (25 mL) on each tortilla, leaving 1 inch (2.5 cm) edge.

Add remaining 6 ingredients to remaining cranberry mixture. Mix well. Spoon across centre of each tortilla. Fold sides over filling. Roll up from bottom to enclose. Makes 4 wraps.

1 wrap: 428 Calories; 13.4 g Total Fat (6.4 g Mono, 3.6 g Poly, 3 g Sat); 39 mg Cholesterol; 59 g Carbohydrate; 7 g Fibre; 22 g Protein; 472 mg Sodium

Pictured on page 53.

Potato Cakes Benny

Poached eggs top cheesy mushroom potatoes. An all-in-one breakfast or light lunch!

Hard margarine (or butter)	1 tbsp.	15 mL
Chopped fresh white mushrooms	1 cup	250 mL
Garlic clove, minced (or 1/4 tsp., 1 mL, powder)	1	1
Mashed potatoes (about 3 medium, uncooked)	2 cups	500 mL
Large egg, fork-beaten	1	1
Chopped fresh chives (or 1/2 tsp., 2 mL, dried)	2 tsp.	10 mL
Pepper	1/4 tsp.	1 mL
All-purpose flour	1/4 cup	60 mL
Paprika	1/4 tsp.	1 mL
Cooking oil	2 tsp.	10 mL
Grated medium Cheddar cheese	1 cup	250 mL
Water		
White vinegar	1 tsp.	5 mL
Large eggs	8	8

Melt margarine in small frying pan on medium-high. Add mushrooms and garlic. Cook for 2 to 3 minutes, stirring often, until mushrooms are softened. Transfer to medium bowl.

Add next 4 ingredients. Stir well. Shape mixture into 8 patties, using about 1/4 cup (60 mL) for each.

Combine flour and paprika in small shallow dish. Press both sides of each patty into flour mixture until coated.

Heat cooking oil in large frying pan on medium-high. Add patties. Cook for 1 to 2 minutes per side until golden. Transfer to baking sheet.

Sprinkle cheese over each patty. Cover to keep warm.

Pour water into large saucepan until 3 inches (7.5 cm) deep. Add vinegar. Stir. Bring to a boil on medium. Reduce heat to medium-low. Water should continue to simmer.

(continued on next page)

Break eggs, 1 at a time, into shallow dish. Slip each egg into water until all eggs are submerged (see Note). Cook each egg for 2 to 3 minutes until white is set and yolk reaches desired doneness. Remove each cooked egg with slotted spoon. Place 1 egg on top of each patty. Transfer 2 egg-topped potato cakes to each of 4 plates. Serves 4.

1 serving: 477 Calories; 26.7 g Total Fat (10.4 g Mono, 2.9 g Poly, 10.6 g Sat); 516 mg Cholesterol; 34 g Carbohydrate; 2 g Fibre; 25 g Protein; 368 mg Sodium

Note: Use a stove-top egg poacher, if desired.

Pictured on page 71.

Grilled Veggie Quesadillas

Something for everyone! Adults will enjoy the colourful vegetables. Kids will like the oozy cheese. Serve with salsa and sour cream.

Fat-free Italian dressing	2 tbsp.	30 mL
Mild pickled banana peppers (optional)	1 tbsp.	15 mL
Olive (or cooking) oil	1 tsp.	5 mL
Garlic clove, minced (or 1/4 tsp., 1 mL, powder)	1	1
Medium zucchini, quartered lengthwise	1	1
Small red pepper, quartered, seeds and ribs removed	1	1
Whole wheat flour tortillas (9 inch, 22 cm, diameter)	4	4
Grated sharp Cheddar cheese	2 cups	500 mL
Sliced green onions	2	2

Combine first 4 ingredients in medium bowl.

Add zucchini and red pepper. Stir until coated. Preheat two-sided grill for 5 minutes. Place vegetables in single layer on greased grill. Close lid. Cook for about 7 minutes until tender-crisp and lightly browned. Dice vegetables.

Scatter vegetables, cheese and green onions over half of each tortilla. Fold other half over filling. Press down lightly. Cook tortillas, 1 or 2 at a time, on greased grill for 3 to 4 minutes until grill marks appear.

Cut each quesadilla into 3 wedges. Serves 4.

1 serving: 440 Calories; 22.7 g Total Fat (6.7 g Mono, 1.4 g Poly, 13 g Sat); 63 mg Cholesterol; 40 g Carbohydrate; 6 g Fibre; 22 g Protein; 798 mg Sodium

Crab-Stuffed Zucchini

What to do with a bountiful harvest? Stuff it with an elegant crab filling. Garlic and dill add the perfect accent.

Medium zucchini, halved lengthwise	3	3
Hard margarine (or butter)	2 tbsp.	30 mL
Finely chopped onion	1/2 cup	125 mL
Garlic cloves, minced (or 1/2 tsp., 2 mL, powder)	2	2
Can of crabmeat, drained, cartilage removed, flaked	6 oz.	170 g
Grated Swiss cheese	1/2 cup	125 mL
Crumbled feta cheese (about 1 1/2 oz., 43 g)	1/3 cup	75 mL
Large egg, fork-beaten	1	1
All-purpose flour	1 tbsp.	15 mL
Chopped fresh parsley (or 3/4 tsp., 4 mL, flakes)	1 tbsp.	15 mL
Chopped fresh dill (or 1/2 tsp., 2 mL, dill weed)	2 tsp.	10 mL
Paprika	1 tsp.	5 mL
Pepper	1/4 tsp.	1 mL

Scoop out pulp from each zucchini half, leaving 1/2 inch (12 mm) thick shells. Arrange shells in single layer on greased baking sheet. Chop pulp.

Melt margarine in small frying pan on medium-high. Add onion and garlic. Cook for 3 to 5 minutes, stirring often, until onion starts to soften. Add zucchini pulp. Stir. Transfer to medium bowl.

Add remaining 9 ingredients. Stir well. Spoon into zucchini shells. Bake in 375°F (190°C) oven for about 30 minutes until filling is set. Makes 6 stuffed zucchini.

1 stuffed zucchini: 150 Calories; 9.7 g Total Fat (4 g Mono, 0.7 g Poly, 4.1 g Sat); 53 mg Cholesterol; 6 g Carbohydrate; 2 g Fibre; 10 g Protein; 369 mg Sodium

Pictured on page 53.

Fruit-Full French Toast

Your efforts will be fruitful as raves are sure to come your way when you make this delightful dish.

Orange marmalade	1/4 cup	60 mL
Thick whole wheat bread slices (with crusts)	6	6
Chopped dried apricot	1/2 cup	125 mL
Dried cranberries	1/4 cup	60 mL
Large eggs	4	4
Milk	3/4 cup	175 mL
Applesauce	1/2 cup	125 mL
Vanilla	1/2 tsp.	2 mL
Ground cinnamon	1/2 tsp.	2 mL
Fresh raspberries	1 cup	250 mL
Fresh blueberries	1/2 cup	125 mL
Sliced natural almonds, toasted (see Tip, page 21), optional	2 tbsp.	30 mL
Icing (confectioner's) sugar (optional)	1 tsp.	5 mL

Spread marmalade on 1 side of each bread slice. Cut slices in half diagonally.

Scatter apricot and cranberries in greased 9 x 13 inch (22 x 33 cm) pan. Arrange bread slices, marmalade side-up, in single layer on top of fruit.

Beat eggs and milk with whisk in medium bowl.

Add applesauce, vanilla and cinnamon. Stir well. Carefully pour over bread. Cover. Chill overnight. Bake, uncovered, in 450ºF (230ºC) oven for 20 to 25 minutes until edges are golden.

Scatter raspberries, blueberries and almonds, in order given, over top.

Sprinkle with icing sugar. Serves 6.

1 serving: 302 Calories; 6.3 g Total Fat (2.4 g Mono, 1.1 g Poly, 1.8 g Sat); 145 mg Cholesterol; 54 g Carbohydrate; 7 g Fibre; 12 g Protein; 368 mg Sodium

Pictured on page 71.

Ratatouille Pie

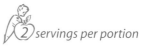 *servings per portion*

Traditional ratatouille wrapped with rice in a phyllo crust. Impressive!

Diced eggplant	3 cups	750 mL
Diced zucchini (with peel)	3 cups	750 mL
Salt	1 tbsp.	15 mL
Cooking oil	1 tbsp.	15 mL
Chopped onion	1 cup	250 mL
Garlic cloves, minced (or 1/2 tsp., 2 mL, powder)	2	2
Dried thyme	1/2 tsp.	2 mL
Dried basil	1/2 tsp.	2 mL
Dried whole oregano	1/4 tsp.	1 mL
Pepper	1/4 tsp.	1 mL
Can of diced tomatoes, drained	14 oz.	398 mL
Diced green pepper	1 cup	250 mL
Frozen phyllo pastry sheets, thawed according to package directions	10	10
Cooked long grain white rice (about 1 cup, 250 mL, uncooked)	3 cups	750 mL
Hard margarine (or butter), melted	1 tbsp.	15 mL

Put eggplant and zucchini into large bowl. Sprinkle with salt. Stir. Let stand for 1 hour. Drain. Rinse with cold water. Drain. Gently squeeze to remove excess liquid. Set aside.

Heat cooking oil in large frying pan on medium. Add next 6 ingredients. Cook for about 5 minutes, stirring often, until onion starts to soften.

Add eggplant and zucchini, tomatoes and green pepper. Stir. Cook for about 5 minutes, stirring occasionally, until green pepper is tender-crisp. Mixture will be quite dry. Cool.

Work with pastry sheets 1 at a time. Keep remaining sheets covered with damp tea towel to prevent drying. Spray 1 side of sheet with cooking spray. Fold into thirds lengthwise to make 4 inch (10 cm) strip. Place in greased 9 inch (22 cm) springform pan, allowing strip to hang over edge. Spray second pastry sheet with cooking spray. Fold into thirds lengthwise. Lay over first pastry strip at an angle, slightly overlapping. Repeat with 3 more pastry sheets and cooking spray until entire pan is covered (see Diagram 1). Gently press pastry to fit in pan, forming shell.

(continued on next page)

Press 1/2 of rice firmly in bottom of pastry shell. Spread 1/2 of vegetable mixture evenly over rice (see Diagram 2). Fold remaining pastry sheets. Cover filling, overlapping at an angle. Layer remaining rice and vegetable mixture. Fold overhanging pastry over filling toward centre of pie. Filling will not be completely covered.

Brush pastry with margarine. Bake in 350ºF (175ºC) oven for about 1 hour until pastry is crisp and golden. Let stand for 15 minutes. Cuts into 8 wedges.

1 wedge: 246 Calories; 5.2 g Total Fat (2.4 g Mono, 1.7 g Poly, 0.8 g Sat); 0 mg Cholesterol; 45 g Carbohydrate; 3 g Fibre; 6 g Protein; 1102 mg Sodium

Pictured on page 72.

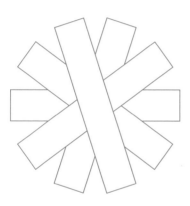

Diagram 1

Diagram 2

Calico Rice Creole

4 servings per portion

Vegetables and rice in a spicy tomato sauce—this will remind you of jambalaya, without the meat! Add more cayenne pepper if you like lots of heat.

Cooking oil	1 tbsp.	15 mL
Chopped red onion	2 cups	500 mL
Garlic cloves, minced (or 1 tsp., 5 mL, powder)	4	4
Cajun seasoning	1 tbsp.	15 mL
Ground cumin	1 tsp.	5 mL
Cayenne pepper	1/8 tsp.	0.5 mL
Can of diced tomatoes (with juice)	28 oz.	796 mL
Can of mixed beans, rinsed and drained	19 oz.	540 mL
Prepared vegetable broth	2 cups	500 mL
Frozen kernel corn	2 cups	500 mL
Chopped red pepper	2 cups	500 mL
Chopped celery	1 cup	250 mL
Chopped carrot	1 cup	250 mL
Worcestershire sauce	1 tbsp.	15 mL
Long grain white rice	1/2 cup	125 mL
Chopped fresh (or frozen, thawed) green beans	1 1/2 cups	375 mL
Chopped fresh parsley (or 1 1/2 tsp., 7 mL, flakes)	2 tbsp.	30 mL

Heat cooking oil in large pot or Dutch oven on medium. Add onion. Cook for 5 to 10 minutes, stirring often, until softened.

Add next 4 ingredients. Heat and stir for about 1 minute until fragrant.

Add next 8 ingredients. Stir. Bring to a boil on high. Reduce heat to medium-low. Cover. Simmer for 30 minutes, stirring occasionally.

Add rice. Stir. Cover. Simmer for about 20 minutes, without stirring, until rice is almost tender.

Add green beans. Stir. Cover. Simmer for about 7 minutes until green beans are tender-crisp.

Add parsley. Stir gently. Serves 6.

1 serving: 292 Calories; 4.4 g Total Fat (1.8 g Mono, 1.4 g Poly, 0.5 g Sat); 0 mg Cholesterol; 57 g Carbohydrate; 8 g Fibre; 11 g Protein; 877 mg Sodium

Pictured on page 72.

Sweet Potato Pork Tenders

Sweet apple, spicy cinnamon and a nutty topping. If it weren't for the pork, your family could mistake this for dessert!

All-purpose flour	1 tbsp.	15 mL
Cornstarch	1 tbsp.	15 mL
Garlic salt	1/4 tsp.	1 mL
Pepper	1/8 tsp.	0.5 mL
Pork tenderloin, trimmed of fat and cut into 3/4 inch (2 cm) pieces	1 lb.	454 g
Cooking oil	1 tbsp.	15 mL
Medium cooking apples (such as McIntosh), peeled, cores removed, cut into 1/2 inch (12 mm) pieces	2	2
Ground cinnamon	1/8 tsp.	0.5 mL
Can of sweet potatoes, drained	19 oz.	540 mL
Brown sugar, packed	1 tsp.	5 mL
Ground ginger	1/4 tsp.	1 mL
Ground nutmeg	1/8 tsp.	0.5 mL
PECAN CRUMBLE TOPPING		
Brown sugar, packed	1/3 cup	75 mL
All-purpose flour	3 tbsp.	50 mL
Hard margarine (or butter)	3 tbsp.	50 mL
Chopped pecans	1/4 cup	60 mL

Combine first 4 ingredients in large resealable freezer bag. Add pork. Seal bag. Toss until coated.

Heat cooking oil in large frying pan on medium-high. Add pork. Cook for about 3 minutes, stirring often, until browned. Transfer with slotted spoon to ungreased 2 quart (2 L) shallow baking dish.

Heat and stir apple and cinnamon in same large frying pan for about 1 minute, scraping any brown bits from bottom of pan, until apple is tender-crisp. Add to pork. Stir. Spread evenly in baking dish.

Mash next 4 ingredients in large bowl until smooth. Spread evenly on top of pork mixture.

Pecan Crumble Topping: Combine brown sugar and flour in small bowl. Cut in margarine until mixture resembles fine crumbs. Add pecans. Stir. Makes about 3/4 cup (175 mL) topping. Sprinkle evenly over sweet potato mixture. Bake, uncovered, in 350ºF (175ºC) oven for about 30 minutes until heated through and topping is golden. Serves 4.

1 serving: 533 Calories; 22.8 g Total Fat (13.2 g Mono, 3.9 g Poly, 4.2 g Sat); 72 mg Cholesterol; 57 g Carbohydrate; 3 g Fibre; 26 g Protein; 273 mg Sodium

Chickpea Spinach Curry

 2 servings per portion

Add a little colour to your day with this mild curry dish. Nice with rice.

Ingredient	Imperial	Metric
Cooking oil	1 tbsp.	15 mL
Chopped onion	1 cup	250 mL
Curry powder	1 1/2 tbsp.	25 mL
Garlic cloves, minced (or 1/2 tsp., 2 mL, powder)	2	2
Cans of chickpeas (garbanzo beans), 19 oz. (540 mL) each, rinsed and drained	2	2
Can of plum tomatoes (with juice)	28 oz.	796 mL
Cubed peeled yam (or sweet potato)	2 cups	500 mL
Low-sodium prepared chicken broth	1/2 cup	125 mL
Granulated sugar	1/2 tsp.	2 mL
Garlic and herb no-salt seasoning (such as Mrs. Dash)	1/2 tsp.	2 mL
Pepper	1/4 tsp.	1 mL
Fresh spinach, stems removed, lightly packed	2 cups	500 mL
Low-fat plain yogurt	3 tbsp.	50 mL

Heat cooking oil in large pot or Dutch oven on medium. Add onion. Cook for 5 to 10 minutes, stirring often, until softened.

Add curry powder and garlic. Heat and stir for about 1 minute until fragrant.

Add next 7 ingredients. Stir. Bring to a boil on medium-high. Reduce heat to medium-low. Cover. Simmer for about 35 minutes, stirring occasionally, until yam is tender.

Add spinach and yogurt. Stir. Cook for 1 to 2 minutes, stirring occasionally, until spinach is wilted. Serves 6.

1 serving: 268 Calories; 5.1 g Total Fat (1.9 g Mono, 1.8 g Poly, 0.5 g Sat); 0 mg Cholesterol; 48 g Carbohydrate; 8 g Fibre; 11 g Protein; 491 mg Sodium

1. Potato Cakes Benny, page 62
2. Fruit-Full French Toast, page 65
3. Apricot Breakfast Drink, page 11

Stuffed Roasted Peppers

 *3 servings per portion*

Plump, whole red peppers stuffed with delicious lentils and rice. A little topping sprinkled over stuffing adds a nice touch.

Large red peppers	4	4
Cooking oil	2 tsp.	10 mL
Finely chopped zucchini (with peel)	1 1/2 cups	375 mL
Finely chopped onion	1 cup	250 mL
Bacon slices, cooked crisp and crumbled	4	4
Can of brown lentils, rinsed and drained	19 oz.	540 mL
Can of diced tomatoes, drained and juice reserved	14 oz.	398 mL
Cooked brown rice (about 1/3 cup, 75 mL, uncooked)	1 cup	250 mL
Pepper	1/4 tsp.	1 mL
Grated Parmesan cheese	1/3 cup	75 mL
Chopped fresh basil (or 1 1/2 tsp., 7 mL, dried)	2 tbsp.	30 mL

Slice 1/2 inch (12 mm) from top of each red pepper. Set tops aside. Remove seeds and ribs. Trim bottom of each pepper so it will sit flat, being careful not to cut into cavity. Place peppers in greased 3 quart (3 L) casserole.

Heat cooking oil in large frying pan on medium. Add zucchini and onion. Cook for 5 to 10 minutes, stirring often, until onion is softened.

Add next 5 ingredients. Stir. Cook for about 5 minutes, stirring occasionally, until heated through. Spoon into prepared peppers. Replace tops. Pour reserved tomato juice over and around peppers in casserole. Bake, uncovered, in 350°F (175°C) oven for 35 to 40 minutes until peppers are tender-crisp.

Discard tops. Combine Parmesan cheese and basil in small bowl. Sprinkle over peppers. Serves 4.

1 serving: 294 Calories; 6.9 g Total Fat (3.2 g Mono, 1.7 g Poly, 1.5 g Sat); 5 mg Cholesterol; 48 g Carbohydrate; 9 g Fibre; 14 g Protein; 444 mg Sodium

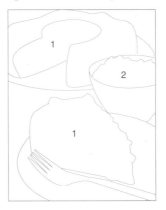

1. Ratatouille Pie, page 66
2. Calico Rice Creole, page 68

Bean And Turkey Bake

 *servings per portion*

This one's sure to be gobbled up quickly! Serve with rice or mashed potatoes.

Frozen french-style green beans	6 cups	1.5 L
Water		
Salt	1/2 tsp.	2 mL
Cooking oil	2 tsp.	10 mL
Lean ground turkey	1 lb.	454 g
Chopped onion	1/2 cup	125 mL
All-purpose flour	2 tsp.	10 mL
Can of condensed mushroom soup	10 oz.	284 mL
Low-sodium soy sauce	1 tsp.	5 mL
Fresh bean sprouts	3 cups	750 mL
Hard margarine (or butter)	2 tbsp.	30 mL
Fine dry bread crumbs	1/2 cup	125 mL

Cook green beans in water and salt in medium saucepan until tender-crisp. Drain. Cover to keep warm.

Heat cooking oil in large frying pan on medium-high. Add ground turkey and onion. Scramble-fry for 5 to 10 minutes until turkey is no longer pink.

Add flour. Stir. Add soup and soy sauce. Heat and stir for about 2 minutes until boiling.

Add green beans and bean sprouts. Stir. Spread evenly in ungreased 2 quart (2 L) shallow baking dish.

Melt margarine in small saucepan. Add bread crumbs. Mix well. Sprinkle evenly over turkey mixture. Bake, uncovered, in 350ºF (175ºC) oven for about 30 minutes until heated through and crumbs are golden. Serves 4.

1 serving: 467 Calories; 24.4 g Total Fat (10.1 g Mono, 6.6 g Poly, 5.7 g Sat); 90 mg Cholesterol; 36 g Carbohydrate; 5 g Fibre; 29 g Protein; 965 mg Sodium

BEAN AND CHICKEN BAKE: Omit lean ground turkey. Use same amount of lean ground chicken.

Leek And Potato Cod

No harm in letting the news "leek" out that dinner's cooking! Reel your family into the kitchen with the aroma of this zesty dilled dish.

Cooking oil	1 tbsp.	15 mL
Thinly sliced leek (white part only)	1 1/2 cups	375 mL
Thinly sliced red pepper	1 cup	250 mL
Thinly sliced baby potato	2 cups	500 mL
Low-sodium prepared chicken broth	1 1/2 cups	375 mL
Lemon juice	2 tbsp.	30 mL
Dijon mustard (with whole seeds)	2 tsp.	10 mL
Grated lemon zest	1 tsp.	5 mL
Cod fillets (about 1 lb., 454 g), any small bones removed	4	4
Chopped fresh dill (or 3/4 tsp., 4 mL, dill weed)	1 tbsp.	15 mL
Pepper, sprinkle		

Heat cooking oil in large frying pan on medium. Add leek and red pepper. Cook for 5 to 10 minutes, stirring often, until leek is softened. Spread evenly in pan.

Layer potato slices on top of leek mixture.

Combine next 4 ingredients in small bowl. Pour over potato. Cover. Cook for 8 to 10 minutes until potato is tender.

Place fillets in single layer on top of potato. Sprinkle with dill and pepper. Cover. Cook on medium-low for 8 to 10 minutes, depending on thickness of fillets, until fish flakes easily when tested with fork. Serves 4.

1 serving: 229 Calories; 4.7 g Total Fat (2.2 g Mono, 1.6 g Poly, 0.5 g Sat); 49 mg Cholesterol; 23 g Carbohydrate; 3 g Fibre; 24 g Protein; 355 mg Sodium

Squash Mushroom Lasagne

Sweet squash and carrots add a depth of flavour to earthy mushrooms in this scrumptious dish. Good cold too!

ONION CREAM SAUCE		
Cooking oil	1 tsp.	5 mL
Chopped onion	1/2 cup	125 mL
Garlic cloves, minced (or 1/2 tsp., 2 mL, powder)	2	2
All-purpose flour	1/4 cup	60 mL
Can of skim evaporated milk	13 1/2 oz.	385 mL
Milk	1 cup	250 mL
Prepared vegetable broth	1/2 cup	125 mL
Sliced fresh white mushrooms	3 cups	750 mL
Grated carrot	1 cup	250 mL
Grated butternut squash	1 cup	250 mL
Lemon pepper	1 tsp.	5 mL
Dried whole oregano	1/2 tsp.	2 mL
1% cottage cheese	1 1/2 cups	375 mL
Grated Parmesan cheese	1/4 cup	60 mL
Large eggs	2	2
Oven-ready lasagna noodles	9	9
Grated part-skim mozzarella cheese	1 cup	250 mL
Chopped fresh parsley, for garnish	2 tbsp.	30 mL

Onion Cream Sauce: Heat cooking oil in medium saucepan on medium. Add onion and garlic. Cook for 5 to 10 minutes, stirring often, until onion is softened.

Add flour. Heat and stir for 1 minute. Slowly add evaporated milk and milk, stirring constantly. Heat and stir for 5 to 10 minutes until boiling and thickened. Remove from heat. Makes about 2 1/2 cups (625 mL) cream sauce. Set aside.

Measure broth into large frying pan. Bring to a boil on medium-high. Add mushrooms. Heat and stir for 2 minutes.

(continued on next page)

Add next 4 ingredients. Cook, uncovered, for 5 to 10 minutes, stirring often, until liquid is evaporated. Remove from heat. Let stand for 10 minutes.

Add next 3 ingredients. Stir well.

Layer ingredients in greased 9 x 13 inch (22 x 33 cm) pan as follows:

1. 1/2 cup (125 mL) Onion Cream Sauce, spread evenly in pan
2. 3 noodles
3. 1/2 of vegetable mixture
4. 2/3 cup (150 mL) cream sauce
5. 3 noodles
6. Remaining vegetable mixture
7. 2/3 cup (150 mL) cream sauce
8. Remaining noodles
9. Remaining cream sauce, spread evenly on top

Sprinkle with mozzarella cheese. Cover with greased foil. Bake in 350°F (175°C) oven for 45 minutes. Discard foil. Bake for about 15 minutes until noodles are tender and mozzarella cheese is golden. Let stand for 15 minutes.

Garnish with parsley. Cuts into 8 pieces.

1 piece: 251 Calories; 6.7 g Total Fat (2.1 g Mono, 0.6 g Poly, 3.3 g Sat); 71 mg Cholesterol; 27 g Carbohydrate; 2 g Fibre; 21 g Protein; 548 mg Sodium

Shrimp And Asparagus Pasta

A feast for the eyes before you even lift a fork. Serve with a crisp salad.

Fettuccine	13 oz.	370 g
Boiling water	10 cups	2.5 L
Salt	1 1/4 tsp.	6 mL
Olive (or cooking) oil	1 tbsp.	15 mL
Chopped red onion	1 cup	250 mL
Can of diced tomatoes, drained	14 oz.	398 mL
Granulated sugar	1/2 tsp.	2 mL
Salt	1/4 tsp.	1 mL
Pepper	1/4 tsp.	1 mL
Fresh asparagus, trimmed of tough ends and cut into 1 inch (2.5 cm) pieces	1/2 lb.	225 g
Frozen uncooked medium shrimp (peeled and deveined), thawed	1 lb.	454 g
Chopped fresh parsley	2 tbsp.	30 mL
Grated Parmesan cheese (optional)	2 tbsp.	30 mL
Lemon juice	1 tbsp.	15 mL

Cook fettuccine in boiling water and salt in large uncovered pot or Dutch oven for 12 to 15 minutes, stirring occasionally, until tender but firm. Drain. Return to same pot. Cover to keep warm.

Heat olive oil in large frying pan on medium. Add onion. Cook for 5 to 10 minutes, stirring often, until softened.

Add next 4 ingredients. Stir. Bring to a boil.

Add asparagus. Stir. Cook for about 3 minutes until asparagus is almost tender-crisp.

Add shrimp. Stir. Cook for about 2 minutes until shrimp turn pink and asparagus is tender-crisp. Add to fettuccine.

Add remaining 3 ingredients. Toss gently. Remove to large serving dish. Serves 4.

1 serving: 520 Calories; 6.8 g Total Fat (3 g Mono, 1.6 g Poly, 1 g Sat); 129 mg Cholesterol; 82 g Carbohydrate; 5 g Fibre; 32 g Protein; 449 mg Sodium

Pictured on page 89.

Eggplant Pasta Bake

 *servings per portion*

Whole wheat pasta adds a nutty flavour to this rich, tomatoey dish. Scrumptious.

Whole wheat penne (or other tube) pasta	**2 cups**	**500 mL**
Boiling water	**10 cups**	**2.5 L**
Salt	**1 1/4 tsp.**	**6 mL**
Eggplant, peeled and cut lengthwise into 1/4 inch (6 mm) slices	**2**	**2**
Salt, sprinkle		
Olive (or cooking) oil	**1 tbsp.**	**15 mL**
Chopped onion	**1 cup**	**250 mL**
Pasta sauce	**2 3/4 cups**	**675 mL**
Roma (plum) tomatoes, chopped	**6**	**6**
Basil pesto	**1/4 cup**	**60 mL**
Grated Parmesan cheese	**1/2 cup**	**125 mL**
Grated part-skim mozzarella cheese	**1/2 cup**	**125 mL**

Cook pasta in boiling water and salt in large uncovered pot or Dutch oven for 10 to 12 minutes, stirring occasionally, until tender but firm. Drain. Return to same pot. Cover to keep warm.

Sprinkle both sides of each eggplant slice with salt. Place on wire rack set in baking sheet with sides. Let stand for 20 minutes. Rinse slices with cold water. Pat dry with paper towels. Spray both sides of each slice with cooking spray. Preheat electric grill for 5 minutes or gas barbecue to medium (see Note). Cook slices on greased grill for 2 to 3 minutes per side until golden. Transfer to large plate. Cut into 1 inch (2.5 cm) pieces.

Heat olive oil in large frying pan on medium. Add onion. Cook for 5 to 10 minutes, stirring often, until softened.

Add eggplant, pasta and next 3 ingredients. Stir well. Spread evenly in greased 3 quart (3 L) casserole.

Sprinkle with both cheeses. Bake, uncovered, in 350ºF (175ºC) oven for 30 to 40 minutes until heated through and cheese is golden. Serves 6.

1 serving: 413 Calories; 16.5 g Total Fat (8.3 g Mono, 2.6 g Poly, 4.5 g Sat); 13 mg Cholesterol; 57 g Carbohydrate; 10 g Fibre; 15 g Protein; 829 mg Sodium

Note: If preferred, cook eggplant slices in 3 batches in 1 tbsp. (15 mL) olive (or cooking) oil in large frying pan on medium for 3 to 5 minutes per side until golden.

Broccoli Macaroni Bake

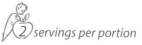

Macaroni and cheese that's fancy enough for company. This one will soon be a favourite!

Broccoli florets	**4 cups**	**1 L**
Boiling water		
Ice water		
Elbow macaroni	**1 1/2 cups**	**375 mL**
Boiling water	**8 cups**	**2 L**
Salt	**1 tsp.**	**5 mL**
Hard margarine (or butter)	**1 tbsp.**	**15 mL**
Finely chopped onion	**1 cup**	**250 mL**
Chopped red pepper	**1 cup**	**250 mL**
Chopped low-fat deli ham	**1 cup**	**250 mL**
All-purpose flour	**1/3 cup**	**75 mL**
Milk	**4 cups**	**1 L**
Grated light sharp Cheddar cheese	**2 cups**	**500 mL**
Chopped fresh parsley	**1/4 cup**	**60 mL**
Dijon mustard	**2 tsp.**	**10 mL**
Garlic and herb (or Italian) no-salt seasoning (such as Mrs. Dash)	**1 tsp.**	**5 mL**
Pepper	**1/4 tsp.**	**1 mL**
Hard margarine (or butter)	**1 tbsp.**	**15 mL**
Fine dry bread crumbs	**1/4 cup**	**60 mL**

Cook broccoli in boiling water in large saucepan for about 5 minutes until bright green. Drain. Immediately plunge into ice water in large bowl. Let stand for about 10 minutes until cold. Drain. Set aside.

Cook macaroni in boiling water and salt in large uncovered pot or Dutch oven for 8 to 10 minutes, stirring occasionally, until tender but firm. Drain. Transfer to medium bowl. Set aside.

Melt first amount of margarine in same large pot on medium. Add onion, red pepper and ham. Cook for 5 to 10 minutes, stirring often, until onion is softened.

Add flour. Heat and stir for 1 minute. Slowly add milk, stirring constantly. Heat and stir for 5 to 10 minutes until boiling and thickened. Remove from heat.

Add next 5 ingredients. Stir until cheese is melted. Add broccoli and macaroni. Stir until coated. Spread evenly in greased 2 1/2 quart (2.5 L) casserole.

(continued on next page)

Melt second amount of margarine in small saucepan on medium. Add bread crumbs. Mix well. Sprinkle over top of macaroni mixture. Bake in 350ºF (175ºC) oven for about 30 minutes until heated through. Serves 6.

1 serving: 487 Calories; 21.4 g Total Fat (7.6 g Mono, 1.5 g Poly, 10.9 g Sat); 60 mg Cholesterol; 47 g Carbohydrate; 4 g Fibre; 28 g Protein; 825 mg Sodium

Zucchini Tomato Spaghetti

2 servings per portion

Feta and garlic add a delightful nip to this simple pasta dish. Serve with warm rolls.

Whole wheat spaghetti	**13 oz.**	**370 g**
Boiling water	**10 cups**	**2.5 L**
Salt	**1 1/4 tsp.**	**6 mL**
Olive (or cooking) oil	**1 tbsp.**	**15 mL**
Medium zucchini (with peel), chopped	**4**	**4**
Garlic cloves, minced (or 1/2 tsp., 2 mL, powder)	**2**	**2**
Roma (plum) tomatoes, quartered lengthwise	**4**	**4**
Light feta cheese, cubed (about 3/4 cup, 175 mL)	**4 1/2 oz.**	**125 g**
Chopped fresh parsley	**1/4 cup**	**60 mL**
Lemon juice	**1 tbsp.**	**15 mL**
Pepper	**1/4 tsp.**	**1 mL**

Cook spaghetti in boiling water and salt in large uncovered pot or Dutch oven for 10 to 12 minutes, stirring occasionally, until tender but firm. Drain. Return to same pot. Cover to keep warm.

Heat olive oil in large frying pan on medium. Add zucchini and garlic. Cook for 5 to 10 minutes, stirring occasionally, until zucchini is softened.

Add tomato. Heat and stir for about 3 minutes until tomato just starts to soften. Add to spaghetti.

Add remaining 4 ingredients. Toss gently. Serves 6.

1 serving: 328 Calories; 8.2 g Total Fat (2.9 g Mono, 0.8 g Poly, 3.8 g Sat); 19 mg Cholesterol; 55 g Carbohydrate; 8 g Fibre; 14 g Protein; 257 mg Sodium

Creamy Mushroom Pasta

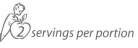servings per portion

Tender pasta snuggles with earthy mushrooms, smoky ham and sweet peas in a creamy, cheesy sauce. Delicious!

Package of dried porcini mushrooms	3/4 oz.	22 g
Boiling water		
Medium bow (or other) pasta	1 1/2 cups	375 mL
Boiling water	8 cups	2 L
Salt	1 tsp.	5 mL
Cooking oil	1 tbsp.	15 mL
Sliced brown (or white) mushrooms	3 cups	750 mL
Chopped low-fat deli ham	1 cup	250 mL
All-purpose flour	2 tbsp.	30 mL
Milk	2 cups	500 mL
Low-sodium prepared chicken broth	1/2 cup	125 mL
Dijon mustard	1 tbsp.	15 mL
Pepper	1/4 tsp.	1 mL
Frozen peas	1 cup	250 mL
Chopped fresh parsley	1/4 cup	60 mL
Grated light sharp Cheddar cheese	2/3 cup	150 mL

Put porcini mushrooms into small bowl. Pour boiling water over top until covered. Let stand for about 20 minutes until softened. Drain. Rinse with cold water. Squeeze to remove excess liquid. Discard stems. Thinly slice caps.

Cook pasta in boiling water and salt in large uncovered pot or Dutch oven for 12 to 15 minutes, stirring occasionally, until tender but firm. Drain. Return to same pot. Cover to keep warm.

Heat cooking oil in large frying pan on medium-high. Add porcini mushrooms, brown mushrooms and ham. Stir. Cook for about 5 minutes, stirring occasionally, until mushrooms start to brown.

Add flour. Heat and stir for 1 minute. Slowly add milk, broth, mustard and pepper, stirring constantly. Heat and stir for about 5 minutes until boiling and thickened.

(continued on next page)

Add peas and parsley. Heat and stir for about 5 minutes until peas are heated through. Remove from heat.

Add cheese. Stir until melted. Add to pasta. Stir until coated. Serves 4.

1 serving: 503 Calories; 14.4 g Total Fat (5.7 g Mono, 2.3 g Poly, 5.1 g Sat); 39 mg Cholesterol; 65 g Carbohydrate; 5 g Fibre; 28 g Protein; 870 mg Sodium

Tomato And Chickpea Pasta

Bright red tomato and deep green spinach make this meatless pasta dish an attractive entrée. A hearty meal.

Medium bow (or other) pasta	2 1/2 cups	625 mL
Boiling water	10 cups	2.5 L
Salt	1 1/4 tsp.	6 mL
Olive (or cooking) oil	1 tbsp.	15 mL
Cherry tomatoes, halved	12 oz.	340 g
Chili paste (sambal oelek)	1/2 tsp.	2 mL
Garlic cloves, minced (or 1/2 tsp., 2 mL, powder)	2	2
Can of chickpeas (garbanzo beans), rinsed and drained	19 oz.	540 mL
Fresh spinach, stems removed, lightly packed	3 cups	750 mL
Crumbled light feta cheese (about 4 oz., 113 g)	3/4 cup	175 mL

Cook pasta in boiling water and salt in large uncovered pot or Dutch oven for 12 to 15 minutes, stirring occasionally, until tender but firm. Drain. Return to same pot. Cover to keep warm.

Heat olive oil in large frying pan on medium. Add next 3 ingredients. Heat and stir for about 2 minutes until fragrant.

Add chickpeas and spinach. Heat and stir for 3 to 4 minutes until spinach is wilted. Add to pasta. Toss.

Add cheese. Toss well. Serves 4.

1 serving: 414 Calories; 13 g Total Fat (4.5 g Mono, 1.6 g Poly, 5.6 g Sat); 29 mg Cholesterol; 58 g Carbohydrate; 6 g Fibre; 18 g Protein; 550 mg Sodium

Pepper Mushroom Ravioli

servings per portion

Mushrooms and colourful peppers in a white wine cream sauce perfectly complement tender ravioli.

Ingredient	Imperial	Metric
Cooking oil	1 tbsp.	15 mL
Sliced fresh white mushrooms	2 cups	500 mL
Chopped red pepper	1 cup	250 mL
Chopped yellow pepper	1 cup	250 mL
Garlic cloves, minced (or 1/2 tsp., 2 mL, powder)	2	2
Dry white (or alcohol-free) wine	1/3 cup	75 mL
Low-sodium prepared chicken (or prepared vegetable) broth	1/3 cup	75 mL
Light sour cream	2 tbsp.	30 mL
Finely shredded basil (or 1 1/2 tsp., 7 mL, dried)	2 tbsp.	30 mL
Pepper	1/4 tsp.	1 mL
Package of fresh cheese (or your favourite) ravioli	11 oz.	300 g
Shaved Parmesan cheese	1/3 cup	75 mL

Heat cooking oil in large frying pan on medium. Add next 4 ingredients. Cook for 5 to 10 minutes, stirring occasionally, until peppers are softened.

Add wine. Stir. Bring to a boil. Boil gently for about 5 minutes, stirring occasionally, until wine is almost evaporated.

Add broth. Bring to a boil. Add sour cream, basil and pepper. Stir. Reduce heat to low. Cover to keep warm.

Cook ravioli according to package directions. Drain. Add to mushroom mixture. Stir until coated. Spoon onto each of 4 plates.

Scatter Parmesan cheese over each. Serves 4.

1 serving: 283 Calories; 13.3 g Total Fat (3.1 g Mono, 1.3 g Poly, 2.6 g Sat); 53 mg Cholesterol; 24 g Carbohydrate; 2 g Fibre; 15 g Protein; 415 mg Sodium

Sun-Dried Tomato Frittata

A delicious weekend brunch. Great with toast and juice.

Penne (or other tube) pasta	1 1/2 cups	375 mL
Boiling water	8 cups	2 L
Salt	1 tsp.	5 mL
Cooking oil	1 tbsp.	15 mL
Medium zucchini (with peel), chopped	2	2
Finely chopped onion	1 cup	250 mL
Sun-dried tomatoes in oil, drained and chopped	1/2 cup	125 mL
Chopped fresh thyme leaves (or 1/4 tsp., 1 mL, dried)	1 1/2 tsp.	7 mL
Pepper	1/4 tsp.	1 mL
Large eggs	8	8
Milk	1/4 cup	60 mL
Grated Parmesan cheese	1 tbsp.	15 mL
Grated sharp white Cheddar cheese	3/4 cup	175 mL

Cook pasta in boiling water and salt in large uncovered pot or Dutch oven for 10 to 12 minutes, stirring occasionally, until tender but firm. Drain. Return to same pot. Cover to keep warm.

Heat cooking oil in large frying pan on medium. Add zucchini and onion. Cook for 5 to 10 minutes, stirring often, until onion is softened.

Add pasta and next 3 ingredients. Heat and stir for about 5 minutes until heated through. Spread evenly in pan.

Beat eggs, milk and Parmesan cheese with whisk in medium bowl. Pour over pasta mixture. Reduce heat to medium-low. Cover. Cook for 3 to 5 minutes until bottom is golden and top is almost set. Remove cover.

Sprinkle with Cheddar cheese. Broil 4 inches (10 cm) from heat in oven (see Note) for about 2 minutes until Cheddar cheese is melted and frittata is set. Cuts into 8 wedges. Serves 4.

1 serving: 547 Calories; 24.7 g Total Fat (9.5 g Mono, 3.3 g Poly, 8.9 g Sat); 456 mg Cholesterol; 53 g Carbohydrate; 4 g Fibre; 28 g Protein; 349 mg Sodium

Note: To avoid damaging frying pan handle in oven, wrap handle with foil before placing under broiler.

Spicy Sweet Chicken Stew

Sweet raisins and dates mingle nicely in this spicy curry stew. Lots of sauce to serve over potatoes, noodles or rice.

All-purpose flour	3 tbsp.	50 mL
Bone-in chicken thighs, skin removed	1 3/4 lbs.	790 g
Cooking oil	1 tbsp.	15 mL
Thinly sliced onion	1 cup	250 mL
Cinnamon stick (4 inches, 10 cm)	1	1
Ground cumin	2 tsp.	10 mL
Ground coriander	2 tsp.	10 mL
Turmeric	1/2 tsp.	2 mL
Pepper	1/2 tsp.	2 mL
Low-sodium prepared chicken broth	3 cups	750 mL
Medium carrots, cut into 1/4 inch (6 mm) pieces	2	2
Red medium pepper, seeds and ribs removed, cut into 1/4 inch (6 mm) pieces	1	1
Medium zucchini (with peel), cut into 1/4 inch (6 mm) pieces	2	2
Medium tomatoes, peeled (see Tip, page 38), chopped	2	2
Dark raisins	1 cup	250 mL
Chopped pitted dates	1/2 cup	125 mL
Water	1/4 cup	60 mL
All-purpose flour	2 tbsp.	30 mL

Measure first amount of flour into large resealable freezer bag. Add chicken. Seal bag. Toss until coated.

Heat cooking oil in large pot or Dutch oven on medium. Add chicken. Cook for 3 to 4 minutes per side until browned. Transfer to large plate. Cover to keep warm.

Cook onion in same large pot for 5 to 10 minutes, stirring often, until softened.

Add next 5 ingredients. Heat and stir for about 1 minute until fragrant.

(continued on next page)

Slowly add broth, stirring constantly and scraping any brown bits from bottom of pot. Add chicken, carrot and red pepper. Stir. Bring to a boil. Reduce heat to medium-low. Cover. Simmer for 15 minutes. Increase heat to medium. Cook, uncovered, for 10 to 15 minutes until chicken is no longer pink inside.

Add next 4 ingredients. Stir. Cook for about 10 minutes, stirring occasionally, until vegetables are tender-crisp and raisins and dates are softened. Discard cinnamon stick. Transfer chicken and vegetables with slotted spoon to large serving bowl. Cover to keep warm. Bring broth mixture to a boil.

Stir water into second amount of flour in small cup until smooth. Slowly add to broth mixture, stirring constantly. Heat and stir for 2 to 3 minutes until boiling and thickened. Spoon onto chicken and vegetables. Serves 6.

1 serving: 332 Calories; 7.7 g Total Fat (2.9 g Mono, 2 g Poly, 1.4 g Sat); 69 mg Cholesterol; 49 g Carbohydrate; 6 g Fibre; 21 g Protein; 340 mg Sodium

Pictured on page 90.

If a recipe calls for less than an entire can of tomato paste, freeze unopened can for 30 minutes. Open both ends and push contents through one end. Slice off only what you need. Freeze remaining paste in resealable freezer bag or plastic wrap for future use.

Curried Pork Stew

 *3 servings per portion*

A pottage of chunky vegetables smothered in a thick, spicy sauce. Its wonderful aroma will make everyone scurry to the curry in a hurry to eat!

Cooking oil	1 tbsp.	15 mL
Pork stew meat	1 lb.	454 g
Curry powder	1 1/2 tbsp.	25 mL
Chopped carrot	2 cups	500 mL
Chopped onion	1 1/2 cups	375 mL
Low-sodium prepared chicken broth	1 1/2 cups	375 mL
Chopped yellow turnip	1 cup	250 mL
Chopped celery	1/2 cup	125 mL
Tomato paste (see Tip, page 87)	1/4 cup	60 mL
Bay leaves	2	2
Pepper	1/4 tsp.	1 mL

Heat cooking oil in large pot or Dutch oven on medium. Add pork. Cook for about 10 minutes, stirring occasionally, until browned.

Add curry powder. Heat and stir for about 1 minute until fragrant.

Add remaining 8 ingredients. Stir. Bring to a boil on medium-high. Reduce heat to medium-low. Cover. Simmer for about 1 hour, stirring occasionally, until pork is tender. Remove cover. Bring to a boil on medium. Boil gently for about 10 minutes until sauce is thickened. Discard bay leaves. Serves 4.

1 serving: 400 Calories; 24.7 g Total Fat (11.2 g Mono, 3.4 g Poly, 7.4 g Sat); 81 mg Cholesterol; 22 g Carbohydrate; 5 g Fibre; 24 g Protein; 419 mg Sodium

1. Shrimp And Asparagus Pasta, page 78
2. Minted Beef And Noodles, page 46

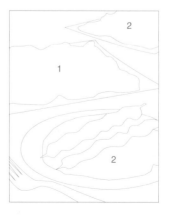

Hearty Beef Stew

2 servings per portion

Rich, dark and delicious. Serve with thick bread slices or crusty rolls. Equally good over egg noodles.

Cooking oil	1 tbsp.	15 mL
Beef stew meat	1 1/2 lbs.	680 g
Can of diced tomatoes (with juice)	28 oz.	796 mL
Chopped onion	1 1/2 cups	375 mL
Chopped carrot	1 1/2 cups	375 mL
Chopped parsnip	1 cup	250 mL
Dry red (or alcohol-free) wine	3/4 cup	175 mL
Chopped celery	1/2 cup	125 mL
Worcestershire sauce	1 tbsp.	15 mL
Garlic and herb no-salt seasoning (such as Mrs. Dash)	1/2 tsp.	2 mL
Bay leaves	2	2
Pepper	1/2 tsp.	2 mL
Water	3 tbsp.	50 mL
All-purpose flour	3 tbsp.	50 mL

Heat cooking oil in large frying pan on medium-high. Add beef in 2 batches. Cook for about 7 minutes per batch, stirring occasionally, until browned. Transfer to greased 3 quart (3 L) casserole.

Add next 10 ingredients. Stir. Cover. Cook in 325ºF (160ºC) oven for about 1 1/2 hours until vegetables are softened and beef is almost tender.

Stir water into flour in small cup until smooth. Slowly add to beef mixture, stirring constantly. Return to oven. Cook, uncovered, for about 30 minutes, stirring once, until beef is tender and sauce is boiling and thickened. Serves 6.

1 serving: 322 Calories; 12.1 g Total Fat (5.4 g Mono, 1.3 g Poly, 4 g Sat); 59 mg Cholesterol; 22 g Carbohydrate; 4 g Fibre; 26 g Protein; 355 mg Sodium

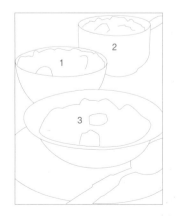

1. Spicy Sweet Chicken Stew, page 86
2. Barley Beef Stew, page 99
3. Minted Lamb And Pea Braise, page 94

Roasted Pepper Goulash

2 servings per portion

Deliciously tender pork with mellow roasted peppers in lots of creamy sauce. Serve over egg noodles.

Large green pepper	1	1
Large red pepper	1	1
Large orange (or yellow) pepper	1	1
All-purpose flour	1/3 cup	75 mL
Garlic and herb no-salt seasoning (such as Mrs. Dash)	2 tsp.	10 mL
Lemon pepper	1 tsp.	5 mL
Boneless pork loin roast, cut into 1/4 inch (6 mm) slices and then into thin strips	1 1/2 lbs.	680 g
Cooking oil	3 tbsp.	50 mL
Large onion, thinly sliced	1	1
Garlic clove, minced (or 1/4 tsp., 1 mL, powder)	1	1
Water	1/3 cup	75 mL
Paprika	2 tbsp.	30 mL
Can of diced tomatoes (with juice)	14 oz.	398 mL
Can of condensed vegetable broth	10 oz.	284 mL
Granulated sugar	1 tsp.	5 mL
Garlic and herb no-salt seasoning (such as Mrs. Dash)	1/2 tsp.	2 mL
Light sour cream	1 cup	250 mL
All-purpose flour	2 tbsp.	30 mL
Finely chopped fresh parsley (or 1 1/2 tsp., 7 mL, flakes)	2 tbsp.	30 mL

Place peppers on ungreased baking sheet. Broil 4 inches (10 cm) from heat in oven for about 10 minutes, turning often, until skins are blistered and blackened. Transfer to large bowl. Cover with plastic wrap. Let sweat for about 15 minutes until cool enough to handle. Remove skins. Cut peppers in half. Discard seeds and ribs, reserving any liquid. Strain liquid through sieve into small bowl. Cut peppers into strips. Set aside.

Measure first amounts of flour, seasoning and lemon pepper into large resealable freezer bag. Add pork. Seal bag. Toss until coated.

(continued on next page)

Heat cooking oil in large pot or Dutch oven on medium-high. Cook pork in 2 batches for 5 to 10 minutes per batch, stirring often, until browned. Transfer with slotted spoon to paper towels to drain.

Cook onion, garlic and water in same large pot on medium for about 5 minutes, stirring often and scraping any brown bits from bottom of pot, until onion is softened.

Add paprika. Stir. Add pork, reserved liquid from peppers and next 4 ingredients. Stir. Reduce heat to medium-low. Cover. Simmer for about 1 1/2 hours, stirring occasionally, until pork is tender.

Beat sour cream and second amount of flour with whisk in small bowl until smooth. Add small amount of hot pork mixture. Stir well. Add to pork mixture in pot. Stir well.

Add pepper strips and parsley. Heat and stir on medium for about 5 minutes until sauce is boiling and slightly thickened. Serves 6.

1 serving: 430 Calories; 26.1 g Total Fat (12.9 g Mono, 4.5 g Poly, 9.2 g Sat); 79 mg Cholesterol; 22 g Carbohydrate; 3 g Fibre; 27 g Protein; 444 mg Sodium

Chilies and hot peppers contain capsaicin in seeds and ribs. Removing the seeds and ribs will reduce the heat. Wear rubber gloves when handling chilies or peppers and avoid touching your eyes. Wash your hands well afterwards.

Minted Lamb And Pea Braise

A traditional combination, simmered to minty perfection in a succulent stew.

Lamb stew meat	1 lb.	454 g
All-purpose flour	2 tbsp.	30 mL
Cooking oil	1 tbsp.	15 mL
Cooking oil	1 tsp.	5 mL
Small onions, quartered	2	2
Small carrots, cut into 3/4 inch (2 cm)	4	4
pieces		
Spiced apple cider	1 cup	250 mL
Frozen peas	1 cup	250 mL
Chopped fresh mint leaves	1/4 cup	60 mL

Put lamb into large resealable freezer bag. Add flour. Seal bag. Toss until coated.

Heat first amount of cooking oil in large saucepan on medium-high. Cook lamb in 2 batches for 5 to 6 minutes per batch, stirring occasionally, until browned. Transfer to medium bowl. Cover to keep warm.

Heat second amount of cooking oil in same large saucepan on medium. Add onion. Cook for 5 to 10 minutes, stirring often, until softened.

Add lamb, carrot and apple cider. Stir. Bring to a boil on medium-high. Reduce heat to medium-low. Cover. Simmer for about 1 1/2 hours, stirring occasionally, until lamb is tender. Remove cover. Bring to a boil on medium. Boil gently for about 5 minutes, stirring occasionally, until sauce is thickened.

Add peas and mint. Stir. Reduce heat to medium-low. Simmer, uncovered, for about 5 minutes until peas are heated through. Serves 4.

1 serving: 408 Calories; 24.4 g Total Fat (10.7 g Mono, 3.1 g Poly, 8.8 g Sat); 78 mg Cholesterol; 23 g Carbohydrate; 4 g Fibre; 24 g Protein; 130 mg Sodium

Pictured on page 90.

Mediterranean Hot Pot

 *servings per portion*

A colourful dish with a full-bodied rosemary and tomato sauce everyone's sure to love.

Cooking oil	**1 tbsp.**	**15 mL**
Boneless, skinless chicken thighs, halved	**1 lb.**	**454 g**
Bacon slices, cooked crisp and crumbled	**4**	**4**
Can of diced tomatoes (with juice)	**28 oz.**	**796 mL**
Chopped red onion	**1 cup**	**250 mL**
Chopped red pepper	**1 cup**	**250 mL**
Fresh rosemary sprigs	**2**	**2**
Garlic cloves, minced (or 1/2 tsp., 2 mL, powder)	**2**	**2**
Granulated sugar	**1/2 tsp.**	**2 mL**
Pepper	**1/4 tsp.**	**1 mL**
Chopped kalamata olives (Greek)	**1/4 cup**	**60 mL**
Cubed light feta cheese (about 1 1/2 oz., 43 g)	**1/3 cup**	**75 mL**
Chopped fresh parsley (or 1 1/2 tsp., 7 mL, flakes)	**2 tbsp.**	**30 mL**

Heat cooking oil in large pot or Dutch oven on medium-high. Add chicken. Cook for 5 to 10 minutes, turning occasionally, until browned.

Add next 8 ingredients. Stir. Bring to a boil. Reduce heat to medium-low. Cover. Simmer for about 30 minutes, stirring occasionally, until chicken is no longer pink inside.

Add olives. Stir. Simmer, uncovered, for 1 to 2 minutes until heated through. Discard rosemary sprigs.

Sprinkle with cheese and parsley. Do not stir. Cover. Simmer for about 2 minutes until cheese is softened. Serves 4.

1 serving: 345 Calories; 18.1 g Total Fat (6.9 g Mono, 3.4 g Poly, 6 g Sat); 117 mg Cholesterol; 17 g Carbohydrate; 3 g Fibre; 29 g Protein; 698 mg Sodium

Pork And Apricot Braise

 2 servings per portion

Deliciously sweet apricot sauce makes this stew fancy enough for company. Beautiful colour and a hint of spiciness—it's sure to satisfy.

Cooking oil	1 tbsp.	15 mL
Pork stew meat	1 lb.	454 g
Ground cumin	2 tsp.	10 mL
Ground ginger	1 tsp.	5 mL
Dried crushed chilies	1/2 tsp.	2 mL
Chopped carrot	2 cups	500 mL
Low-sodium prepared chicken broth	1 cup	250 mL
Water	1 cup	250 mL
Chopped celery	1/2 cup	125 mL
Chopped dried apricot	1/2 cup	125 mL
Dry onion soup mix, stir before measuring	3 tbsp.	50 mL
Frozen peas	1 cup	250 mL
Chopped fresh parsley (or 2 1/4 tsp., 11 mL, flakes)	3 tbsp.	50 mL
Liquid honey	2 tbsp.	30 mL
Grated orange zest	1/2 tsp.	2 mL
Water (or orange juice)	2 tbsp.	30 mL
Cornstarch	1 tbsp.	15 mL

Heat cooking oil in large pot or Dutch oven on medium. Add pork. Cook for about 15 minutes, stirring occasionally, until browned.

Add next 3 ingredients. Heat and stir for about 1 minute until fragrant.

Add next 6 ingredients. Stir. Bring to a boil. Reduce heat to medium-low. Cover. Simmer for about 1 1/2 hours, stirring occasionally, until pork and carrot are tender.

Add next 4 ingredients. Stir. Bring to a boil on medium.

Stir water into cornstarch in small cup until smooth. Add to pork mixture. Heat and stir for 1 to 2 minutes until peas are tender-crisp and sauce is boiling and thickened. Serves 4.

1 serving: 494 Calories; 25.3 g Total Fat (11.6 g Mono, 3.5 g Poly, 7.6 g Sat); 81 mg Cholesterol; 43 g Carbohydrate; 6 g Fibre; 26 g Protein; 1361 mg Sodium

Sausage Ragoût

2 servings per portion

A delightful tomato-based dish with plenty of spicy sausage and tender vegetables. Serve with fresh brown bread to soak up the sauce.

Hot Italian sausages	1 lb.	454 g
Cooking oil	1 tsp.	5 mL
Chopped onion	1 cup	250 mL
Finely grated, peeled gingerroot (or 3/4 tsp., 4 mL, ground ginger)	1 tbsp.	15 mL
Garlic cloves, minced (or 1/2 tsp., 2 mL, powder)	2	2
Paprika	2 tsp.	10 mL
Dried crushed chilies	1/2 tsp.	2 mL
Ground cinnamon	1/4 tsp.	1 mL
Sliced carrot	1 1/2 cups	375 mL
Diced peeled potato	1 1/2 cups	375 mL
Low-sodium prepared chicken broth	2 cups	500 mL
Can of mixed beans, rinsed and drained	19 oz.	540 mL
Tomato sauce	1 cup	250 mL
Chopped fresh basil	2 tbsp.	30 mL

Randomly poke several holes with fork into each sausage. Heat cooking oil in large pot or Dutch oven on medium. Add sausages. Cook for about 10 minutes, turning occasionally, until browned. Transfer to paper towel-lined plate. Cover to keep warm. Discard drippings, reserving about 1 tbsp. (15 mL) in pot.

Add onion. Cook for 5 to 10 minutes, stirring often, until softened.

Add next 5 ingredients. Heat and stir for about 1 minute until fragrant.

Add carrot and potato. Heat and stir on medium-high for 1 minute.

Slowly add broth, stirring constantly and scraping any brown bits from bottom of pot. Add sausages. Bring to a boil. Reduce heat to medium-low. Cover. Simmer for about 10 minutes until carrot is almost tender. Transfer sausages with slotted spoon to cutting board. Cut into 1/2 inch (12 mm) slices. Return to carrot mixture.

Add beans and tomato sauce. Stir. Cook on medium-high for about 5 minutes, stirring occasionally, until sauce is boiling and thickened.

Add basil. Heat and stir for 1 minute to blend flavours. Serves 4.

1 serving: 425 Calories; 19.4 g Total Fat (8.7 g Mono, 3 g Poly, 6.4 g Sat); 45 mg Cholesterol; 44 g Carbohydrate; 8 g Fibre; 21 g Protein; 1402 mg Sodium

Chicken Vegetable Hot Pot

 *2 servings per portion*

Rich, earthy flavours and wholesome vegetables abound in this sweet 'n' spicy stew.

Chinese dried mushrooms, stems removed	8	8
Boiling water		
Water	1 tbsp.	15 mL
Cornstarch	1 tbsp.	15 mL
Cooking oil	2 tsp.	10 mL
Medium onion, cut into thin wedges	1	1
Garlic cloves, minced (or 1/2 tsp., 2 mL, powder)	2	2
Dried crushed chilies	1/2 tsp.	2 mL
Boneless, skinless chicken breast halves, thinly sliced (see Tip, page 101)	1 lb.	454 g
Low-sodium prepared chicken broth	3 cups	750 mL
Sweet chili sauce	2 tbsp.	30 mL
Low-sodium soy sauce	1 tbsp.	15 mL
Shredded suey choy (Chinese cabbage)	2 cups	500 mL
Sliced red pepper	1 cup	250 mL
Rice vinegar	1 tbsp.	15 mL
Sesame oil, for flavour	1/2 tsp.	2 mL
Rice vermicelli	8 oz.	225 g
Boiling water		

Put mushrooms into small bowl. Pour boiling water over top until covered. Let stand for about 20 minutes until softened. Drain. Thinly slice. Set aside.

Stir water into cornstarch in small cup until smooth. Set aside.

Heat cooking oil in large pot or Dutch oven on medium. Add next 3 ingredients. Cook for about 5 minutes, stirring often, until onion is tender-crisp.

Add chicken. Cook for 5 to 10 minutes, stirring occasionally, until chicken is no longer pink inside.

Add next 3 ingredients. Stir. Cover. Cook for about 5 minutes, stirring occasionally, until boiling.

(continued on next page)

Add next 4 ingredients. Stir. Cover. Cook for about 2 minutes until cabbage and red pepper are tender-crisp. Stir cornstarch mixture. Add to chicken mixture. Add mushrooms. Heat and stir for about 1 minute until sauce is boiling and slightly thickened.

Put vermicelli into large bowl. Pour boiling water over top until covered. Cover. Let stand for about 5 minutes until vermicelli is tender. Drain. Spoon into each of 4 bowls. Spoon chicken mixture onto vermicelli. Serves 4.

1 serving: 465 Calories; 5.8 g Total Fat (2.1 g Mono, 1.5 g Poly, 0.8 g Sat); 66 mg Cholesterol; 69 g Carbohydrate; 4 g Fibre; 34 g Protein; 732 mg Sodium

Barley Beef Stew

Beef and barley are always good in soup. Now try them together with some colourful veggies in this tasty stew.

Cooking oil	**1 tbsp.**	**15 mL**
Beef stew meat	**1 1/2 lbs.**	**680 g**
Low-sodium prepared beef broth	**3 cups**	**750 mL**
Chopped onion	**1 cup**	**250 mL**
Fennel bulb (white part only), thinly sliced	**1**	**1**
Sliced red pepper	**2 cups**	**500 mL**
Pearl barley	**1/2 cup**	**125 mL**
Chopped fresh oregano leaves (or 3/4 tsp., 4 mL, dried)	**1 tbsp.**	**15 mL**
Pepper	**1/4 tsp.**	**1 mL**
Fresh spinach, stems removed, lightly packed	**2 cups**	**500 mL**

Heat cooking oil in large pot or Dutch oven on medium. Add beef. Cook for about 10 minutes, stirring occasionally, until browned.

Add broth, onion and fennel. Stir. Bring to a boil. Reduce heat to medium-low. Cover. Simmer for about 1 1/2 hours, stirring occasionally, until beef is tender.

Add next 4 ingredients. Stir. Cover. Simmer for about 45 minutes, stirring occasionally, until barley is tender.

Add spinach. Heat and stir for about 1 minute until spinach is wilted. Serves 6.

1 serving: 323 Calories; 12.6 g Total Fat (5.6 g Mono, 1.3 g Poly, 4.2 g Sat); 63 mg Cholesterol; 24 g Carbohydrate; 3 g Fibre; 29 g Protein; 444 mg Sodium

Pictured on page 90.

Beef And Eggplant Stew

 4 servings per portion

Deep colour and rich flavour make this stew a real winner for dinner! Serve with buns or ciabatta bread.

Olive (or cooking) oil	2 tsp.	10 mL
Beef stew meat	1 lb.	454 g
Olive (or cooking) oil	2 tsp.	10 mL
Cubed eggplant	4 cups	1 L
Chopped onion	1 1/2 cups	375 mL
Can of diced tomatoes (with juice)	14 oz.	398 mL
Dry red (or alcohol-free) wine	3/4 cup	175 mL
Tomato paste (see Tip, page 87)	1/4 cup	60 mL
Can of artichoke hearts, drained and quartered	14 oz.	398 mL
Kalamata olives (Greek)	1/4 cup	60 mL
Chopped fresh mint leaves (or 1 1/2 tsp., 7 mL, dried)	2 tbsp.	30 mL

Heat first amount of olive oil in large pot or Dutch oven on medium-high. Add beef. Cook for 10 to 15 minutes, stirring occasionally, until browned. Transfer to large bowl. Cover to keep warm.

Add second amount of olive oil to same large pot. Reduce heat to medium. Add eggplant and onion. Cook for 5 to 10 minutes, stirring often, until onion is softened.

Add tomatoes, wine and tomato paste. Stir. Bring to a boil. Add beef. Stir. Reduce heat to medium-low. Cover. Simmer for about 1 1/2 hours, stirring occasionally, until beef is very tender. Remove cover. Bring to a boil on medium. Boil gently for about 10 minutes, stirring occasionally, until sauce is thickened.

Add remaining 3 ingredients. Stir. Cook for 3 to 5 minutes, stirring occasionally, until heated through. Serves 4.

1 serving: 382 Calories; 15.7 g Total Fat (8.1 g Mono, 1.1 g Poly, 4.8 g Sat); 63 mg Cholesterol; 26 g Carbohydrate; 7 g Fibre; 30 g Protein; 474 mg Sodium

Beef, Broccoli And Apple Stir-Fry *3 servings per portion*

Beef and broccoli with a sweet apple twist. Perfect with coconut rice.

GINGER MARINADE

Dry sherry	3 tbsp.	50 mL
Low-sodium soy sauce	3 tbsp.	50 mL
Granulated sugar	1 tbsp.	15 mL
Finely grated, peeled gingerroot (or 1/4 tsp., 1 mL, ground ginger)	1 tsp.	5 mL
Rib-eye steak, thinly sliced (see Tip, below)	1/2 lb.	225 g
Cooking oil	1 tsp.	5 mL
Cooking oil	1 tsp.	10 mL
Broccoli florets	2 cups	500 mL
Tart medium cooking apple (such as Granny Smith), peeled, core removed, thinly sliced	1	1
Green onions, cut into 1 inch (2.5 cm) pieces	4	4

Ginger Marinade: Combine first 4 ingredients in medium bowl. Makes about 1/2 cup (125 mL) marinade. Add beef. Stir until coated. Marinate in refrigerator for 30 minutes, stirring occasionally.

Heat wok or large frying pan on medium-high until very hot. Add first amount of cooking oil. Add beef with marinade. Stir-fry for about 3 minutes until beef is browned. Transfer to separate medium bowl.

Add second amount of cooking oil to same wok. Add remaining 3 ingredients. Stir-fry for about 3 minutes until broccoli is tender-crisp. Add beef mixture. Stir-fry for about 1 minute until heated through. Serves 2.

1 serving: 420 Calories; 23.4 g Total Fat (10.7 g Mono, 2.2 g Poly, 7.9 g Sat); 60 mg Cholesterol; 24 g Carbohydrate; 4 g Fibre; 27 g Protein; 823 mg Sodium

Pictured on page 107.

To slice meat easily, freeze for about 30 minutes. If using frozen, partially thaw before slicing.

Cashew Vegetable Stir-Fry

An appealing mix of tender-crisp vegetables and crunchy cashews. Ginger and hoisin flavours linger delightfully on the palate. Serve with thick Shanghai noodles or steamed jasmine rice.

Water	1 tbsp.	15 mL
Cornstarch	2 tsp.	10 mL
Chinese dried mushrooms, stems removed	12	12
Boiling water		
Cooking oil	2 tsp.	10 mL
Large onion, cut into thin wedges	1	1
Fresh chili pepper, finely chopped (see Tip, page 93)	1	1
Garlic cloves, minced (or 1/2 tsp., 2 mL, powder)	2	2
Finely grated, peeled gingerroot (or 1/8 tsp., 0.5 mL, ground ginger)	1/2 tsp.	2 mL
Snow peas, trimmed	2 cups	500 mL
Red medium peppers, seeds and ribs removed, cut into thin strips	2	2
Green onions, cut into 1 inch (2.5 cm) pieces	12	12
Medium carrot, cut julienne (see Note)	1	1
Oyster sauce	2 tbsp.	30 mL
Hoisin sauce	2 tbsp.	30 mL
Liquid honey	1 tbsp.	15 mL
Finely shredded fresh basil	2 tbsp.	30 mL
Raw cashews, toasted (see Tip, page 21)	1/3 cup	75 mL

Stir water into cornstarch in small cup until smooth. Set aside.

Put mushrooms into small bowl. Pour boiling water over top until covered. Let stand for about 20 minutes until softened. Drain. Thinly slice. Set aside.

Heat wok or large frying pan on medium-high until very hot. Add cooking oil. Add next 4 ingredients. Stir-fry for about 2 minutes until fragrant.

Add next 4 ingredients. Stir-fry for 2 minutes.

Combine next 3 ingredients in separate small cup. Add to snow pea mixture. Add mushrooms. Stir-fry for 2 to 3 minutes until vegetables are tender-crisp. Stir cornstarch mixture. Add to vegetables. Stir-fry for about 1 minute until sauce is boiling and thickened.

Add basil and cashews. Stir-fry for about 1 minute until heated through. Serves 6.

(continued on next page)

1 serving: 176 Calories; 5.8 g Total Fat (3.2 g Mono, 1.3 g Poly, 0.9 g Sat);
0 mg Cholesterol; 29 g Carbohydrate; 4 g Fibre; 5 g Protein; 572 mg Sodium

Pictured on page 108.

Note: To julienne vegetables, cut into 1/8 inch (3 mm) strips that resemble matchsticks.

Beefy Orange Stir-Fry

2 servings per portion

Sweet citrus and tender-crisp snow peas make this beefy dish hard to resist. Serve with brown rice for a complete meal.

Water	**1 tbsp.**	**15 mL**
Cornstarch	**2 tsp.**	**10 mL**
Black bean sauce (pourable)	**2 tbsp.**	**30 mL**
Liquid honey	**1 tbsp.**	**15 mL**
Sesame oil, for flavour (optional)	**1/2 tsp.**	**2 mL**
Cooking oil	**2 tsp.**	**10 mL**
Beef top sirloin steak, thinly sliced (see Tip, page 101)	**1/2 lb.**	**225 g**
Snow peas, trimmed	**2 cups**	**500 mL**
Medium oranges, segmented	**4**	**4**
Sesame seeds, toasted (see Tip, page 21)	**2 tsp.**	**10 mL**

Stir water into cornstarch in small cup until smooth. Add next 3 ingredients. Stir. Set aside.

Heat wok or large frying pan on medium-high until very hot. Add cooking oil. Add beef. Stir-fry for about 2 minutes until beef starts to brown.

Add snow peas. Stir-fry for about 2 minutes until peas are tender-crisp.

Stir cornstarch mixture. Add to beef mixture. Add orange segments. Stir gently until heated through and sauce is slightly thickened. Remove to large serving dish.

Sprinkle with sesame seeds. Serves 4.

1 serving: 248 Calories; 9 g Total Fat (4.2 g Mono, 1.5 g Poly, 2.4 g Sat);
28 mg Cholesterol; 29 g Carbohydrate; 4 g Fibre; 15 g Protein; 345 mg Sodium

Pictured on page 108.

Choy Sum Pork Stir-Fry

3 servings per portion

A tasty mixture of pork and greens seasoned with a pungent marinade.

FIVE-SPICE MARINADE

Low-sodium soy sauce	2 tbsp.	30 mL
Garlic cloves, minced (or 3/4 tsp., 4 mL, powder)	3	3
Finely grated, peeled gingerroot (or 1/2 tsp., 2 mL, ground ginger)	2 tsp.	10 mL
Granulated sugar	2 tsp.	10 mL
Chinese five-spice powder	1/4 tsp.	1 mL
Pork tenderloin, trimmed of fat and thinly sliced (see Tip, page 101)	1/2 lb.	225 g
Cooking oil .	1 tsp.	5 mL
Coarsely chopped choy sum (or Chinese broccoli), stems trimmed 1 inch (2.5 cm) from end	4 cups	1 L
Sugar snap peas, trimmed	1 cup	250 mL
Green onions, cut into 2 inch (5 cm) pieces	12	12
Sesame seeds, toasted (see Tip, page 21)	1 tsp.	5 mL

Five-Spice Marinade: Combine first 5 ingredients in small bowl. Makes about 2 tbsp. (30 mL) marinade.

Put pork into medium resealable freezer bag. Add marinade. Seal bag. Turn until coated. Marinate in refrigerator for 1 hour, turning occasionally.

Heat wok or large frying pan on medium-high until very hot. Add cooking oil. Add pork with marinade. Stir-fry for 3 minutes.

Add next 3 ingredients. Stir-fry for 3 to 5 minutes until vegetables are tender-crisp. Remove to medium serving dish.

Sprinkle with sesame seeds. Serves 4.

1 serving: 134 Calories; 4.2 g Total Fat (1.9 g Mono, 0.9 g Poly, 1 g Sat); 35 mg Cholesterol; 10 g Carbohydrate; 2 g Fibre; 15 g Protein; 327 mg Sodium

Chicken Pineapple Noodles

Sweet 'n' sour and just a little spicy!

2 servings per portion

Medium rice stick noodles	4 1/2 oz.	125 g
Boiling water		
Cooking oil	1 tbsp.	15 mL
Boneless, skinless chicken breast halves,	1 lb.	454 g
thinly sliced (see Tip, page 101)		
Garlic cloves, minced (or 1/2 tsp., 2 mL,	2	2
powder)		
Dried crushed chilies	1/2 tsp.	2 mL
Fresh (or frozen, thawed) green beans,	2 1/4 cups	550 mL
cut into 1 1/2 inch (3.8 cm) pieces		
Thinly sliced red pepper	1 1/2 cups	375 mL
Can of pineapple tidbits, drained	14 oz.	398 mL
Lime juice	1/4 cup	60 mL
Chopped fresh cilantro or parsley	3 tbsp.	50 mL
Low-sodium soy sauce	2 tbsp.	30 mL
Liquid honey	2 tbsp.	30 mL
Fish sauce	1 tsp.	5 mL
Coarsely chopped unsalted peanuts,	2 tbsp.	30 mL
toasted (see Tip, page 21)		

Put noodles into large bowl. Pour boiling water over top until covered. Let stand for 10 to 15 minutes until softened. Drain. Set aside.

Heat wok or large frying pan on medium-high until very hot. Add cooking oil. Add next 3 ingredients. Stir-fry for about 3 minutes until chicken starts to brown.

Add green beans and red pepper. Stir-fry for about 3 minutes until vegetables are tender-crisp.

Add noodles and next 6 ingredients. Stir-fry for about 1 minute until heated through. Remove to large serving dish.

Sprinkle with peanuts. Serves 4.

1 serving: 415 Calories; 8.3 g Total Fat (3.7 g Mono, 2.3 g Poly, 1.1 g Sat); 66 mg Cholesterol; 55 g Carbohydrate; 4 g Fibre; 32 g Protein; 347 mg Sodium

Shrimp And Pea Stir-Fry

A colourful combination in a light, minty sauce. Serve over rice.

Cooking oil	2 tsp.	10 mL
Small onion, cut into thin wedges	1	1
Sugar snap peas, trimmed	2 cups	500 mL
Frozen uncooked medium shrimp (peeled and deveined), thawed	1 lb.	454 g
Julienned carrot (see Note)	1 cup	250 mL
Chopped fresh mint leaves	3 tbsp.	50 mL
Sweet chili sauce	3 tbsp.	50 mL
Lime juice	1 tbsp.	15 mL

Heat wok or large frying pan on medium-high until very hot. Add cooking oil. Add onion. Stir-fry for about 2 minutes until onion starts to brown.

Add sugar snap peas. Stir-fry for about 2 minutes until peas are tender-crisp.

Add remaining 5 ingredients. Stir-fry for 3 to 5 minutes until shrimp turn pink and carrots are tender-crisp. Serves 4.

1 serving: 176 Calories; 4.1 g Total Fat (1.6 g Mono, 1.4 g Poly, 0.5 g Sat); 129 mg Cholesterol; 15 g Carbohydrate; 3 g Fibre; 20 g Protein; 314 mg Sodium

Pictured on page 108.

Note: To julienne vegetables, cut into 1/8 inch (3 mm) strips that resemble matchsticks.

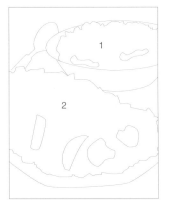

1. Chicken Vegetable Fried Rice, page 111
2. Beef, Broccoli And Apple Stir-Fry, page 101

Chicken Zucchini Stir-Fry

Refreshing lemon and dill add a lively splash and dash of flavour to tender chicken and mild zucchini. Very tasty!

Cooking oil	2 tsp.	10 mL
Boneless, skinless chicken breast halves, thinly sliced (see Tip, page 101)	1 lb.	454 g
Medium zucchini (with peel), cut julienne (see Note)	1	1
Frozen peas	2/3 cup	150 mL
Lemon juice	1 tbsp.	15 mL
Chopped fresh dill (or 1/2 tsp., 2 mL, dill weed)	2 tsp.	10 mL
Garlic cloves, minced (or 1/2 tsp., 2 mL, powder)	2	2
Pepper	1/8 tsp.	0.5 mL

Heat wok or large frying pan on medium-high until very hot. Add cooking oil. Add chicken. Stir-fry for about 3 minutes until chicken starts to brown.

Add remaining 6 ingredients. Stir-fry for about 5 minutes until chicken is no longer pink inside and zucchini is tender-crisp. Serves 4.

1 serving: 175 Calories; 4.4 g Total Fat (1.8 g Mono, 1.2 g Poly, 0.7 g Sat); 66 mg Cholesterol; 6 g Carbohydrate; 2 g Fibre; 27 g Protein; 30 mg Sodium

Note: To julienne vegetables, cut into 1/8 inch (3 mm) strips that resemble matchsticks.

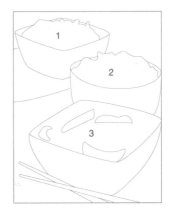

1. Beefy Orange Stir-Fry, page 103
2. Shrimp And Pea Stir-Fry, page 106
3. Cashew Vegetable Stir-Fry, page 102

Mushroom Noodle Stir-Fry

2 servings per portion

An interesting fusion of flavours in a light, creamy sauce. Definitely for mushroom lovers!

Milk	**1/2 cup**	**125 mL**
Cornstarch	**2 tsp.**	**10 mL**
Package of fresh Chinese egg noodles (10 1/2 oz., 300 g, size)	**1/2**	**1/2**
Boiling water	**2 cups**	**500 mL**
Cooking oil	**1 tbsp.**	**15 mL**
Sliced brown (or white) mushrooms	**4 cups**	**1 L**
Garlic cloves, minced (or 1/2 tsp., 2 mL, powder)	**2**	**2**
Frozen peas	**1 cup**	**250 mL**
Prepared vegetable (or low-sodium prepared chicken) broth	**1/2 cup**	**125 mL**
Pepper	**1/4 tsp.**	**1 mL**
Grated Parmesan cheese	**1/3 cup**	**75 mL**
Chopped fresh parsley (or 2 1/4 tsp., 11 mL, flakes)	**3 tbsp.**	**50 mL**

Stir milk into cornstarch in small cup until smooth. Set aside.

Cook noodles in boiling water in large uncovered saucepan for 1 minute. Stir to loosen noodles. Drain. Return to same saucepan. Cover to keep warm.

Heat wok or large frying pan on medium-high until very hot. Add cooking oil. Add mushrooms and garlic. Stir-fry for about 4 minutes until mushrooms start to brown.

Add peas, broth and pepper. Stir-fry for 1 minute. Stir cornstarch mixture. Add to mushroom mixture. Stir-fry for about 1 minute until sauce is boiling and thickened. Add noodles. Stir-fry for about 1 minute until heated through.

Add Parmesan cheese and parsley. Toss well. Serves 4.

1 serving: 193 Calories; 7.5 g Total Fat (3.1 g Mono, 1.5 g Poly, 2.4 g Sat); 21 mg Cholesterol; 22 g Carbohydrate; 4 g Fibre; 11 g Protein; 333 mg Sodium

Chicken Vegetable Fried Rice

A colourful blend with delicious smoky flavour. A meal all by itself!

Cooking oil	1 tbsp.	15 mL
Boneless, skinless chicken breast halves, thinly sliced (see Tip, page 101)	12 oz.	340 g
Chopped green pepper	1 cup	250 mL
Chopped red pepper	1 cup	250 mL
Frozen peas	1 cup	250 mL
Can of sliced water chestnuts, drained	8 oz.	227 mL
Thinly sliced green onion	1/2 cup	125 mL
Chopped low-fat deli ham	1/2 cup	125 mL
Low-sodium soy sauce	1 1/2 tbsp.	25 mL
Hoisin sauce	1 tbsp.	15 mL
Sweet chili sauce	1 tbsp.	15 mL
Cold cooked long grain white rice (about 2/3 cup, 150 mL, uncooked)	2 cups	500 mL

Heat wok or large frying pan on medium-high until very hot. Add cooking oil. Add chicken. Stir-fry for 3 to 5 minutes until chicken is no longer pink inside.

Add next 6 ingredients. Stir-fry for 2 to 3 minutes until peppers are tender-crisp.

Combine next 3 ingredients in small cup. Add to chicken mixture. Stir.

Add rice. Stir-fry for about 5 minutes until heated through and liquid is almost evaporated. Serves 6.

1 serving: 272 Calories; 5.2 g Total Fat (2.4 g Mono, 1.2 g Poly, 1 g Sat); 41 mg Cholesterol; 36 g Carbohydrate; 3 g Fibre; 20 g Protein; 448 mg Sodium

Pictured on page 107.

Pork And Apple Stir-Fry

 *servings per portion*

A delicious combination that's ready in just minutes. Serve over spaetzle, egg noodles or oven-roasted potatoes.

Water	**1 tbsp.**	**15 mL**
Cornstarch	**1 tbsp.**	**15 mL**
Apple juice	**1/3 cup**	**75 mL**
Low-sodium soy sauce	**1 tbsp.**	**15 mL**
Liquid honey	**1 tbsp.**	**15 mL**
Pepper	**1/8 tsp.**	**0.5 mL**
Cooking oil	**1 tbsp.**	**15 mL**
Pork tenderloin, trimmed of fat and thinly sliced (see Tip, page 101)	**3/4 lb.**	**340 g**
Chopped green cabbage	**2 1/2 cups**	**625 mL**
Medium cooking apples (such as McIntosh), peeled, cores removed, sliced	**2**	**2**
Chopped pecans, toasted (see Tip, page 21)	**1/3 cup**	**75 mL**

Stir water into cornstarch in small bowl until smooth. Add next 4 ingredients. Stir.

Heat wok or large frying pan on medium-high until very hot. Add cooking oil. Add pork. Stir-fry for 2 to 3 minutes until pork starts to brown.

Add cabbage and apple. Stir-fry for about 2 minutes until cabbage just starts to soften. Stir cornstarch mixture. Add to pork mixture. Stir-fry for about 1 minute until sauce is boiling and thickened.

Add pecans. Stir well. Serves 4.

1 serving: 292 Calories; 15.2 g Total Fat (8.4 g Mono, 3.3 g Poly, 2.4 g Sat); 47 mg Cholesterol; 20 g Carbohydrate; 2 g Fibre; 20 g Protein; 170 mg Sodium

Sweet Tofu And Vegetables

servings per portion

A sweet and spicy combination that's great served with noodles.

Low-sodium soy sauce	1 tbsp.	15 mL
Liquid honey	1 tbsp.	15 mL
Dry sherry	1 tbsp.	15 mL
Cornstarch	2 tsp.	10 mL
Chili paste (sambal oelek)	1 tsp.	5 mL
Package of extra-firm tofu, drained and cut into 1/2 inch (1.2 cm) cubes	12 1/4 oz.	350 g
Peanut (or cooking) oil	1 tbsp.	15 mL
Snow peas, trimmed	2 cups	500 mL
Coarsely chopped suey choy (Chinese cabbage)	2 cups	500 mL
Thinly sliced green pepper	1 cup	250 mL
Green onions, cut into 1 inch (2.5 cm) pieces	4	4
Garlic clove, minced (or 1/4 tsp., 1 mL, powder)	1	1

Combine first 5 ingredients in medium bowl. Add tofu. Stir gently.

Heat wok or large frying pan on medium-high until very hot. Add peanut oil. Add remaining 5 ingredients. Stir-fry for 1 minute. Add tofu mixture. Stir gently for 3 to 4 minutes until sauce is boiling and thickened and vegetables are tender-crisp. Serves 4.

1 serving: 235 Calories; 11.4 g Total Fat (3.3 g Mono, 5.6 g Poly, 1.7 g Sat); 0 mg Cholesterol; 20 g Carbohydrate; 3 g Fibre; 17 g Protein; 144 mg Sodium

To increase the intake of soy (a high-quality plant protein source) in your diet, use soy milk in smoothies, have a soy burger instead of a hamburger or add cubed tofu to stir-fries.

Pork And Spinach Stir-Fry

A fragrant stir-fry that's made for pasta!

Cooking oil	1 tbsp.	15 mL
Boneless pork loin chops, trimmed of fat and thinly sliced (see Tip, page 101)	3/4 lb.	340 g
Fresh asparagus, trimmed of tough ends and cut into 1 inch (2.5 cm) pieces	1/2 lb.	225 g
Lemon juice	1 tbsp.	15 mL
Garlic cloves, minced (or 1/2 tsp., 2 mL, powder)	2	2
Chili paste (sambal oelek)	1/2 tsp.	2 mL
Pepper	1/8 tsp.	0.5 mL
Fresh spinach, stems removed, lightly packed	3 cups	750 mL
Finely shredded fresh basil	2 tbsp.	30 mL
Grated Parmesan cheese	2 tbsp.	30 mL

Heat wok or large frying pan on medium-high until very hot. Add cooking oil. Add pork. Stir-fry for 2 minutes.

Add next 5 ingredients. Stir-fry for about 2 minutes until asparagus is tender-crisp.

Add spinach and basil. Stir-fry for about 1 minute until spinach is just wilted. Remove to medium serving dish.

Sprinkle with Parmesan cheese. Serves 4.

1 serving: 227 Calories; 13.9 g Total Fat (6.4 g Mono, 2.2 g Poly, 4.1 g Sat); 52 mg Cholesterol; 5 g Carbohydrate; 2 g Fibre; 21 g Protein; 132 mg Sodium

Tomato Fennel Risotto

Fennel, lemon and dill are refreshing additions to this creamy dish. Fabulous with fish.

Low-sodium prepared chicken (or prepared vegetable) broth	3 cups	750 mL
Cooking oil	2 tsp.	10 mL
Fennel bulb (white part only), thinly sliced	1	1
Finely chopped onion	3/4 cup	175 mL
Arborio (or short grain white) rice	1 cup	250 mL
Dry white (or alcohol-free) wine	1/4 cup	60 mL
Medium tomatoes, peeled (see Tip, page 38) and chopped	2	2
Medium zucchini (with peel), diced	1/2	1/2
Chopped fresh dill (or 3/4 tsp., 4 mL, dill weed)	1 tbsp.	15 mL
Lemon juice	2 tsp.	10 mL
Pepper	1/8 tsp.	0.5 mL

Bring broth to a boil in medium saucepan on medium-high. Reduce heat to low. Cover to keep warm.

Heat cooking oil in large saucepan on medium. Add fennel and onion. Cook for about 7 minutes, stirring occasionally, until fennel is softened.

Add rice. Stir. Add wine. Heat and stir for about 1 minute until wine is almost absorbed.

Add tomato and 1 cup (250 mL) warm broth. Heat and stir for about 6 minutes until broth is almost absorbed. Add 1 cup (250 mL) warm broth. Heat and stir for 8 to 10 minutes until broth is almost absorbed.

Add zucchini and remaining broth. Heat and stir for about 10 minutes until broth is almost absorbed and zucchini is tender-crisp.

Add remaining 3 ingredients. Stir well. Serves 6.

1 serving: 175 Calories; 1.9 g Total Fat (1 g Mono, 0.6 g Poly, 0.2 g Sat); 0 mg Cholesterol; 33 g Carbohydrate; 1 g Fibre; 5 g Protein; 331 mg Sodium

Marinated Mushrooms

Always good! These tender mushrooms with a chili pepper bite are perfect with pasta or roasted meats. Add another chili for more heat.

Fresh chili peppers (with seeds), chopped	2	2
Cooking oil	1 cup	250 mL
White wine vinegar	1/3 cup	75 mL
Granulated sugar	1 tbsp.	15 mL
Garlic cloves, minced (or 3/4 tsp., 4 mL, powder)	3	3
Salt	1 tsp.	5 mL
Pepper	1/2 tsp.	2 mL
Small mushrooms	1 1/2 lbs.	680 g
Diced red pepper	1 cup	250 mL

Combine first 7 ingredients in large saucepan. Heat and stir on medium for about 5 minutes until boiling and sugar is dissolved.

Add mushrooms. Cook for about 5 minutes, stirring often, until mushrooms are softened.

Add red pepper. Cook for 3 to 5 minutes, stirring occasionally, until red pepper is tender-crisp. Drain. Serves 8.

1 serving: 163 Calories; 14.8 g Total Fat (8.5 g Mono, 4.4 g Poly, 1.1 g Sat); 0 mg Cholesterol; 8 g Carbohydrate; 2 g Fibre; 2 g Protein; 153 mg Sodium

Potato Pan Cake

Shredded potato and onion baked in a pan and cut like a cake. Almost too easy.

Cold water		
Potatoes, peeled	2 lbs.	900 g
Large eggs	2	2
Finely chopped onion	1/2 cup	125 mL
Garlic and herb no-salt seasoning (such as Mrs. Dash)	1/2 tsp.	2 mL
Pepper	1/4 tsp.	1 mL
Hot milk	1 cup	250 mL

(continued on next page)

Pour cold water into large bowl until about 1/2 full. Grate potatoes into water (to prevent browning), adding more water if necessary to keep covered.

Combine next 4 ingredients in separate large bowl. Drain potato. Squeeze to remove excess water. Add to egg mixture. Stir well.

Slowly add hot milk, stirring constantly until potato is coated. Spread evenly in greased 9 x 9 inch (22 x 22 cm) pan. Bake, uncovered, in 375ºF (190ºC) oven for about 1 hour until golden. Let stand for 5 minutes before cutting. Cuts into 9 pieces.

1 piece: 82 Calories; 1.5 g Total Fat (0.5 g Mono, 0.2 g Poly, 0.6 g Sat); 49 mg Cholesterol; 14 g Carbohydrate; 1 g Fibre; 4 g Protein; 32 mg Sodium

Stir-Fried Honey Greens

Tender-crisp vegetables glisten with a gently sweet honey sauce.

Hoisin sauce	**1 tbsp.**	**15 mL**
Liquid honey	**1 tbsp.**	**15 mL**
Cornstarch	**2 tsp.**	**10 mL**
Cooking oil	**1 tsp.**	**5 mL**
Chopped bok choy	**3 cups**	**750 mL**
Fresh asparagus, trimmed of tough ends and cut into 2 inch (5 cm) pieces	**1 lb.**	**454 g**

Combine hoisin sauce, honey and cornstarch in small cup.

Heat wok or large frying pan on medium-high until very hot. Add cooking oil. Add bok choy and asparagus. Stir-fry for 4 to 5 minutes until vegetables are tender-crisp. Stir cornstarch mixture. Add to vegetable mixture. Stir-fry for about 1 minute until sauce is boiling and thickened. Serves 6.

1 serving: 48 Calories; 1 g Total Fat (0.5 g Mono, 0.3 g Poly, 0.1 g Sat); 0 mg Cholesterol; 9 g Carbohydrate; 1 g Fibre; 2 g Protein; 91 mg Sodium

To maintain the nutrients in your fresh vegetables, steam or cook them with as little water as possible. Use the nutrient-rich cooking water in your gravies and sauces.

Two-Potato Scallop

One potato, two potato—there's a treat for you in store.
Taste it once, it's very nice, and then come have some more!

Hard margarine (or butter)	1/4 cup	60 mL
All-purpose flour	2 tbsp.	30 mL
Milk	2 cups	500 mL
Grated Parmesan cheese	3 tbsp.	50 mL
Ground thyme	1/4 tsp.	1 mL
Pepper (white is best)	1/4 tsp.	1 mL
Potatoes, peeled and very thinly sliced	1 lb.	454 g
Sweet potatoes (or yams), peeled and very thinly sliced	1 lb.	454 g
Chopped onion	1/2 cup	125 mL

Melt margarine in medium saucepan on medium. Add flour. Heat and stir for 1 minute.

Slowly add milk, Parmesan cheese, thyme and pepper, stirring constantly. Heat and stir for about 7 minutes until boiling and thickened.

Layer 1/2 of potato, 1/2 of sweet potato and 1/2 of onion, in order given, in greased 2 quart (2 L) casserole. Pour 1/2 of milk mixture evenly over top. Repeat with remaining potato, sweet potato, onion and milk mixture. Bake in 375°F (190°C) oven for about 1 hour until potatoes are tender. Serves 6.

1 serving: 261 Calories; 10.3 g Total Fat (5.8 g Mono, 1 g Poly, 2.9 g Sat); 6 mg Cholesterol; 36 g Carbohydrate; 3 g Fibre; 7 g Protein; 210 mg Sodium

Dilled Zucchini

Tender-crisp zucchini accented with orange and dill. A palette of green that needs to be seen!

Hard margarine (or butter)	2 tsp.	10 mL
Medium zucchini (with peel), cut julienne (see Note)	3	3
Orange juice	2 tbsp.	30 mL
Cornstarch	1 tsp.	5 mL
Chopped fresh dill (or 3/4 tsp., 4 mL, dill weed)	1 tbsp.	15 mL
Pepper, sprinkle		

(continued on next page)

Melt margarine in medium frying pan on medium-high. Add zucchini. Cook for about 3 minutes, stirring often, until tender-crisp.

Stir orange juice into cornstarch in small cup until smooth. Add to zucchini mixture, stirring constantly. Heat and stir until boiling and thickened.

Add dill and pepper. Heat and stir for another minute. Serves 4.

1 serving: 38 Calories; 2.1 g Total Fat (1.3 g Mono, 0.3 g Poly, 0.4 g Sat); 0 mg Cholesterol; 4 g Carbohydrate; 2 g Fibre; 1 g Protein; 26 mg Sodium

Note: To julienne vegetables, cut into 1/8 inch (3 mm) strips that resemble matchsticks.

Marinated Celery

Crisp celery marinated in a tangy vinaigrette makes a tasty addition to a barbecue meal.

Celery ribs, cut diagonally into 1/2 inch (12 mm) pieces	**2 lbs.**	**900 g**
Water		
Cooking oil	**1/3 cup**	**75 mL**
Red wine vinegar	**1/3 cup**	**75 mL**
Roasted red peppers, drained, blotted dry, finely chopped	**1/4 cup**	**60 mL**
Granulated sugar	**2 tbsp.**	**30 mL**
Dry mustard	**1 tsp.**	**5 mL**
Dijon mustard	**1/2 tsp.**	**2 mL**

Put celery into large pot or Dutch oven. Add water. Cover. Bring to a boil on medium-high. Boil gently for 1 minute. Drain. Rinse with cold water until cold. Drain well.

Combine all 6 ingredients in large bowl. Add celery. Stir until coated. Cover. Chill for 4 hours. Drain. Serves 8.

1 serving: 68 Calories; 4.9 g Total Fat (2.8 g Mono, 1.5 g Poly, 0.4 g Sat); 0 mg Cholesterol; 6 g Carbohydrate; 2 g Fibre; 1 g Protein; 100 mg Sodium

Polynesian Sweet Potatoes

Almost sweet enough to be dessert. Serve with roast beef or pork.

Hard margarine (or butter)	1/2 tsp.	2 mL
Chopped pecans	2 1/2 tbsp.	37 mL
Medium unsweetened coconut	2 tbsp.	30 mL
Sweet potatoes (or yams), peeled	2 1/2 lbs.	1.1 kg
Mashed banana (about 1 medium)	1/3 cup	75 mL
Orange juice	1/4 cup	60 mL
Brown sugar, packed	2 tbsp.	30 mL
Salt	1/2 tsp.	2 mL
Maple (or maple-flavoured) syrup	2 tbsp.	30 mL

Melt margarine in small frying pan on medium. Add pecans. Heat and stir for 1 minute. Add coconut. Heat and stir for 2 to 5 minutes until fragrant and coconut is golden. Set aside.

Randomly poke several holes with fork into each sweet potato. Wrap each with paper towel. Microwave on high (100%) for 18 to 20 minutes, turning potatoes at halftime, until tender. Discard paper towels. Slice each potato in half lengthwise. Scoop flesh into large bowl. Discard skins.

Add next 4 ingredients. Mash well. Spread evenly in ungreased 1 1/2 quart (1.5 L) shallow baking dish. Sprinkle pecan mixture evenly over top. Bake in 325ºF (160ºC) oven for 15 to 20 minutes until heated through.

Drizzle with syrup. Serves 6.

1 serving: 179 Calories; 4 g Total Fat (1.6 g Mono, 0.7 g Poly, 1.4 g Sat); 0 mg Cholesterol; 35 g Carbohydrate; 3 g Fibre; 2 g Protein; 216 mg Sodium

 Set reasonable goals when changing eating habits in order to improve your health. For example, add one fruit to your diet every other day until you are more in line with the recommendations of Canada's Food Guide.

Stir-Fried Red Cabbage

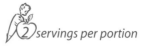

2 servings per portion

Savoury Chinese five-spice powder and tart apple add interest to simple cabbage. Satisfyingly crunchy!

White vinegar	2 tbsp.	30 mL
Water	2 tbsp.	30 mL
Cornstarch	1 tsp.	5 mL
Chinese five-spice powder	1/2 tsp.	2 mL
Cooking oil	1 tbsp.	15 mL
Hard margarine (or butter)	1 tbsp.	15 mL
Shredded red cabbage, lightly packed	6 cups	1.5 L
Tart medium cooking apple (such as Granny Smith), with peel, core removed, grated	1/2	1/2
Apple jelly	3 tbsp.	50 mL

Combine first 4 ingredients in small cup. Set aside.

Heat cooking oil and margarine in wok or large frying pan on medium-high until very hot. Add cabbage. Stir-fry for 5 to 10 minutes until tender-crisp.

Add apple and jelly. Stir-fry for 1 minute. Stir cornstarch mixture. Add to cabbage mixture. Heat and stir for 1 to 2 minutes until sauce is boiling and thickened. Serves 6.

1 serving: 91 Calories; 4.5 g Total Fat (2.6 g Mono, 1 g Poly, 0.6 g Sat); 0 mg Cholesterol; 13 g Carbohydrate; 2 g Fibre; 1 g Protein; 35 mg Sodium

Asparagus Vinaigrette

Pickled asparagus spears accented with pretty pimiento. A pleasant, summery dish.

Fresh asparagus, trimmed of tough ends	**1 lb.**	**454 g**
Boiling water		
Ice water		
PIMIENTO MARINADE		
White vinegar	**1/3 cup**	**75 mL**
Jar of sliced pimiento (do not drain)	**2 oz.**	**57 mL**
Cooking oil	**3 tbsp.**	**50 mL**
Sweet pickle relish	**3 tbsp.**	**50 mL**
Salt	**1 tsp.**	**5 mL**
Granulated sugar	**1 tsp.**	**5 mL**
Cayenne pepper	**1/8 tsp.**	**0.5 mL**
Garlic powder	**1/8 tsp.**	**0.5 mL**

Partially cook asparagus in boiling water in large saucepan for about 5 minutes until bright green. Drain. Immediately plunge into ice water in large bowl. Let stand for about 10 minutes until cold. Drain. Transfer to ungreased 3 quart (3 L) shallow baking dish.

Pimiento Marinade: Combine all 8 ingredients in small bowl. Makes about 1 cup (250 mL) marinade. Pour over asparagus. Turn asparagus until coated. Cover with plastic wrap. Chill for at least 3 hours. Drain. Serves 4.

1 serving: 90 Calories; 5.5 g Total Fat (3.1 g Mono, 1.7 g Poly, 0.4 g Sat); 0 mg Cholesterol; 10 g Carbohydrate; 2 g Fibre; 2 g Protein; 393 mg Sodium

Red Pepper Brussels Sprouts

Bacon and red pepper add delicious flavour to attractive, crisp Brussels sprouts.

Brussels sprouts (about 1 1/2 lbs., 680 g)	**3 cups**	**750 mL**
Water		
Bacon slices, diced	**4**	**4**
Finely chopped red pepper	**1/2 cup**	**125 mL**
Finely chopped onion	**1/4 cup**	**60 mL**
Hard margarine (or butter)	**2 tbsp.**	**30 mL**
Brown sugar, packed	**1 tsp.**	**5 mL**
Lemon pepper	**1/2 tsp.**	**2 mL**

(continued on next page)

Cook Brussels sprouts in water in large saucepan until tender-crisp. Drain. Cover to keep warm.

Cook bacon in medium frying pan on medium until crisp. Transfer with slotted spoon to paper towels to drain. Discard drippings, reserving about 2 tsp. (10 mL) in pan.

Heat reserved drippings. Add red pepper and onion. Cook for 5 to 10 minutes, stirring often, until onion is softened.

Add margarine, brown sugar and lemon pepper. Heat and stir for about 1 minute until margarine is melted. Add Brussels sprouts. Stir gently until coated. Serves 4.

1 serving: 176 Calories; 9.5 g Total Fat (5.3 g Mono, 1.2 g Poly, 2.4 g Sat); 5 mg Cholesterol; 19 g Carbohydrate; 7 g Fibre; 8 g Protein; 284 mg Sodium

Creamy Mashed Yams

Sweet, creamy yam to serve with ham. Delicious!

Yams (or sweet potatoes), peeled and cubed	**2 lbs.**	**900 g**
Water		
Low-fat plain yogurt	**1/4 cup**	**60 mL**
Grated Parmesan cheese	**1/4 cup**	**60 mL**
Chopped fresh parsley (or 2 1/4 tsp., 11 mL, flakes)	**3 tbsp.**	**50 mL**
Granulated sugar	**1 tsp.**	**5 mL**
Ground nutmeg	**1/8 tsp.**	**0.5 mL**
Pepper	**1/8 tsp.**	**0.5 mL**

Cook yam in water in large saucepan until tender. Drain.

Add remaining 6 ingredients. Mash well. Serves 8.

1 serving: 163 Calories; 1.4 g Total Fat (0.3 g Mono, 0.1 g Poly, 0.8 g Sat); 3 mg Cholesterol; 34 g Carbohydrate; 5 g Fibre; 4 g Protein; 79 mg Sodium

Zucchini Cakes

Golden patties of grated zucchini and onion pleasantly seasoned with Italian herbs. Serve these instead of hash brown potatoes for brunch.

Large egg	1	1
Grated zucchini (with peel), lightly packed	2 1/2 cups	625 mL
Fine dry bread crumbs	1 1/4 cups	300 mL
Finely chopped onion	1/4 cup	60 mL
Italian no-salt seasoning (such as Mrs. Dash)	1 1/2 tsp.	7 mL
Dry mustard	1/4 tsp.	1 mL
All-purpose flour	1/4 cup	60 mL
Cooking oil	1/4 cup	60 mL

Beat egg with fork in large bowl. Add next 5 ingredients. Stir well. Shape mixture into 8 patties, using 1/4 cup (60 mL) for each.

Dredge both sides of each patty in flour in shallow dish.

Heat 2 tbsp. (30 mL) cooking oil in large frying pan on medium. Add 4 patties. Cook for about 2 minutes per side until golden. Remove to large serving plate. Cover to keep warm. Repeat with remaining cooking oil and patties. Makes 8 zucchini cakes. Serves 4.

1 serving: 340 Calories; 18 g Total Fat (9.8 g Mono, 5.1 g Poly, 1.9 g Sat); 54 mg Cholesterol; 37 g Carbohydrate; 3 g Fibre; 8 g Protein; 492 mg Sodium

1. Poppy Seed Fruit Bowl, page 23
2. Creamy Raspberry Cooler, page 12
3. Fruit-Full Muffins, page 148

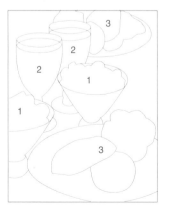

Mediterranean Green Beans

A fragrant, colourful mix that's good any time.

Fresh (or frozen, thawed) green beans	1/2 lb.	225 g
Medium onion, cut into 1/4 inch (6 mm) slices	1	1
Chopped green pepper	1/2 cup	125 mL
Chopped red pepper	1/2 cup	125 mL
Water	1/2 cup	125 mL
Olive (or cooking) oil	2 tbsp.	30 mL
Dried basil	1/2 tsp.	2 mL
Ground cumin	1/4 tsp.	1 mL
Pepper	1/8 tsp.	0.5 mL

Put first 4 ingredients into ungreased 8 x 8 inch (20 x 20 cm) pan.

Combine remaining 5 ingredients in small bowl. Pour over vegetables. Toss until coated. Cover with foil. Bake in 400°F (205°C) oven for 25 to 30 minutes until green beans are tender-crisp. Stir. Drain. Serves 6.

1 serving: 67 Calories; 4.7 g Total Fat (3.4 g Mono, 0.4 g Poly, 0.6 g Sat); 0 mg Cholesterol; 6 g Carbohydrate; 1 g Fibre; 1 g Protein; 4 mg Sodium

Pictured on page 126.

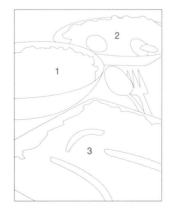

1. Beet Coleslaw, page 22
2. Grilled Mixed Veggies, page 128
3. Mediterranean Green Beans, above

Grilled Mixed Veggies

 3 servings per portion

Combine the goodness of vegetables with smoky barbecue flavour. Delicious!

Medium zucchini (with peel), cut into 1/4 inch (6 mm) slices	3	3
Small red pepper, seeds and ribs removed, cut into 1 inch (2.5 cm) pieces	1	1
Small yellow pepper, seeds and ribs removed, cut into 1 inch (2.5 cm) pieces	1	1
Halved fresh white mushrooms	1 cup	250 mL
Sliced red onion	1/2 cup	125 mL
Olive (or cooking) oil	4 tsp.	20 mL
Dried whole oregano	2 tsp.	10 mL
Lemon juice	1 tsp.	5 mL
No-salt seasoning (such as Mrs. Dash)	1 tsp.	5 mL
Pepper	1/2 tsp.	2 mL

Preheat gas barbecue to medium. Combine all 10 ingredients in large bowl. Transfer to barbecue basket. Place basket on grill. Cook for 25 to 30 minutes, turning basket occasionally, until vegetables are tender-crisp. Serves 4.

1 serving: 91 Calories; 5.1 g Total Fat (3.4 g Mono, 0.6 g Poly, 0.7 g Sat); 0 mg Cholesterol; 11 g Carbohydrate; 4 g Fibre; 3 g Protein; 7 mg Sodium

Pictured on page 126.

Minted Carrots

Carrots need never be boring again!

Water	2/3 cup	150 mL
White vinegar	1/3 cup	75 mL
Granulated sugar	2 tbsp.	30 mL
Coarse ground pepper	1 tsp.	5 mL
Large carrots	3	3
Chopped fresh mint leaves	2 tbsp.	30 mL

(continued on next page)

Combine first 4 ingredients in large bowl.

Peel carrots with vegetable peeler into thin strips. Chop strips. Add to vinegar mixture. Stir until coated. Cover. Chill for at least 3 hours. Drain.

Add mint. Toss. Serves 8.

1 serving: 23 Calories; 0.1 g Total Fat (0 g Mono, 0 g Poly, 0 g Sat); 0 mg Cholesterol; 6 g Carbohydrate; 1 g Fibre; 0 g Protein; 13 mg Sodium

Lemon Butter Fiddleheads

Even though fiddleheads, with their earthy flavour, are only available for a short season each year, they make an interesting and tasty side dish for dinner.

Fresh fiddleheads (see Note)	**1 lb.**	**454 g**
Water		
Butter (not margarine)	**2 tbsp.**	**30 mL**
Garlic clove, minced (or 1/4 tsp., 1 mL, powder)	**1**	**1**
Lemon juice	**1 tbsp.**	**15 mL**
Maple (or maple-flavoured) syrup	**1 tbsp.**	**15 mL**
Grated lemon zest	**1/4 tsp.**	**1 mL**
Pepper	**1/8 tsp.**	**0.5 mL**

Cook fiddleheads in water in medium saucepan until tender-crisp. Drain.

Melt butter in large frying pan on medium-low. Add garlic. Heat and stir for about 1 minute until fragrant.

Add remaining 4 ingredients. Heat and stir for 1 minute to blend flavours. Add fiddleheads. Stir until coated. Serves 4.

1 serving: 90 Calories; 6.2 g Total Fat (1.7 g Mono, 0.2 g Poly, 3.6 g Sat); 16 mg Cholesterol; 8 g Carbohydrate; 2 g Fibre; 3 g Protein; 62 mg Sodium

Note: To clean fresh fiddleheads, gently rub them between your hands to remove any loose or dry scales. Trim and discard ends. Rinse well.

LEMON BUTTER GREEN BEANS: Omit fiddleheads. Use same amount of fresh green beans.

Lentil Rice Pilaf

 *2 servings per portion*

Warming curry with a hint of sweet honey makes this rice especially nice.

Cooking oil	1 tbsp.	15 mL
Thinly sliced onion	2 cups	500 mL
Chopped red pepper	1 cup	250 mL
Liquid honey	1 tbsp.	15 mL
Curry powder	1 tbsp.	15 mL
Garlic cloves, minced (or 1/2 tsp., 2 mL, powder)	2	2
Garlic and herb no-salt seasoning (such as Mrs. Dash)	1/4 tsp.	1 mL
Pepper	1/4 tsp.	1 mL
Low-sodium prepared chicken (or prepared vegetable) broth	2 1/4 cups	550 mL
Can of lentils, rinsed and drained	19 oz.	540 mL
Basmati rice, rinsed well	1 cup	250 mL
Fresh spinach, stems removed, lightly packed	2 cups	500 mL

Heat cooking oil in large pot or Dutch oven on medium. Add onion. Cook for 10 to 15 minutes, stirring often, until caramelized.

Add next 6 ingredients. Stir well.

Add broth, lentils and rice. Stir. Bring to a boil. Reduce heat to medium-low. Cover. Simmer for 15 minutes without stirring.

Add spinach. Stir. Cover. Remove from heat. Let stand for 5 to 10 minutes until rice is tender and liquid is absorbed. Serves 4.

1 serving: 374 Calories; 4.7 g Total Fat (2.2 g Mono, 1.4 g Poly, 0.4 g Sat); 0 mg Cholesterol; 71 g Carbohydrate; 7 g Fibre; 14 g Protein; 551 mg Sodium

Strawberries With Orange Custard ③ servings per portion

A not-too-sweet treat that's fancy enough for company and simple enough for dessert any day.

Icing (confectioner's) sugar	2 tbsp.	30 mL
Orange-flavoured liqueur (such as Grand Marnier), or orange juice	2 tbsp.	30 mL
Thickly sliced fresh strawberries	6 cups	1.5 L
ORANGE CUSTARD		
Granulated sugar	1/2 cup	125 mL
Cornstarch	1 tbsp.	15 mL
All-purpose flour	1 tbsp.	15 mL
Milk	1 1/2 cups	375 mL
Egg yolks (large)	2	2
Grated orange zest	2 tsp.	10 mL

Combine icing sugar and liqueur in medium bowl. Add strawberries. Stir gently until coated. Cover. Chill for 1 hour.

Orange Custard: Combine sugar, cornstarch and flour in medium saucepan. Slowly add milk, stirring constantly until smooth. Heat and stir on medium for about 10 minutes until boiling and thickened. Remove from heat.

Beat egg yolks with fork in small bowl. Add 3 tbsp. (50 mL) hot milk mixture. Stir. Slowly add to hot milk mixture in saucepan, stirring constantly. Heat and stir on medium-low for 2 minutes.

Add orange zest. Stir. Transfer to small bowl. Cover with plastic wrap directly on surface to prevent skin from forming. Chill for about 3 hours until cold. Makes about 1 2/3 cups (400 mL) custard. Spoon strawberry mixture into each of 4 bowls. Spoon custard onto each. Serves 4.

1 serving: 299 Calories; 4.6 g Total Fat (1.4 g Mono, 0.9 g Poly, 1.5 g Sat); 112 mg Cholesterol; 57 g Carbohydrate; 6 g Fibre; 6 g Protein; 55 mg Sodium

KIWI WITH ORANGE CUSTARD: Omit strawberries. Use same amount of sliced kiwifruit.

Fruited Ginger Cake

A gently spiced cake dotted with tasty bits of fruit and nuts. Perfect for tea time.

Orange pekoe tea bag	1	1
Boiling water	1 cup	250 mL
Dark raisins	1 1/2 cups	375 mL
Brown sugar, packed	1 cup	250 mL
Chopped mixed glazed fruit	1/2 cup	125 mL
Large egg	1	1
Applesauce	1/2 cup	125 mL
Chopped walnuts (or almonds)	1/3 cup	75 mL
Minced crystallized ginger	1/4 cup	60 mL
Hard margarine (or butter), melted	1/4 cup	60 mL
All-purpose flour	2 cups	500 mL
Baking powder	1 tsp.	5 mL
Baking soda	1/4 tsp.	1 mL
Salt	1/4 tsp.	1 mL
Ground cinnamon	1/4 tsp.	1 mL
Ground nutmeg	1/8 tsp.	0.5 mL

Place tea bag in heatproof medium bowl. Pour boiling water over top. Cover. Let steep for 5 minutes. Squeeze and discard tea bag.

Add raisins, brown sugar and glazed fruit. Stir. Cover. Let stand for 1 to 2 hours until raisins are softened.

Combine next 5 ingredients in large bowl.

Add raisin mixture and remaining 6 ingredients. Stir until just moistened. Spread evenly in greased 9 x 9 inch (22 x 22 cm) pan. Bake in 350ºF (175ºC) oven for about 45 minutes until wooden pick inserted in centre comes out clean. Cuts into 9 pieces.

1 piece: 422 Calories; 9.2 g Total Fat (4.4 g Mono, 2.6 g Poly, 1.6 g Sat); 24 mg Cholesterol; 83 g Carbohydrate; 3 g Fibre; 6 g Protein; 237 mg Sodium

Banana Date Waffles

It doesn't get much better than this—unless, of course, you add a dollop of whipped topping!

Brown sugar, packed	1/3 cup	75 mL
2% evaporated milk	3 tbsp.	50 mL
Hard margarine (or butter)	2 tbsp.	30 mL
Medium bananas, cut into 1/4 inch (6 mm) slices	3	3
Chopped pitted dates	1/4 cup	60 mL
Ready-made fresh (or frozen, thawed) waffles	4	4
Pecan pieces, toasted (see Tip, page 21)	1/4 cup	60 mL

Heat and stir first 3 ingredients in large frying pan on medium for about 3 minutes until margarine is melted and sugar is dissolved.

Add banana and dates. Cook for 3 to 5 minutes, stirring gently, until heated through. Reduce heat to low. Cover to keep warm.

Heat waffles according to package directions. Place 1 waffle on each of 4 plates. Spoon banana mixture onto each.

Sprinkle with pecans. Serves 4.

1 serving: 397 Calories; 14.8 g Total Fat (8.4 g Mono, 3 g Poly, 2.5 g Sat); 10 mg Cholesterol; 66 g Carbohydrate; 3 g Fibre; 5 g Protein; 381 mg Sodium

While 100% fruit juice is a good alternative to whole fruits, choose juice that contains pulp to ensure you are getting the benefit of fruit fibre.

Mango Yogurt Swirl

An icy-fresh dessert made with creamy yogurt sweetened with honey.

Cans of sliced mango with syrup **(14 oz., 398 mL, each), do not drain**	**2**	**2**
Lime juice	**2 tbsp.**	**30 mL**
Low-fat plain yogurt	**1 cup**	**250 mL**
Liquid honey	**1/2 cup**	**125 mL**

Process mango with syrup and lime juice in blender or food processor until smooth. Spread evenly in ungreased 2 quart (2 L) shallow baking dish.

Combine yogurt and honey in small bowl. Randomly spoon onto mango mixture. Swirl knife through both mixtures to create marble effect. Cover. Freeze overnight until firm. Scoop into 4 bowls. Serves 4.

1 serving: 379 Calories; 1.3 g Total Fat (0.4 g Mono, 0.1 g Poly, 0.7 g Sat); 4 mg Cholesterol; 95 g Carbohydrate; 2 g Fibre; 4 g Protein; 91 mg Sodium

Pear Cranberry Crumble

Sweet, golden crumble topping invites you to discover delicately sauced fruit. Perfect with frozen yogurt.

Fresh pears, peeled, cores removed, sliced	**3**	**3**
Bag of fresh (or frozen) cranberries	**12 oz.**	**340 g**
Brown sugar, packed	**1/2 cup**	**125 mL**
Minute tapioca	**3 tbsp.**	**50 mL**
Lemon juice	**2 tsp.**	**10 mL**
CRUMBLE TOPPING		
Rolled oats (not instant)	**2/3 cup**	**150 mL**
All-bran cereal	**2/3 cup**	**150 mL**
Brown sugar, packed	**1/3 cup**	**75 mL**
Ground ginger	**1/2 tsp.**	**2 mL**
Ground cinnamon	**1/4 tsp.**	**1 mL**
Hard margarine (or butter), cut up	**1/2 cup**	**125 mL**

(continued on next page)

Combine first 5 ingredients in medium bowl. Spread evenly in greased 2 quart (2 L) shallow baking dish.

Crumble Topping: Combine first 5 ingredients in large bowl. Cut in margarine until mixture resembles coarse crumbs. Sprinkle evenly over pear mixture. Bake in 375°F (190°C) oven for 40 to 45 minutes until pear is tender and topping is browned. Let stand for 15 minutes before serving. Serves 6.

1 serving: 397 Calories; 17.2 g Total Fat (10.7 g Mono, 1.9 g Poly, 3.5 g Sat); 0 mg Cholesterol; 63 g Carbohydrate; 8 g Fibre; 3 g Protein; 275 mg Sodium

Pictured on front cover.

PLUM CRANBERRY CRUMBLE: Omit pears. Use 1 1/2 lbs. (680 g) fresh prune plums, pitted and sliced.

Baked Stuffed Apples

 *servings per portion*

Tender apples filled with a zesty fruit and nut stuffing. Serve with a scoop of low-fat ice cream or frozen yogurt for a simple, sweet treat.

Coarsely chopped pecans, toasted (see Tip, page 21)	1/2 cup	125 mL
Golden raisins	1/2 cup	125 mL
Brown sugar, packed	1/2 cup	125 mL
Diced mixed peel	1/4 cup	60 mL
Hard margarine (or butter), softened	3 tbsp.	50 mL
Grated orange zest	2 tsp.	10 mL
Ground cinnamon	1/2 tsp.	2 mL
Large tart cooking apples (such as Granny Smith), with peel	6	6
Apple juice	1/2 cup	125 mL

Combine first 7 ingredients in medium bowl.

Carefully remove cores from apples with apple corer, leaving apples whole. Carefully cut around hole in each apple with knife to make hole twice as large. Score peel of each apple in several places (to prevent peel from shrinking). Place apples in greased 3 quart (3 L) shallow baking dish. Spoon pecan mixture into centre of each apple, piling excess on top. Cover top of each with small piece of foil.

Pour apple juice into baking dish around apples. Bake, uncovered, in 350°F (175°C) oven for about 1 hour until apples are tender. Makes 6 stuffed apples.

1 stuffed apple: 350 Calories; 13.4 g Total Fat (8.2 g Mono, 2.5 g Poly, 1.9 g Sat); 0 mg Cholesterol; 61 g Carbohydrate; 5 g Fibre; 2 g Protein; 78 mg Sodium

Anise Rum Pears

Golden pears glisten with caramel-coloured syrup. A wonderful blend of flavours to awaken the taste buds! Serve with low-fat ice cream or frozen yogurt.

Fresh medium pears	4	4
Water	2 cups	500 mL
Brown sugar, packed	3/4 cup	175 mL
Spiced rum	1/3 cup	75 mL
Ground ginger	1 tsp.	5 mL
Whole green cardamom, bruised (see Tip, below)	4	4
Star anise	2	2

Carefully remove cores from pears with apple corer, leaving pears whole (see Note). Peel pears.

Combine remaining 6 ingredients in medium saucepan. Cook on medium for about 5 minutes, stirring occasionally, until sugar is dissolved. Carefully lay pears on side in rum mixture. Bring to a boil. Reduce heat to medium-low. Simmer, uncovered, for about 20 minutes, occasionally turning pears with wooden spoon or rubber spatula, until tender. Remove pears with slotted spoon to medium bowl. Cover to keep warm. Bring rum mixture to a boil on high. Boil gently, uncovered, for about 15 minutes until reduced to about 2/3 cup (150 mL). Discard cardamom and star anise. Place 1 pear on each of 4 dessert plates. Drizzle rum mixture over each. Serves 4.

1 serving: 265 Calories; 0.1 g Total Fat (0 g Mono, 0 g Poly, 0 g Sat); 0 mg Cholesterol; 57 g Carbohydrate; 4 g Fibre; 0 g Protein; 21 mg Sodium

Note: Core pears from bottom with apple corer. A grapefruit knife or melon baller also works well. Cut a small slice from bottom of each pear so they will stand upright on plates.

To bruise cardamom, pound pods with mallet or press with flat side of wide knife to "bruise," or crack them open slightly.

Mixed Berry Sorbet

A vibrant, raspberry-coloured, icy dessert. Refreshing after a full meal. Serve with fresh berries or sliced kiwifruit.

Water	**1 1/4 cups**	**300 mL**
Granulated sugar	**1/4 cup**	**60 mL**
Frozen mixed berries	**2 cups**	**500 mL**
Water	**3 tbsp.**	**50 mL**
Orange-flavoured liqueur (such as Grand Marnier)	**2 tbsp.**	**30 mL**
Lemon juice	**2 tsp.**	**10 mL**
Egg whites (large)	**2**	**2**

Heat and stir first amount of water and sugar in small saucepan on medium for about 2 minutes until sugar is dissolved. Bring to a boil on medium-high. Boil gently for 10 minutes. Cool.

Combine berries and second amount of water in medium saucepan. Cook on medium for about 3 minutes, stirring occasionally, until berries are softened and broken up. Press through sieve into medium bowl. Discard seeds. Add berries to sugar mixture.

Add liqueur and lemon juice. Stir well. Spread evenly in ungreased 1 1/2 quart (1.5 L) shallow baking dish. Freeze for about 2 hours until almost firm.

Beat egg whites in separate medium bowl until soft peaks form. Scrape frozen berry mixture into egg whites. Fold until no white streaks remain. Spread evenly in same baking dish. Freeze for about 2 hours until firm. Scrape mixture into blender or food processor. Process until smooth. Spread evenly in same baking dish. Cover. Freeze for about 2 hours until firm. Serves 4.

1 serving: 118 Calories; 0.3 g Total Fat (0 g Mono, 0.1 g Poly, 0 g Sat); 0 mg Cholesterol; 24 g Carbohydrate; 3 g Fibre; 2 g Protein; 28 mg Sodium

Pictured on page 143.

Rhubarb "Pie"

*servings per portion*

Crisp, golden phyllo blankets gently sweet rhubarb sauce. Just sweet enough. Beautiful!

Fresh (or frozen) rhubarb, cut into 1/2 inch (12 mm) pieces	**6 cups**	**1.5 L**
Granulated sugar	**1 cup**	**250 mL**
Water	**1/4 cup**	**60 mL**
Grated orange zest	**1 tsp.**	**5 mL**
Ground cinnamon	**1/2 tsp.**	**2 mL**
Frozen phyllo pastry sheets, thawed according to package directions	**6**	**6**
Icing (confectioner's) sugar	**1 tsp.**	**5 mL**

Combine first 5 ingredients in large saucepan. Bring to a boil on medium. Reduce heat to medium-low. Simmer, uncovered, for 12 to 15 minutes, stirring occasionally, until rhubarb starts to break up and sauce is thickened. Spread evenly in ungreased 9 inch (22 cm) deep dish pie plate.

Work with pastry sheets 1 at a time. Keep remaining sheets covered with damp tea towel to prevent drying. Spray 1 side of sheet with cooking spray. Loosely bunch. Place on top of rhubarb mixture near edge of pie plate. Spray second sheet with cooking spray. Loosely bunch. Place on top of rhubarb mixture, touching first sheet. Repeat with remaining sheets until rhubarb mixture is completely covered. Spray top of pastry with cooking spray. Bake in 350ºF (175ºC) oven for about 20 minutes until pastry is crisp and golden. Let stand for 10 minutes.

Sprinkle with icing sugar. Serve warm. Serves 6.

1 serving: 223 Calories; 1.4 g Total Fat (0.3 g Mono, 0.7 g Poly, 0.2 g Sat); 0 mg Cholesterol; 52 g Carbohydrate; 0 g Fibre; 3 g Protein; 149 mg Sodium

Mango Melon Sorbet

A delightfully tangy dessert for a summer barbecue, or for a day when you just need to chill.

Cubed cantaloupe	**2 cups**	**500 mL**
Ripe large mango, cubed	**1**	**1**
Granulated sugar	**1/4 cup**	**60 mL**
Lime juice	**1/4 cup**	**60 mL**

(continued on next page)

Spread cantaloupe in single layer on plastic wrap-lined baking sheet. Freeze for about 1 1/2 hours until firm. Transfer to blender or food processor.

Add remaining 3 ingredients. Process until smooth. Spread evenly in ungreased 1 1/2 quart (1.5 L) shallow baking dish. Cover with plastic wrap. Freeze for about 2 hours until almost firm. Scrape and stir to break up ice crystals. Freeze until firm. Place in refrigerator for 1 hour before serving (to soften slightly). Serves 6.

1 serving: 90 Calories; 0.3 g Total Fat (0.1 g Mono, 0 g Poly, 0 g Sat); 0 mg Cholesterol; 23 g Carbohydrate; 1 g Fibre; 1 g Protein; 6 mg Sodium

Pictured on page 143.

Lime Bananas

A tropical treat that's oh, so sweet. Yum!

Brown sugar, packed	1/3 cup	75 mL
Lime juice	2 tbsp.	30 mL
Grated lime zest	1 tsp.	5 mL
Small bananas, cut into 1 inch (2.5 cm) slices	4	4
Vanilla frozen yogurt	1 cup	250 mL
Sliced almonds, toasted (see Tip, page 21)	2 tbsp.	30 mL

Combine first 3 ingredients in medium frying pan. Add banana. Stir until coated. Cook on medium for 5 to 6 minutes, stirring gently, until banana is softened and sugar is dissolved.

Scoop 1/4 cup (60 mL) frozen yogurt into each of 4 bowls. Spoon banana mixture onto frozen yogurt.

Sprinkle with almonds. Serves 4.

1 serving: 215 Calories; 3.4 g Total Fat (1.6 g Mono, 0.6 g Poly, 0.9 g Sat); 1 mg Cholesterol; 48 g Carbohydrate; 2 g Fibre; 2 g Protein; 17 mg Sodium

Fruity Bread Pudding

Spongy pudding loaded with pear and blueberries and spiced with nutmeg. Delicious warm or cold.

Chopped, peeled fresh pear	**2 cups**	**500 mL**
Fresh (or frozen, thawed) blueberries	**1 cup**	**250 mL**
Day-old bread slices, cut into	**8**	**8**
** 1/2 inch (12 mm) cubes**		
Large eggs	**4**	**4**
Milk	**2 cups**	**500 mL**
Granulated sugar	**1/2 cup**	**125 mL**
Vanilla	**1 tsp.**	**5 mL**
Ground nutmeg	**1/2 tsp.**	**2 mL**
Coarse brown sugar (such as Sugar in	**2 tbsp.**	**30 mL**
** the Raw)**		

Scatter 1 cup (250 mL) pear and 1/2 cup (125 mL) blueberries in greased 2 quart (2 L) shallow baking dish.

Scatter bread cubes evenly over fruit. Scatter remaining pear and blueberries evenly over bread cubes.

Beat next 5 ingredients with whisk in medium bowl. Carefully pour over top. Let stand for 10 minutes.

Sprinkle with brown sugar. Place baking dish in 9 x 13 inch (22 x 33 cm) pan. Pour boiling water into pan until halfway up side of baking dish. Bake, uncovered, in 325ºF (160ºC) oven for about 1 1/4 hours until just set. Carefully remove baking dish from pan. Let stand for 20 minutes before serving. Serves 6.

1 serving: 297 Calories; 5.6 g Total Fat (2.1 g Mono, 0.7 g Poly, 1.9 g Sat); 147 mg Cholesterol; 52 g Carbohydrate; 3 g Fibre; 10 g Protein; 269 mg Sodium

Many fruits are good sources of fibre and vitamins A and C. Eating the skin especially provides the optimum nutritional boost.

Apple Carrot Cake

A delicious, moist cake made with applesauce instead of cooking oil. A twist on tradition, but just as good.

All-purpose flour	**1 1/2 cups**	**375 mL**
Whole wheat flour	**1/2 cup**	**125 mL**
Baking soda	**2 tsp.**	**10 mL**
Ground cinnamon	**1 1/2 tsp.**	**7 mL**
Ground nutmeg	**1/2 tsp.**	**2 mL**
Salt	**1 tsp.**	**5 mL**
Large eggs	**4**	**4**
Grated carrot	**2 cups**	**500 mL**
Grated, peeled cooking apple (such as McIntosh)	**1 1/2 cups**	**375 mL**
Applesauce	**1 cup**	**250 mL**
Granulated sugar	**1 cup**	**250 mL**
Golden raisins	**1 cup**	**250 mL**
APPLE CREAM ICING		
Icing (confectioner's) sugar	**1 cup**	**250 mL**
Block of light cream cheese, softened	**4 oz.**	**125 g**
Hard margarine (or butter), softened	**1/4 cup**	**60 mL**
Frozen concentrated apple juice	**2 tbsp.**	**30 mL**

Measure first 6 ingredients into large bowl. Stir. Make a well in centre.

Combine next 6 ingredients in separate large bowl. Add to well. Stir until just moistened. Spread evenly in greased 9 x 13 inch (22 x 33 cm) pan. Bake in 350ºF (175ºC) oven for about 45 minutes until wooden pick inserted in centre comes out clean. Let stand in pan on wire rack to cool completely.

Apple Cream Icing: Beat all 4 ingredients in medium bowl on medium until smooth. Makes about 1 1/2 cups (375 mL) icing. Spread evenly on top of cake in pan. Cuts into 12 pieces.

1 piece: 342 Calories; 8.2 g Total Fat (3.9 g Mono, 0.9 g Poly, 2.6 g Sat); 78 mg Cholesterol; 63 g Carbohydrate; 3 g Fibre; 6 g Protein; 563 mg Sodium

Pictured on page 36.

Peachsicle Slice

Golden layers of peachy frozen yogurt sandwich vanilla ice cream. Serve with fresh berries or berry coulis (COO-lee).

Orange juice	**2 cups**	**500 mL**
Chopped dried peaches	**1/2 cup**	**125 mL**
Can of sliced peaches in pear juice (do not drain)	**14 oz.**	**398 mL**
Low-fat peach yogurt	**1/2 cup**	**125 mL**
Low-fat vanilla ice cream, softened	**1 1/2 cups**	**375 mL**

Process orange juice and dried peaches in blender or food processor until smooth.

Add canned peaches and yogurt. Process until smooth. Spread 1/2 of mixture evenly in plastic wrap-lined 9 x 5 x 3 inch (22 x 12.5 x 7.5 cm) loaf pan. Freeze for about 3 hours until firm. Chill remaining peach mixture.

Spread ice cream evenly on top of frozen peach mixture. Stir chilled peach mixture. Spread evenly on top of ice cream. Cover. Freeze overnight until firm. Invert onto cutting board. Discard plastic wrap. Cuts into 8 slices (see Note).

1 slice: 173 Calories; 3.2 g Total Fat (0.9 g Mono, 0.2 g Poly, 1.8 g Sat); 12 mg Cholesterol; 36 g Carbohydrate; 3 g Fibre; 3 g Protein; 37 mg Sodium

Pictured on page 143.

Note: To easily cut frozen desserts, dip knife in hot water before cutting each slice.

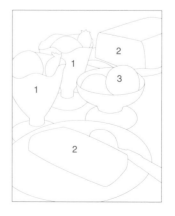

1. Mixed Berry Sorbet, page 137
2. Peachsicle Slice, above
3. Mango Melon Sorbet, page 138

Spiced Eggplant Dip

Chunky dip with flecks of herbs and a subtle chili flavour. Something a little different to serve with tortilla chips.

Eggplant	1	1
Coarse dry bread crumbs	1/2 cup	125 mL
Water	1/4 cup	60 mL
Low-fat plain yogurt	1/3 cup	75 mL
Chopped fresh parsley (or 1 1/2 tsp., 7 mL, flakes)	2 tbsp.	30 mL
Lemon juice	1 tbsp.	15 mL
Sweet chili sauce	1 tbsp.	15 mL
Ground cumin	1/2 tsp.	2 mL
Chili powder	1/4 tsp.	1 mL

Randomly poke several holes with fork into eggplant. Place on greased baking sheet. Bake in 350ºF (175ºC) oven for about 40 minutes until softened. Remove from oven. Let stand on baking sheet for about 10 minutes until cool enough to handle. Cut eggplant in half. Scrape flesh into blender or food processor. Discard peel.

Combine bread crumbs and water in small bowl. Let stand for about 5 minutes until water is absorbed. Add to eggplant.

Add remaining 6 ingredients. Process until smooth. Serves 4.

1 serving: 100 Calories; 1.4 g Total Fat (0.4 g Mono, 0.3 g Poly, 0.4 g Sat); 1 mg Cholesterol; 19 g Carbohydrate; 3 g Fibre; 4 g Protein; 140 mg Sodium

Pictured on page 144.

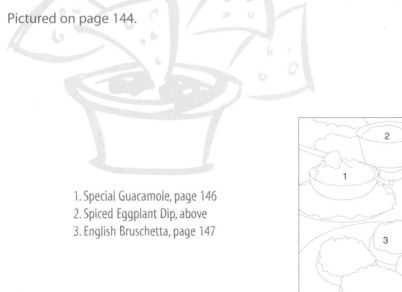

1. Special Guacamole, page 146
2. Spiced Eggplant Dip, above
3. English Bruschetta, page 147

Celery Delight

 2 servings per portion

Reward yourself with a celery snack. A nice change from the traditional process cheese spread filling. De-lish!

Grated carrot	**1 cup**	**250 mL**
Light spreadable cream cheese	**1/2 cup**	**125 mL**
Grated light medium Cheddar cheese	**1/3 cup**	**75 mL**
Light mayonnaise	**2 tbsp.**	**30 mL**
Celery ribs, each cut into 3 pieces	**6**	**6**

Combine first 4 ingredients in small bowl. Spread evenly in each celery piece. Makes 18 pieces. Serves 6.

1 serving: 96 Calories; 6.9 g Total Fat (2.5 g Mono, 0.7 g Poly, 3.2 g Sat); 17 mg Cholesterol; 5 g Carbohydrate; 1 g Fibre; 4 g Protein; 260 mg Sodium

Special Guacamole

Creamy avocado and juicy tomatoes make a delightful dip. Colourful and zesty—perfect for taco chips.

Ripe large avocado	**1**	**1**
Finely chopped green onion	**1 tbsp.**	**15 mL**
Lime juice	**1 tbsp.**	**15 mL**
Finely chopped jalapeño pepper (see Tip, page 93)	**2 tsp.**	**10 mL**
Garlic clove, minced (or 1/4 tsp., 1 mL, powder)	**1**	**1**
Ground cumin	**1/4 tsp.**	**1 mL**
Pepper, sprinkle		
Medium tomatoes, quartered, seeds removed, finely chopped	**2**	**2**

Mash avocado in medium bowl. Add next 6 ingredients. Mix well.

Add tomato. Stir. Serves 6.

1 serving: 76 Calories; 6.3 g Total Fat (3.9 g Mono, 0.8 g Poly, 1 g Sat); 0 mg Cholesterol; 5 g Carbohydrate; 2 g Fibre; 1 g Protein; 8 mg Sodium

Pictured on page 144.

English Bruschetta

servings per portion

Tasty bruschetta made with toasted English muffins and seasoned with a little cumin to make them interesting. "Cumin" get 'em!

Medium tomatoes, quartered, seeds removed, finely chopped	2	2
Finely chopped green onion	2 tbsp.	30 mL
Chopped fresh basil (or 1 1/2 tsp., 7 mL, dried)	2 tbsp.	30 mL
Red wine vinegar	1 tsp.	5 mL
Ground cumin	1/8 tsp.	0.5 mL
Pepper	1/8 tsp.	0.5 mL
Whole wheat English muffins, split	2	2
Grated Parmesan cheese	1/4 cup	60 mL

Combine first 6 ingredients in small bowl.

Toast both halves of each muffin. Place muffins split-side up on ungreased baking sheet. Spoon tomato mixture onto each half.

Sprinkle Parmesan cheese over each. Broil 6 inches (15 cm) from heat in oven for 2 to 3 minutes until Parmesan cheese is melted and starts to brown. Makes 4 bruschetta. Serves 2.

1 serving: 218 Calories; 5.6 g Total Fat (1.4 g Mono, 0.8 g Poly, 2.8 g Sat); 10 mg Cholesterol; 33 g Carbohydrate; 2 g Fibre; 12 g Protein; 478 mg Sodium

Pictured on page 144.

Date Apple Cheese Snack

A sweet, crunchy combination. Add more honey if you like your snacks a little sweeter. Serve on a bed of lettuce.

Large cooking apple (such as McIntosh), with peel, core removed, chopped	1	1
1% cottage cheese	1/2 cup	125 mL
Chopped pitted dates	1/4 cup	60 mL
Pecan pieces, toasted (see Tip, page 21)	2 tbsp.	30 mL
Raw sunflower seeds, toasted (see Tip, page 21)	2 tbsp.	30 mL
Liquid honey	1 tbsp.	15 mL

Combine all 6 ingredients in small bowl. Serves 2.

1 serving: 299 Calories; 10.9 g Total Fat (4.3 g Mono, 4.5 g Poly, 1.4 g Sat); 3 mg Cholesterol; 45 g Carbohydrate; 4 g Fibre; 10 g Protein; 251 mg Sodium

Fruit-Full Muffins

Moist, tender muffins full of tangy rhubarb and cranberries, topped with sweet crumbs. Just as good without the topping.

Large egg	1	1
Chopped fresh (or frozen, thawed) rhubarb	1 1/2 cups	375 mL
Chopped fresh (or frozen, thawed) strawberries	1 1/2 cups	375 mL
Dried cranberries	1 cup	250 mL
Unsweetened applesauce	1 cup	250 mL
Hard margarine (or butter), melted	1/2 cup	125 mL
All-purpose flour	3 cups	750 mL
Brown sugar, packed	1 cup	250 mL
Baking soda	1 tsp.	5 mL
Salt	1/2 tsp.	2 mL
NUTTY TOPPING		
Brown sugar, packed	1/4 cup	60 mL
Ground walnuts	1 tbsp.	15 mL
Ground cinnamon	1/4 tsp.	1 mL

Fork-beat egg in large bowl. Add next 5 ingredients. Stir well.

Measure next 4 ingredients into separate large bowl. Stir. Make a well in centre. Add fruit mixture to well. Stir until just moistened. Grease 12 muffin cups with cooking spray. Fill cups until full.

Nutty Topping: Combine all 3 ingredients in small bowl. Sprinkle evenly over muffins. Bake in 375°F (190°C) oven for 20 to 25 minutes until wooden pick inserted in centre of muffin comes out clean. Let stand in pan for 5 minutes before removing to wire rack to cool. Makes 12 muffins.

1 muffin: 324 Calories; 8.8 g Total Fat (5.3 g Mono, 1.1 g Poly, 1.7 g Sat); 0 mg Cholesterol; 59 g Carbohydrate; 3 g Fibre; 4 g Protein; 312 mg Sodium

Pictured on page 125 and on back cover.

Antipasto

Colourful and chunky. Serve with crisped baguette slices or your favourite crackers. Freezes well.

Cooking oil	2 tbsp.	30 mL
Chopped cauliflower florets	1 cup	250 mL
Finely chopped onion	1/4 cup	60 mL
Small garlic clove, minced	1	1
Diced green pepper	1/2 cup	125 mL
Diced red pepper	1/2 cup	125 mL
Can of mushroom stems and pieces, drained and chopped	10 oz.	284 mL
Ketchup	1 cup	250 mL
Can of sliced ripe olives, drained	4 1/2 oz.	125 mL
Chopped gherkin (or dill pickle)	1/4 cup	60 mL
Gherkin (or dill pickle) juice	2 tbsp.	30 mL
Can of flaked tuna, drained	6 oz.	170 g

Heat cooking oil in large saucepan on medium. Add cauliflower, onion and garlic. Cook for 5 to 10 minutes, stirring often, until onion is softened.

Add green and red pepper. Cook for about 5 minutes, stirring occasionally, until pepper is softened.

Add next 5 ingredients. Stir. Mixture will be very thick. Bring to a boil. Boil gently, uncovered, for 5 minutes, stirring often. Reduce heat to medium-low. Heat and stir for 5 minutes.

Add tuna. Stir well. Remove from heat. Cool. Chill for at least 3 hours until cold. Makes about 3 cups (750 mL). Serves 6.

1 serving: 148 Calories; 5.9 g Total Fat (3.4 g Mono, 1.7 g Poly, 0.5 g Sat); 8 mg Cholesterol; 18 g Carbohydrate; 2 g Fibre; 8 g Protein; 895 mg Sodium

Pictured on front cover.

Measurement Tables

Throughout this book measurements are given in Conventional and Metric measure. To compensate for differences between the two measurements due to rounding, a full metric measure is not always used. The cup used is the standard 8 fluid ounce. Temperature is given in degrees Fahrenheit and Celsius. Baking pan measurements are in inches and centimetres as well as quarts and litres. An exact metric conversion is given below as well as the working equivalent (Standard Measure).

OVEN TEMPERATURES

Fahrenheit (°F)	Celsius (°C)
175°	80°
200°	95°
225°	110°
250°	120°
275°	140°
300°	150°
325°	160°
350°	175°
375°	190°
400°	205°
425°	220°
450°	230°
475°	240°
500°	260°

PANS

Conventional Inches	Metric Centimetres
8x8 inch	20x20 cm
9x9 inch	22x22 cm
9x13 inch	22x33 cm
10x15 inch	25x38 cm
11x17 inch	28x43 cm
8x2 inch round	20x5 cm
9x2 inch round	22x5 cm
10x4 1/2 inch tube	25x11 cm
8x4x3 inch loaf	20x10x7.5 cm
9x5x3 inch loaf	22x12.5x7.5 cm

SPOONS

Conventional Measure	Metric Exact Conversion Millilitre (mL)	Metric Standard Measure Millilitre (mL)
1/8 teaspoon (tsp.)	0.6 mL	0.5 mL
1/4 teaspoon (tsp.)	1.2 mL	1 mL
1/2 teaspoon (tsp.)	2.4 mL	2 mL
1 teaspoon (tsp.)	4.7 mL	5 mL
2 teaspoons (tsp.)	9.4 mL	10 mL
1 tablespoon (tbsp.)	14.2 mL	15 mL

CUPS

1/4 cup (4 tbsp.)	56.8 mL	60 mL
1/3 cup (5 1/3 tbsp.)	75.6 mL	75 mL
1/2 cup (8 tbsp.)	113.7 mL	125 mL
2/3 cup (10 2/3 tbsp.)	151.2 mL	150 mL
3/4 cup (12 tbsp.)	170.5 mL	175 mL
1 cup (16 tbsp.)	227.3 mL	250 mL
4 1/2 cups	1022.9 mL	1000 mL (1 L)

DRY MEASUREMENTS

Conventional Measure Ounces (oz.)	Metric Exact Conversion Grams (g)	Metric Standard Measure Grams (g)
1 oz.	28.3 g	28 g
2 oz.	56.7 g	57 g
3 oz.	85.0 g	85 g
4 oz.	113.4 g	125 g
5 oz.	141.7 g	140 g
6 oz.	170.1 g	170 g
7 oz.	198.4 g	200 g
8 oz.	226.8 g	250 g
16 oz.	453.6 g	500 g
32 oz.	907.2 g	1000 g (1 kg)

CASSEROLES (Canada & Britain)

Standard Size Casserole	Exact Metric Measure
1 qt. (5 cups)	1.13 L
1 1/2 qts. (7 1/2 cups)	1.69 L
2 qts. (10 cups)	2.25 L
2 1/2 qts. (12 1/2 cups)	2.81 L
3 qts. (15 cups)	3.38 L
4 qts. (20 cups)	4.50 L
5 qts. (25 cups)	5.63 L

CASSEROLES (United States)

Standard Size Casserole	Exact Metric Measure
1 qt. (4 cups)	900 mL
1 1/2 qts. (6 cups)	1.35 L
2 qts. (8 cups)	1.80 L
2 1/2 qts. (10 cups)	2.25 L
3 qts. (12 cups)	2.70 L
4 qts. (16 cups)	3.60 L
5 qts. (20 cups)	4.50 L

Recipe Index

Recipe Notes

Recipe Notes

The Company's Coming

story

Jean Paré (pronounced "jeen PAIR-ee") grew up understanding that the combination of family, friends and home cooking is the best recipe for a good life. From her mother, she learned to appreciate good cooking, while her father praised even her earliest attempts in the kitchen. When Jean left home, she took with her a love of cooking, many family recipes and an intriguing desire to read cookbooks as if they were novels!

"never share a recipe you wouldn't use yourself"

In 1963, when her four children had all reached school age, Jean volunteered to cater the 50th Anniversary of the Vermilion School of Agriculture, now Lakeland College, in Alberta, Canada. Working out of her home, Jean prepared a dinner for more than 1,000 people, which launched a flourishing catering operation that continued for over 18 years. During that time, she had countless opportunities to test new ideas with immediate feedback—resulting in empty plates and contented customers! Whether preparing cocktail sandwiches for a house party or serving a hot meal for 1,500 people, Jean Paré earned a reputation for good food, courteous service and reasonable prices.

As requests for her recipes mounted, Jean was often asked the question, "Why don't you write a cookbook?" Jean responded by teaming up with her son, Grant Lovig, in the fall of 1980 to form Company's Coming Publishing Limited. The publication of *150 Delicious Squares* on April 14, 1981 marked the debut of what would soon become one of the world's most popular cookbook series.

The company has grown since those early days when Jean worked from a spare bedroom in her home. Today, she continues to write recipes while working closely with the staff of the Recipe Factory, as the Company's Coming test kitchen is affectionately known. There she fills the role of mentor, assisting with the development of recipes people most want to use for everyday cooking and easy entertaining. Every Company's Coming recipe is *kitchen-tested* before it's approved for publication.

Jean's daughter, Gail Lovig, is responsible for marketing and distribution, leading a team that includes sales personnel located in major cities across Canada. In addition, Company's Coming cookbooks are published and distributed under licence in the United States, Australia and other world markets. Bestsellers many times over in English, Company's Coming cookbooks have also been published in French and Spanish.

Familiar and trusted in home kitchens around the world, Company's Coming cookbooks are offered in a variety of formats. Highly regarded as kitchen workbooks, the softcover Original Series, with its lay-flat plastic comb binding, is still a favourite among readers.

Jean Paré's approach to cooking has always called for *quick and easy recipes* using *everyday ingredients.* That view has served her well. The recipient of many awards, including the Queen Elizabeth Golden Jubilee medal, Jean was appointed a Member of the Order of Canada, her country's highest lifetime achievement honour.

Jean continues to gain new supporters by adhering to what she calls The Golden Rule of Cooking: *"Never share a recipe you wouldn't use yourself."* It's an approach that works—*millions of times over!*